To David and Wendy,

With best wishes.

Subhankar Banerjee

June 23, 2003

ARCTIC NATIONAL WILDLIFE REFUGE

seasons OF *life* AND *land*

A PHOTOGRAPHIC JOURNEY BY SUBHANKAR BANERJEE

PETER MATTHIESSEN

FRAN MAUER

WILLIAM H. MEADOWS

DEBBIE S. MILLER

GEORGE B. SCHALLER

DAVID ALLEN SIBLEY

FOREWORD BY JIMMY CARTER
POEM BY TERRY TEMPEST WILLIAMS

PUBLISHED BY THE MOUNTAINEERS BOOKS WITH A GENEROUS GRANT FROM THE MOUNTAINEERS FOUNDATION, SEATTLE, WASHINGTON

Published by
The Mountaineers Books
1001 SW Klickitat Way,
Suite 201 Seattle, WA 98134

Published simultaneously in Great
Britain by Cordee, 3a DeMontfort
Street, Leicester, England, LE1 7HD

Manufactured in Hong Kong by Midas
Printing (Asia) Ltd.

Project Editor: Kerry I. Smith
Developmental Editors: Deb Easter
and Linda Gunnarson
Editor: Christine Clifton-Thornton
Director of Editorial and Production:
Kathleen Cubley
Cover design: Ani Rucki
Book design and layout: Ani Rucki
Map art and design: Rose Michelle
Taverniti
Map relief: Dee Molenaar

All photographs by Subhankar
Banerjee except as noted. *All images
were taken inside the Arctic National
Wildlife Refuge, with the exception of
some contributers' portraits and those
photographs taken at Arctic Village and
of the Prudhoe Bay industrial complex.
Cover photograph: Flock of willow
ptarmigan over the Hulahula River valley,
snow-capped Brooks Range in the
background*
Half title page: *Muskox herd sleeps on
the snow-covered Canning River delta*
Title page: *Pregnant Porcupine caribou in
the Coleen River valley*
Dedication page: *Nichenthraw Mountain
reflects on an unnamed lake on the East
Fork of the Chandalar River*

Page 171: Poem "Wild Mercy" © Terry
Tempest Williams, 2001. Reprinted
with her permission. First published
in *Arctic Refuge: Circle of Testimony*,
Milkweed Editions, 2001

*Library of Congress Cataloging-in-
Publication Data*
Banerjee, Subhankar.
  Arctic National Wildlife Refuge :
seasons of life and land / Subhankar
Banerjee.— 1st ed.
    p.   cm.
Includes bibliographical references
and index.
  ISBN 0-89886-438-0 (pbk.) —
  ISBN 0-89886-909-9 (hardcover)
  1. Natural history—Alaska—Arctic
National Wildlife Refuge. 2. Natural
history—Alaska—Arctic National
Wildlife Refuge—Pictorial works.
3. Arctic National Wildlife Refuge
(Alaska). 4. Arctic National
Wildlife Refuge (Alaska)—Pictorial
works. I. Title.
  QH105.A4 B36 2003
  508.798'7—dc21

      2002154578

THIS BOOK IS SUPPORTED BY A GENEROUS GRANT FROM

THE MOUNTAINEERS FOUNDATION

THE SUBHANKAR BANERJEE PROJECT WAS MADE POSSIBLE
WITH THE GENEROUS SUPPORT OF:

Blue Earth Alliance

Furthermore: a program of the J. M. Kaplan Fund

Hugh and Jane Ferguson Foundation

Kongsgaard-Goldman Foundation

The Mountaineers Foundation

National Audubon Society

Natural Resources Defense Council

Outside magazine

Tom and Sonya Campion

Sanjeeban Chatterjee

Virendra and Roshila Chaudhary

Ellen Ferguson

Julian Sayers

M. Srikant

Tom Steinburn

Patricia Sunny Walter

THE ACCOMPANYING EXHIBITION IS SPONSORED BY
THE SMITHSONIAN NATIONAL MUSEUM OF NATURAL HISTORY

To the Arctic Refuge animals, plants, land, and sea, who cannot speak for themselves;

and to my Gwich'in and Inupiat friends, for their warm hospitality and compassion,

and for allowing me a window through which to learn about their cultures.

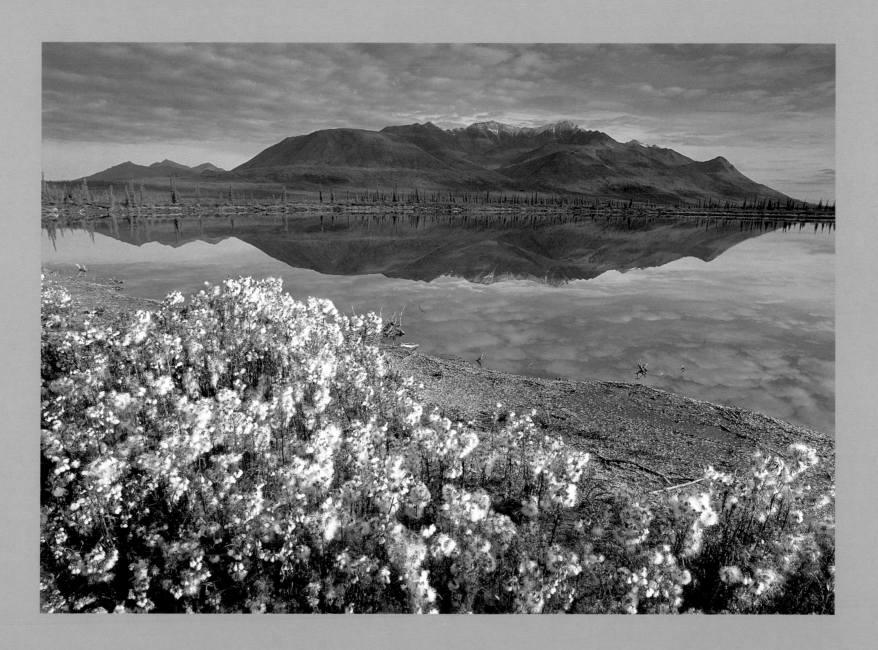

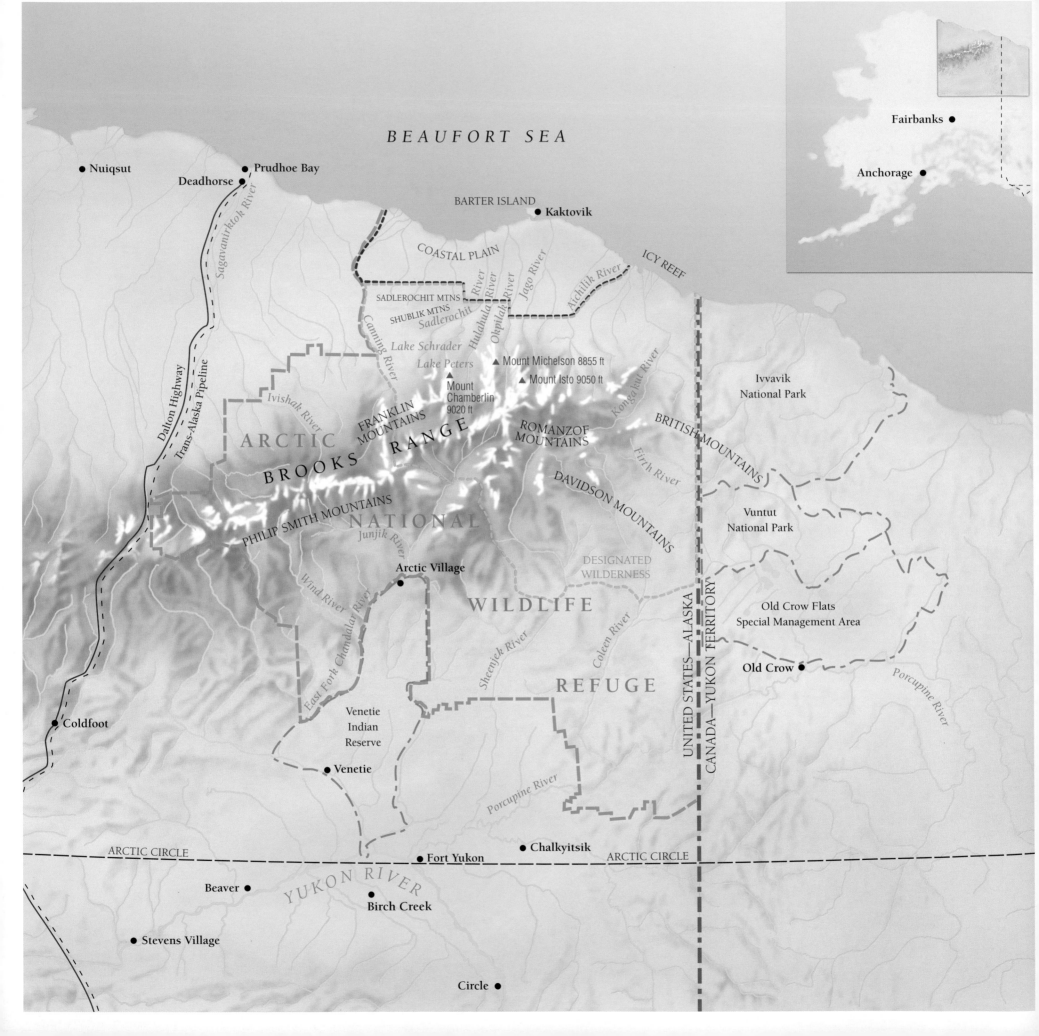

BEAUFORT SEA

Nuiqsut

Prudhoe Bay
Deadhorse

BARTER ISLAND
Kaktovik

COASTAL PLAIN

ICY REEF

SADLEROCHIT MTNS
SHUBLIK MTNS
Sadlerochit

Sagavanirktok River
Canning River
Hulahula River
Okpilak River
Jago River
Aichilik River

Lake Schrader
Lake Peters

▲ Mount Michelson 8855 ft
▲ Mount Isto 9050 ft

Mount
Chamberlin
9020 ft

Konga kut River

Ivishak River

ARCTIC

FRANKLIN
MOUNTAINS

BROOKS RANGE

ROMANZOF
MOUNTAINS

Firth River

BRITISH MOUNTAINS

Ivvavik
National Park

Dalton Highway
Trans-Alaska Pipeline

PHILIP SMITH MOUNTAINS

NATIONAL

DAVIDSON
MOUNTAINS

Vuntut
National Park

Junjik River

Wind River

East Fork Chandalar River

Arctic Village

WILDLIFE

DESIGNATED
WILDERNESS

Old Crow Flats
Special Management Area

Sheenjek River

Coleen River

REFUGE

Venetie
Indian
Reserve

Old Crow

Porcupine River

Venetie

UNITED STATES—ALASKA
CANADA—YUKON TERRITORY

Porcupine River

Coldfoot

Porcupine River

Chalkyitsik

ARCTIC CIRCLE
Fort Yukon
ARCTIC CIRCLE

YUKON RIVER

Beaver

Birch Creek

Stevens Village

Circle

Fairbanks

Anchorage

CONTENTS

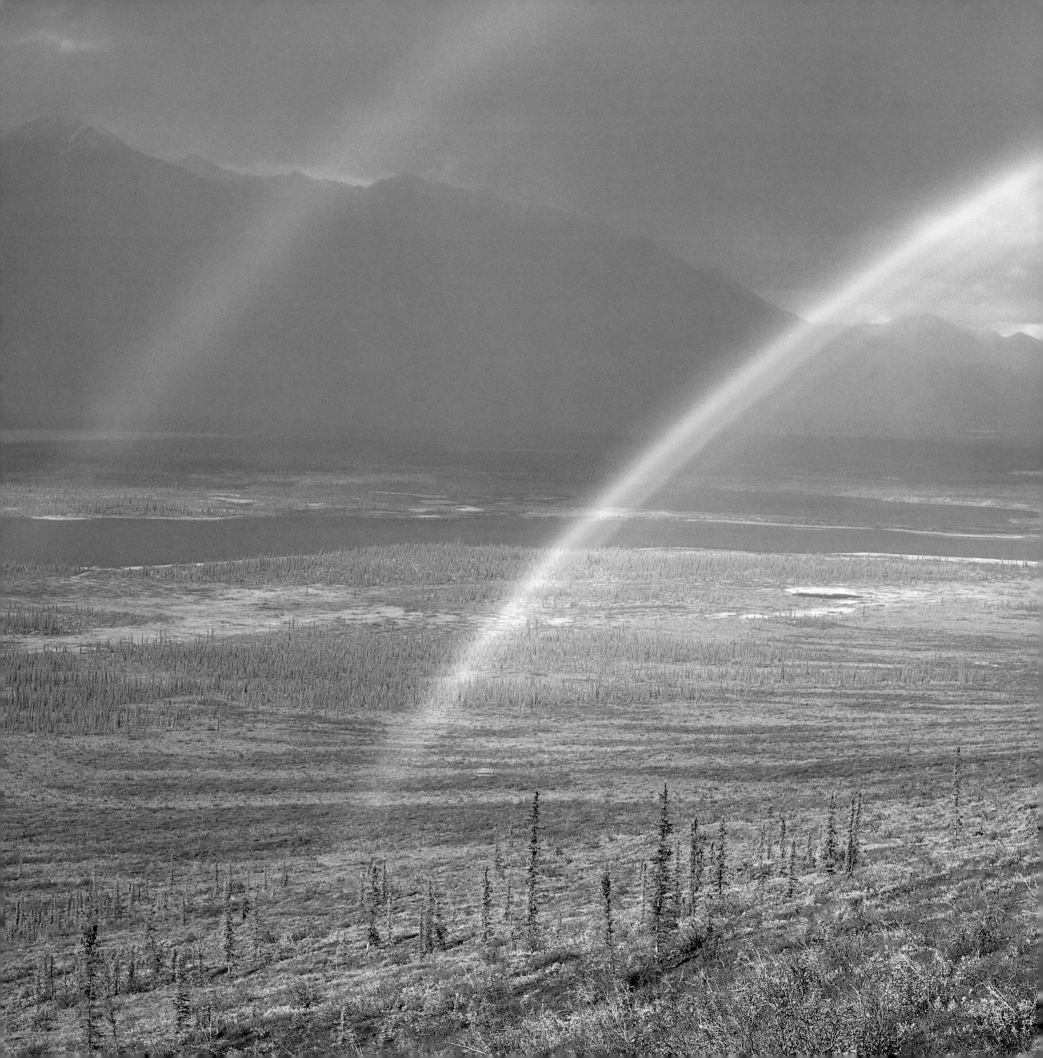

ACKNOWLEDGMENTS

This project has received so much support and good will from so many that I hardly know how to begin expressing my gratitude. In different ways, everyone mentioned here made an important contribution to this book. If I have left anyone out, I hope to be excused for weakness of memory.

Throughout the course of the project I was unable to afford an apartment, health insurance, or any other unrelated expenses. The unconditional and heartfelt generosity of my friends turned this project from a *vision* into *reality*. They provided me with home, food, financial support, logistical support, and guidance. I am indebted to you for life: Tom and Sonya Campion, Sanjeeban Chatterjee, Virendra and Roshila Chaudhary, Ashish and Usree Kirtania, Fran Mauer and Yoriko Freed, Julian Sayers, M. Srikant, and Patricia Sunny Walter.

I would like to express my deepest appreciation to President Jimmy Carter, Peter Matthiessen, George B. Schaller, David Allen Sibley, Fran Mauer, Debbie S. Miller, and William H. Meadows, for contributing wonderful essays to this book, and Terry Tempest Williams for her beautiful poem. I am grateful and tremendously honored to be in your company. And to Edward O. Wilson, Jane Goodall, Barry Lopez, and Robert Redford, for providing thoughtful endorsements for the book.

My most sincere thanks goes to the following people:
The talented staff at The Mountaineers Books for their continuing enthusiasm for this project in the face of the most demanding deadlines imaginable, especially publisher Helen Cherullo, without whose vision, support, and guidance you would not be holding this book in your hands today; art director Ani Rucki for the magnificent design of the book; project editor Kerry Smith, whose skillful management and meticulous organization kept all of the elements of the project on track; editor Christine Clifton-Thornton for her thoughtful and eloquent edits and her willingness to always help; editors Deb Easter, Kathleen Cubley, Linda Gunnerson, and David Emblidge for an excellent job in working with the contributors to bring together the text for the book; and Alison Koop (publicity), Hally Swift (finance), Doug Canfield (sales and marketing), and Elaine Bongiorno (sales and marketing); Fran Mauer for fact checking the content; The Mountaineers club and The Mountaineers Foundation for their unrelenting support of my project: executive director Steve Costie for introducing me to The Mountaineers Books; editor Brad Stracener for graciously agreeing to publish my images and stories in a monthly column in The Mountaineers newsletter in 2001; Donna Osseward of The Mountaineers Foundation for her enthusiasm and strong support of this project; and Kelly McCaffrey for her logistical support; My colleagues at Blue Earth Alliance, a non-profit organization dedicated to supporting photographic documentary projects that educate the public about endangered environments, threatened species, and current social issues: project mentors Natalie Fobes, Phil Borges, Julee Geier, Marita Holdaway, Malcolm Edwards, Kristin Ianniciello, and Judy DeBarros, who gave me advice regarding photography, survival, managing a project of this magnitude, writing grant proposals, and hosting a photo exhibit of my work: Over and above all, for teaching me the essence of the BEA mantra, *shooting from the heart;* Gary Braasch, Robert Glenn Ketchum, Izuro Toki, Steve Kazilowski, and Gary Luhm, fellow photographers and friends, for their invaluable advice; Robert Sullivan, associate director of the Smithsonian National Museum of Natural History (NMNH) in Washington, D.C., for believing in this project at an early stage and agreeing to host and sponsor the accompanying exhibit of my work at the NMNH; and Nancy Lynn and David Harvey, of the American Museum of Natural History in New York,

for agreeing to host this exhibit subsequent to NMNH; Carl Beebe at Prolab in Seattle for the superb job in handling all of my photo processing and duplicating needs throughout the project; Joseph Levine of Calypso Imaging in Santa Clara for a fabulous job handling my printing needs; Bill Jones at Camera Tech for a superb job of fixing my broken cameras and providing helpful advice; Ray Pfortner, Cindy Shogan (Alaska Wilderness League), Adam Kolton (National Wildlife Federation), Chuck Clusen (Natural Resources Defense Council), Stanley Senner (Audubon Alaska), Daniel Taylor (Audubon California), Deborah Williams (Alaska Conservation Foundation), Julie Jessen (Alaska Conservation Foundation), Sam Howe Verhovek *(The New York Times),* Mary Lewis (Jane Goodall Institute), Hans Cole (Jane Goodall Institute), Joyce Deep (Robert Redford's office), Faye Perdue (Carter Center), Norman Shaifer, Reverend James Parks Morton (Interfaith Center of New York), Peggy Harrington (Interfaith Center of New York), Max and Michelle Langstaff, Lee Langstaff, Pat and Wayne Fisher, Robert Childers, Pam Miller (Arctic Connections), Sidney and Barbara Coon, Kaustuve Bhattacharyya and Gees Stein, Amy Schlachtenhaufen, and Karen Fant, who all graciously gave their time and direct support to this project; Patricia Reynolds, Ann Morkill, David Payer, Alan Brackney, Roger Kaye, Richard Voss, Beverly Reitz, and Cathy Curby, of the U.S. Fish and Wildlife Service—Arctic National Wildlife Refuge; and Steve Amstrup, Tony Fishbach, George Durner, of the USGS Biological Sciences Division, and Susanne Klaxdorff, of the USFWS Marine Mammal Management Program, who offered invaluable information, research assistance, guidance, and advice; Dee Molenaar and Michelle Taverniti for creating the beautiful maps that appear in this book; Arctic National Wildlife Refuge, U.S. Geological Survey, Gwich'in Steering Committee, Conservation GIS Support Center, The Wilderness Society, The Alaska Native Language Center, and the Alaska State office of the National Audubon Society for their assistance with the maps; Field guides and friends Robert Thompson (Kaktovik Arctic Adventures), Charlie Swaney and Jimi John (Arctic Village), Jim Campbell and Karol Kasza (Arctic Treks); and pilots Walt Audi (Alaska Flyers) and Kirk Sweetsir (Yukon Air Service), without whose expert assistance I never would have been able to complete this project; Editors Rob Haggart, Michael Roberts, and Mary Turner of *Outside* magazine for publishing my images in an article on the Arctic Refuge by Peter Matthiessen.

I would like to thank my family in India for their spiritual support and unwavering love, even though at times they were worried sick, wondering if I was even alive when they did not hear from me for months at a time while I was in the field: Debdas and Nina Banerjee, Ruma, Abhijit, Debolina and Debopriya Sen, Dipankar, Suktara, Debasish and Ria Banerjee, and Sumit Sen. Thank you, Brooke Tone Boswell, for your love and support.

Finally, I would like to thank all my friends of the far north for your generous and giving hearts: Sarah James, Charlie and Marion Swaney, Robert and Jane Thompson, Walt Audi and Marilyn Trayner (Waldo Arms Hotel), and Nora Agiak for your warm hospitality and generosity during my time at Arctic Village and Kaktovik—these were my homes-away-from-home; and Trimble Gilbert, Evon Peter, Luci Beach, Gideon James, Jimi John, Mike Garnette, and Lilian Garnette, of Arctic Village; and Daniel and Lillian Akootchook, Susie Akootchook, Isaac Akootchook, Ida Akootchook, and Papa Tagrook, of Kaktovik. Forgive me for not being able to mention the names of all the children and elders who filled my heart with joy—but I thank you all.

—Subhankar Banerjee

Opposite • After a rainstorm: Autumn on the southern taiga

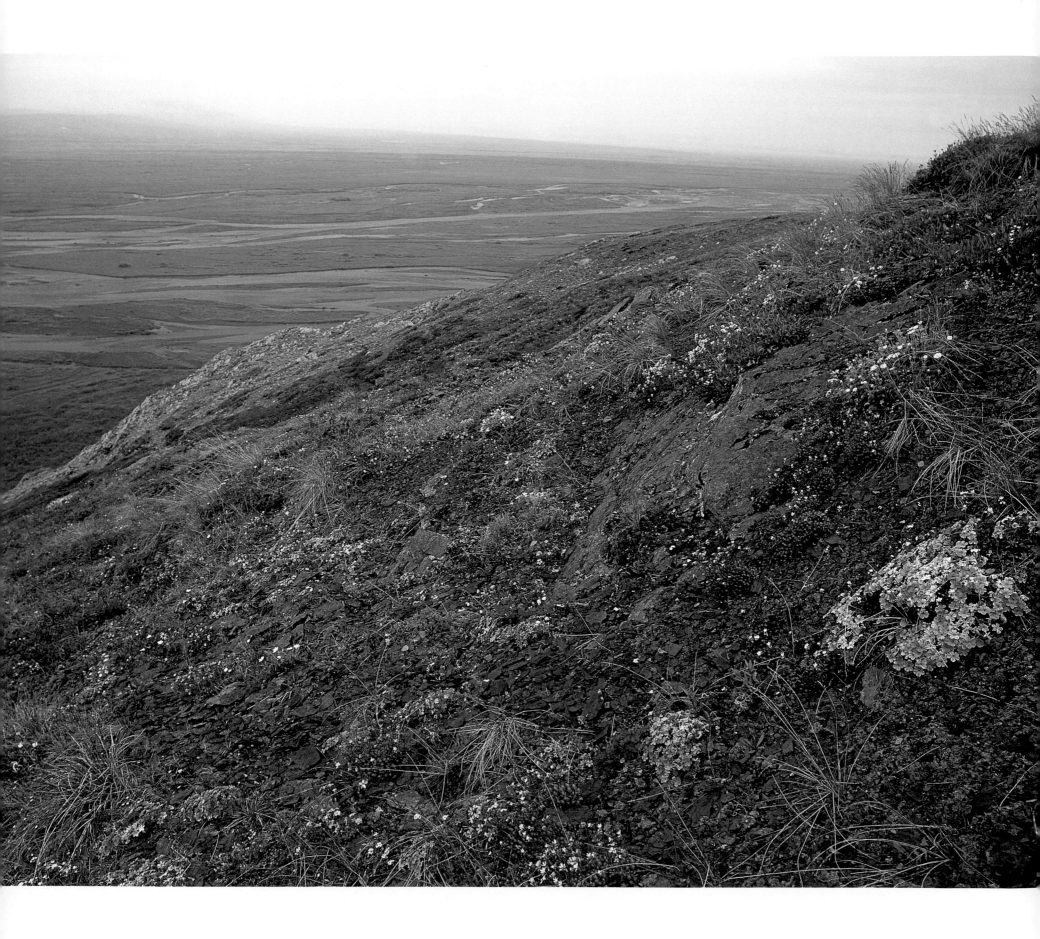

PREFACE

The story of how I came to meet Subhankar Banerjee and be captivated by his vision is one that everyone involved in this project has experienced.

Busy, over-committed, demanding lives were interrupted by phone calls from Subhankar asking for "just a half hour of time" to talk about "an exciting project." He politely challenged efforts to pass him off, or to have him put something in the mail or call back in six months. Eventually, we relented—perhaps because of conscience, or an inability to disappoint—or perhaps because we heard something in his voice that hinted at what we all eventually became passionately involved in.

During my first meeting with Subhankar, I asked him to summarize the ultimate goal that he wanted to achieve with the publication of his book. After a moment's reflection, he replied, "I want to see official, permanent wilderness designation for the coastal plain of the Arctic National Wildlife Refuge." I was impressed by the purity of his selfless vision; I could tell he was sincere.

When he told me of the impressive line-up of writers and environmentalists he had contacted who had verbally agreed to write essays for the book, I asked him why he thought The Mountaineers Books was the right publisher for his project.

Subhankar said he had taken part in The Mountaineers Club photography class and was first published in the organization's membership magazine. The Mountaineers Foundation (among others noted in the sponsorship page) provided funds in support of his travels to the refuge. Subsequently the foundation also provided a generous grant that helped us produce this book on a compressed schedule and that offset costs to make the book financially accessible. "The Mountaineers has supported me from day one. It is my dream to be published by The Mountaineers Books," Subhankar said.

I was standing before someone with no prior publication experience, with an exquisite but small and incomplete collection of images, and only his word that he had commitments from essayists who would provide the authoritative voice for his book. But somehow I knew from the way he told the stories as he showed me each of his images that it was his destiny to bring this off. I told him we were going to publish his book, and we needed to get down to work right away.

Subhankar returned to the Arctic and continued his photographic journey. As it turned out, not one of his contributors backed down from their initial commitment—even though they were on a very challenging schedule driven by an April 2003 exhibit of Subhankar's Arctic Refuge images at the Smithsonian National Museum of Natural History, and the unfolding political urgency to protect this land.

Arctic National Wildlife Refuge: Seasons of Life and Land partners Subhankar's extraordinary photographs with essays from the most articulate voices in the fields of natural history and the environment. Peter Matthiessen, one of the most eminent and lyrical nature writers in the world, reflects on his journey through the refuge with Subhankar, passionately defending the need to preserve this wilderness and the life it shelters. George Schaller, one of the world's foremost wildlife field biologists and a member of the groundbreaking 1956 Murie expedition that helped create the refuge, narrates its history, its biodiversity, and the original vision of the founders. Wildlife biologist Fran Mauer walks us across its magnificent expanse, noting the geological and geographical uniqueness of one of the world's last wild places. David Allen Sibley, the leading national expert in bird identification and behavior and a gifted painter, journeys through the region with Subhankar and explores the prolific bird life and migrations found there. William Meadows, a prominent conservationist and President of The Wilderness Society, writes about the political battles past and present to protect this fragile ecosystem. Debbie Miller, noted Arctic explorer and author, depicts the area's native cultures: the Inupiat Eskimos and the Gwich'in Athabascan Indians. The eloquent Terry Tempest Williams makes a plea for the protection of the refuge coastal plain in her poem "Wild Mercy." And in the foreword, President Jimmy Carter, 2002 Nobel Peace Prize winner, continues his longtime support in the battle to protect the refuge.

All of us who brought this book to life share the dream that many years from now, readers will look back on this classic work and be thankful that wiser heads prevailed to save this land. Do we have the courage to keep this grandeur of nature intact for future generations, or are we going to look for short-term profits and despoil it with industrial development? It is our collective goal to protect the web of life bound by the rhythm of the seasons and migrations of this remarkable land, captured symbolically by Subhankar Banerjee in the subtle shifting of light and the elegant curve of a wing.

HELEN CHERULLO
Publisher, The Mountaineers Books

Opposite • Summer wildflowers in bloom along the Kongakut River valley

jimmy carter

FOREWORD

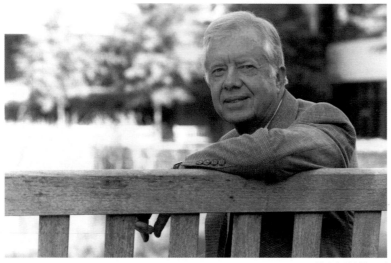

JIMMY CARTER, *the thirty-ninth president of the United States (1977-1981),*

advocated and signed the Alaska National Interest Lands Conservation Act of 1980. He

has consistently opposed drilling for oil in the Arctic National Wildlife Refuge as

fundamentally incompatible with wilderness. In 1982 he founded The Carter Center, a

nongovernmental organization guided by a commitment to human rights and the

alleviation of human suffering. Mr. Carter won the Nobel Peace Prize in 2002 for his

decades of effort in finding peaceful solutions to international conflicts, advancing

democracy and human rights, and promoting economic and social development. He is

the author of sixteen books and the recipient of numerous other awards, including the

highest awards of the National Wildlife Federation, The Wilderness Society, the National

Audubon Society, and the National Parks Conservation Association.

The Arctic National Wildlife Refuge stands alone as America's last truly great wilderness. This magnificent area is as vast as it is wild, from the windswept coastal plain where polar bears and caribou give birth, to the towering Brooks Range where Dall sheep cling to cliffs and wolves howl in the midnight sun.

More than a decade ago, Rosalynn and I had the fortunate opportunity to camp and hike in these regions of the Arctic Refuge. During bright July days, we walked along ancient caribou trails and studied the brilliant mosaic of wildflowers, mosses, and lichens that hugged the tundra. There was a timeless quality about this great land. As the never-setting sun circled above the horizon, we watched muskox, those shaggy survivors of the Ice Age, lumber along braided rivers that meander toward the Beaufort Sea.

One of the most unforgettable and humbling experiences of our lives occurred on the coastal plain. We had hoped to see caribou during our trip, but to our amazement, we witnessed the migration of tens of thousands of caribou with their newborn calves. In a matter of a few minutes, the sweep of tundra before us became flooded with life, with the sounds of grunting animals and clicking hooves filling the air. The dramatic procession of the Porcupine caribou herd was a once-in-a-lifetime wildlife spectacle. We understand firsthand why some have described this special birthplace as "America's Serengeti."

Standing on the coastal plain, I was saddened to think of the tragedy that might occur if this great wilderness was consumed by a web of roads and pipelines, drilling rigs and industrial facilities. Such proposed developments would forever destroy the wilderness character of America's only Arctic Refuge and disturb countless numbers of animals that depend on this northernmost terrestrial ecosystem.

The extraordinary wilderness and wildlife values of the Arctic Refuge have long been recognized by both Republican and Democratic presidents. In 1960, President Dwight D. Eisenhower established the original 8.9 million-acre Arctic National Wildlife Range to preserve its unique wildlife, wilderness, and recreational values. Twenty years later, I signed the Alaska National Interest Lands Conservation Act, monumental legislation that safeguarded more than 100 million acres of national parks, refuges, and forests in Alaska. This law specifically created the Arctic National Wildlife Refuge, doubled the size of the former range, and restricted development in areas that are clearly incompatible with oil exploration.

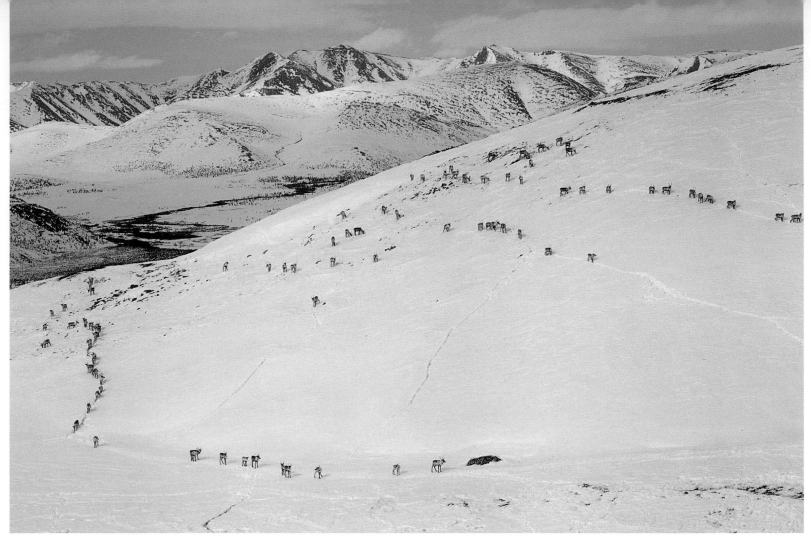

Pregnant porcupine caribou migrate over the Davidson Mountains on the way to the coastal plain.

Since I left office, there have been repeated proposals to open the Arctic Refuge coastal plain to oil drilling. Those attempts have failed because of tremendous opposition by the American people, including the Gwich'in Athabascan Indians of Alaska and Canada, indigenous people whose culture has depended on the Porcupine caribou herd for thousands of years. Having visited many aboriginal peoples around the world, I can empathize with the Gwich'in's struggle to safeguard one of their precious human rights.

We must look beyond the alleged benefits of a short-term economic gain and focus on what is really at stake. At best, the Arctic Refuge might provide 1 to 2 percent of the oil our country consumes each day. We can easily conserve more than that amount by driving more fuel-efficient vehicles. Instead of tearing open the heart of our greatest refuge, we should use our resources more wisely.

This stunning book reveals the greatness of the Arctic Refuge through all its seasons and moods. Subhankar Banerjee's dramatic photographs include summer pictures of the Porcupine caribou herd and some of the many migratory birds that fly to the refuge from six continents. A dedicated photographer, Banerjee spent twenty-nine days in his tent, braving blizzard conditions and minus forty-degree temperatures, to capture pictures of a mother polar bear and her cubs emerging from their winter den. His impassioned photographs of the landscape, wildlife, and indigenous peoples, coupled with insightful essays, give us a strong testament why the Arctic Refuge should always remain off-limits to industrialization.

There are few places on earth as wild and free as the Arctic Refuge. It is a symbol of our natural heritage, a remnant of frontier America that our first settlers once called wilderness. Little of that precious wilderness remains.

It will be a grand triumph for America if we can preserve the Arctic Refuge in its pure, untrammeled state. To leave this extraordinary land alone would be the greatest gift we could pass on to future generations.

Jimmy Carter

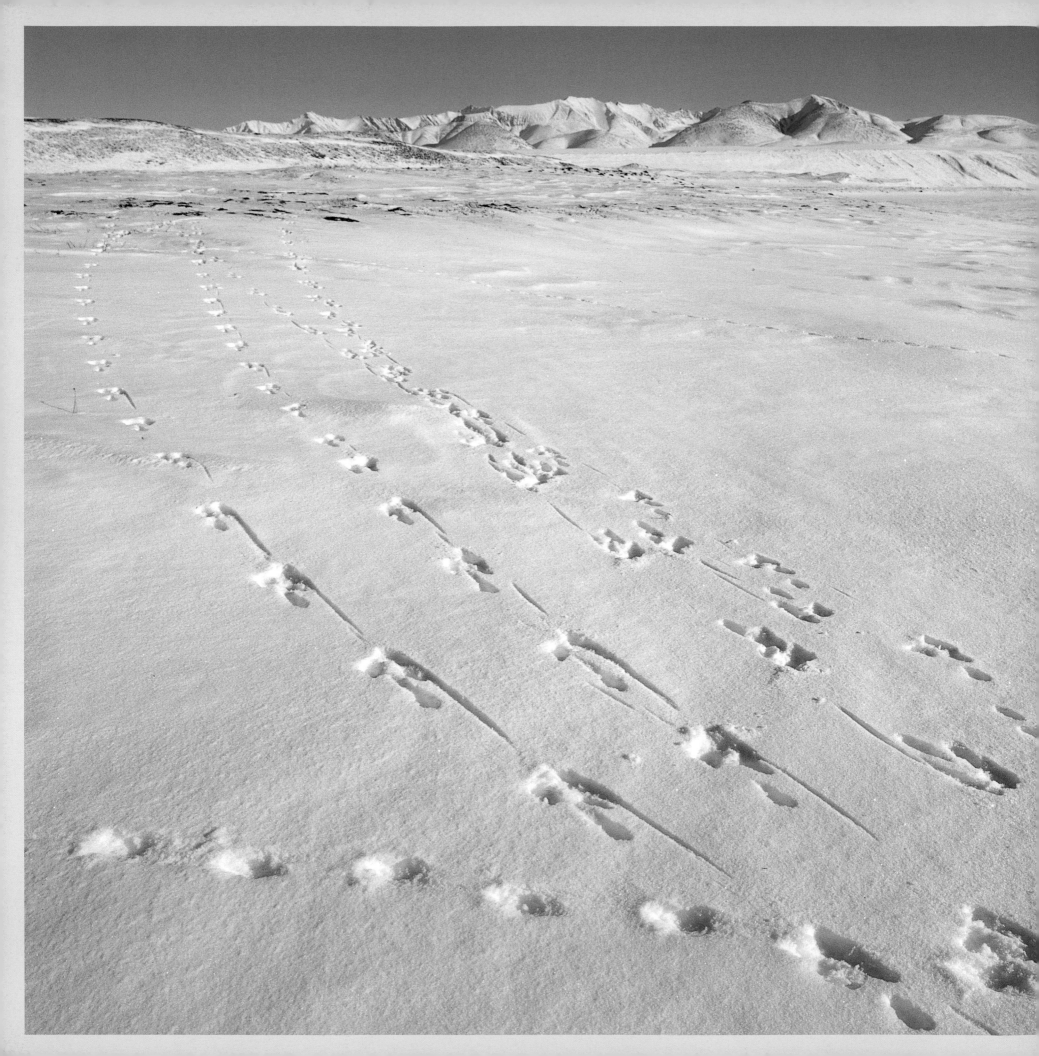

subhankar banerjee

INTRODUCTION

Only if we understand can we care.

Only if we care will we help.

Only if we help shall all be saved.

JANE GOODALL
Founder, The Jane Goodall Institute,
and United Nations Messenger of Peace

I n the far northeastern corner of Alaska lies an Arctic sanctuary, a precious jewel of the circumpolar north: the Arctic National Wildlife Refuge. Over a two-year period I had the remarkable opportunity of living in this vast wilderness. I observed and photographed breathtaking wildlife spectacles during all four seasons— a polar bear mother and her tiny cubs frolicking by their den, a newborn muskox baby walking with its herd, caribou calves born on the coastal plain, birds engaging in courtship and nesting, and large flocks of snow geese flying over the coastal plain. Beyond the abundant wildlife, the refuge has the most beautiful landscape I have ever seen and is so remote and untamed that many peaks, valleys, and lakes are still without names.

One summer evening in the refuge I sat meditating on a nameless hilltop, looking out at the braided Kongakut River valley and the mountains of the Brooks Range beyond, and found amidst its startling beauty a glimpse of hope and faith in the future of humanity. No matter how industrialized our nation gets, no matter how our resource needs change, I believe we will have the moral courage to keep places like the Arctic Refuge free of development so that future citizens of the world will continue to have the opportunity to meet nature in its wildest form. During my time in the Arctic I learned much about nature from my Native friends, the Gwich'in Athabascan Indians and the Inupiat Eskimos. They shared with me their way of life, their relationship to land and animals. They instilled in me their respect and reverence for nature and their resolve to coexist with the natural world instead of trying to conquer it.

I traveled to New York, Washington, D.C., Fairbanks, and other cities to share my stories and learn more about the Arctic Refuge, and I met many wonderful people who helped me. At some point, the dream of creating a book, weaving my images with authoritative voices that

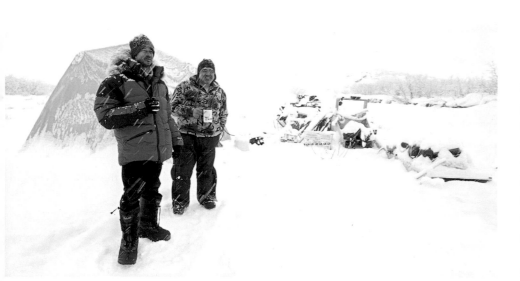

Subhankar Banerjee with Robert Thompson in the Hulahula River valley

Opposite • Wolverine and ptarmigan tracks in the Okpilak River valley

SUBHANKAR BANERJEE *is a freelance photographer specializing in wildlife, environmental, and cultural photography. Born in India in 1967, Banerjee received his bachelor's degree in engineering before moving to the United States where he obtained master's degrees in physics and computer science. Banerjee is the recipient of the Daniel Housberg Wilderness Image Award from the Alaska Conservation Foundation, and his images have appeared in* Outside *magazine and the publications of the National Audubon Society and The Wilderness Society. The Smithsonian National Museum of Natural History, Washington, D.C., has sponsored a solo exhibit of his Arctic Refuge images.*

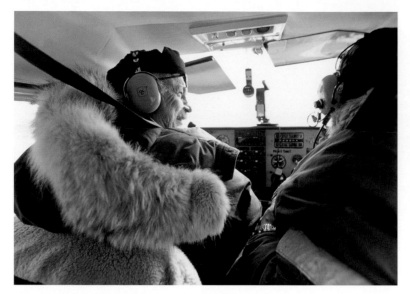

Legendary bush pilot Walt Audi inside his Cessna 206

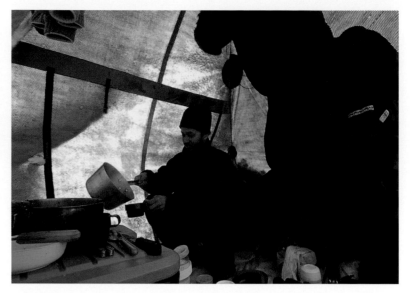

Waiting out a winter blizzard: Drying sleeping bags after thirteen days inside a tent
Photo by Robert Thompson

could best describe the story of this threatened and beautiful land, became my life's work.

My search for these voices brought me in contact with the essayists in this book. I spent time with Fran Mauer and Debbie Miller while at the refuge. I worked with William Meadows to support the 2001–2002 campaign as part of energy legislation to prevent oil drilling on the coastal plain. I met with George Schaller when I gave a presentation at the Wildlife Conservation Society in New York.

Both Peter Matthiessen and David Sibley joined me on two separate expeditions at the refuge. Their first-person accounts of their trips are included in this book.

Based on my work with the Alaska Wilderness League, President Jimmy Carter, an ardent supporter of the protection of the refuge, agreed to write the foreword, and Terry Tempest Williams gave me permission to use her powerful poem about the refuge, "Wild Mercy."

Through images and insightful essays, *Arctic National Wildlife Refuge: Seasons of Life and Land* presents a complete year-round cycle of the landscape, animals, plants, birds, and indigenous peoples of the Arctic National Wildlife Refuge. I have also included eight short stories about my time in the field. My experiences in the refuge were so amazing I wanted to share them with my readers, so they might feel what I felt, see what I saw, as if they were standing right next to me.

The images in the book flow through the seasons, beginning in winter, continuing through the abbreviated yet tremendously prolific spring–summer–autumn, and ending in winter again. The proponents of oil drilling have said that the coastal plain of the refuge is "white and barren;

void of any life" for nine months of the year. This perception exists perhaps because few people have traveled to the refuge outside of the short spring and summer seasons. During the harsh winter months, when the temperature drops to minus forty degrees F or lower, not only does life thrive there, but new life is born. Some of my most powerful photographs were taken during the winter months in the refuge.

The driving forces in my life are my photography and my passion for preserving the refuge, but you might be wondering how a young man from Calcutta ended up taking photographs during Arctic blizzards. The best answer I can give is that, in my life, there are no straight lines. Just as my Inupiat guide, Robert Thompson, and I wandered spontaneously across Alaska's North Slope to find and photograph wildlife and landscapes, the way I arrived in Alaska was by a route I never could have imagined.

But how did I arrive here? I had a grand-uncle who was a well-known painter, and his work inspired the artist in me. Science was the track I followed in school, but my interest in images never went away. I went to New Mexico to pursue graduate studies, and New Mexico worked its magic on me. In India I was a city boy; in the American Southwest I was drawn irresistibly to the wide-open spaces. I joined the Sierra Club and soon found myself hiking frequently in New Mexico's mountains. Nature was now my classroom, and my new path was capturing images of wild things on film. I started with a simple Minolta 35mm SLR camera, taking snapshots. I didn't know it at the time, but a seed had been planted that would change my life. A job at Boeing brought me to Seattle, but really it was the mountain landscape

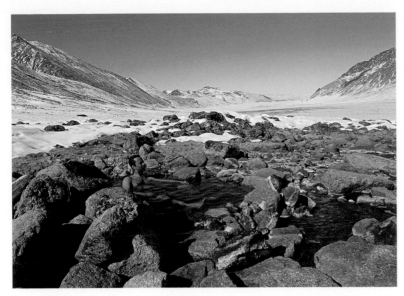

Subhankar Banerjee in a hotspring in Okpilak River valley *Photo by Robert Thompson*

near the city that attracted me to the Northwest. At this point, the idea of switching my career to documenting endangered landscapes and threatened habitats and cultures was spinning around in my head, but it wasn't until 2000 that I took the plunge.

Wild areas, from Florida to the Canadian Rockies, made up my aimless itinerary. Then, while traveling with friends, I saw the polar bears near Churchill in Manitoba, Canada—an arresting moment. But I also saw too many people, each scrambling for pictures.

My entire being became galvanized with the desire to witness polar bears in a wild landscape untrammeled by tourism or industry. Various associates advised me to visit the Arctic National Wildlife Refuge in Alaska. At the time I had no idea how I could meet the daunting costs of working in Alaska on my own. I thought, "It is just a dream." In time, though, my sense of inner necessity became the mother of invention, and I cobbled together initial funds by paring down my expenses in Seattle and by taking on debts that I realized were necessary to complete my project. Later, as my commitment grew, I was able to find some support from organizations, foundations, and individuals, which kept the project alive. At the beginning, though, it was a giant leap of faith.

What is the difference between serendipity and fate? I'm still uncertain, but when I read a 1986 U.S. Fish and Wildlife Service baseline report about wildlife in the Arctic National Wildlife Refuge, I was stunned by the biodiversity of the refuge and how little had been documented photographically. I was inspired by what I read and dreamed of doing a year-round exploration and documentation of the refuge, but roaming the backcountry on my own was obviously out of the question. I wouldn't know where to look; I might not know what I was seeing; and I certainly would not know how to cope with the elements, particularly in winter—which is most of the year. Remember, I'm from Calcutta! Clearly, I needed a guide.

There is an old saying, "When the student is ready, the teacher appears." Robert Thompson, an Inupiat guide, had worked for years with Fish and Wildlife Service biologists. We clicked right from the beginning, even on the telephone. Robert knows the legendary Walt Audi, bush pilot since 1965, and that answered the question of how to get out to the wildest places. March 19, 2001, I arrived in Kaktovik, Robert's village on the northern coast of the Alaskan Arctic. It was the coldest day of the year, minus forty degrees F. I couldn't help thinking, "When is the next plane out of here?" I feared that my enthusiasm had finally gotten me in over my head; freezing to death seemed like a real possibility. With reassurances from Robert and his wife, Jane, I took one baby step at a time and eventually learned to live and work in the Arctic icebox. Much of my time was spent on the north side of the refuge, with Kaktovik as my home base. I learned about and documented Inupiat cultural activities, including the sacred whale hunt. The Inupiat people depend on the bowhead whale for food, and their culture primarily depends on marine life.

I also wanted to learn about the Gwich'in people, who depend on the Porcupine caribou herd for food, clothing, and their cultural identity. I spent time at Arctic Village, a remote Gwich'in village nestled by the bank of the East Fork of the Chandalar River, just outside the southern boundary of the refuge. Charlie Swaney and Jimi John, two of the most active Gwich'in hunters from Arctic Village, graciously took me with them on hunting trips to learn about the Gwich'in way of life, while Sarah James, village chief Evon Peter, traditional chief Trimble Gilbert, Gideon James, Marion Swaney, Lillian Garnette, and others at the village generously shared stories and food with me.

From my childhood in Calcutta to the moment of this book's birth, there was no direct route. Like the zigzag path across the frozen Alaskan landscape that Robert and I followed, I have turned many corners to find innumerable surprises en route. There were times when I was sure I would freeze to death until another cup of hot coffee revived me, times when there was no money and only the richness of fellowship could buy us sufficient hope for another day's work. At those times I took my inspiration from nature itself, from my Native Alaskan friends, and from my abiding sense that, however I got there, the Arctic Refuge had become one of my homes. The privilege of working at the refuge has no price tag, and my book is the best way I have of saying thank you to my Gwich'in and Inupiat friends, to my supporters, to the animals, the plants, the landscape, and the unforgettable Alaskan light.

Subhankar Banerjee

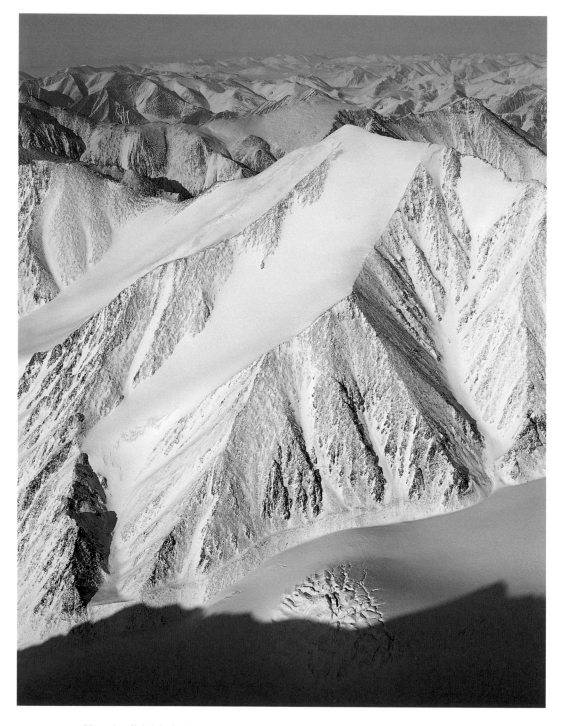

Mount Isto (9,050 feet), the highest peak in the Brooks Range, with Arey Glacier in the foreground

Opposite • McCall Glacier has lost nearly thirty-three feet in depth over the past four decades. It is one of the most extensively studied glaciers in the circumpolar north for signs of climate change due to global warming.

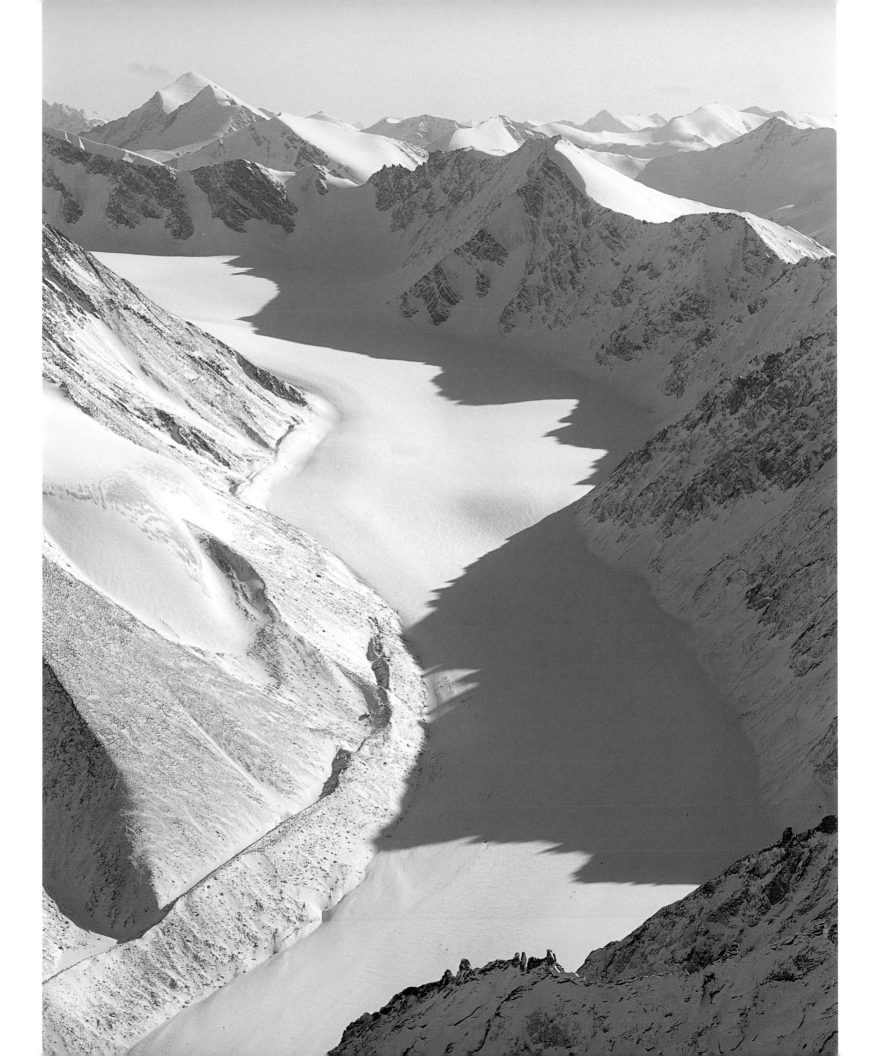

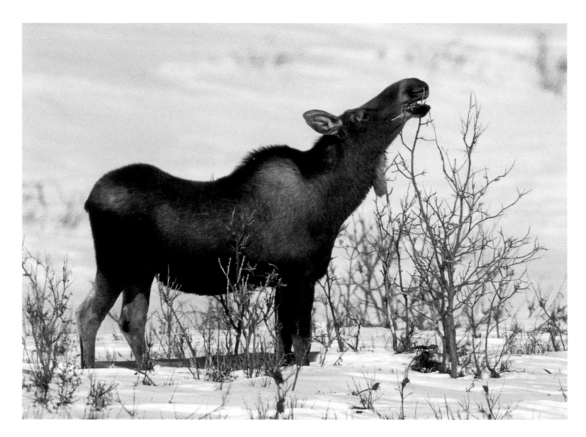

A moose feeds on a willow patch in the Okpilak River valley. In Inupiaq, the language of the Inupiats, Okpilak means "River with no Willows." Scientists say that one of the visible signs of climate change impacts due to global warming is that treelines, especially willow and dwarf birch, are moving north at a rapid pace not seen in the last 8,000 years. According to documents of European travelers in the early 1900s, there was little or no evidence of moose on the North Slope of the Brooks Range. Locals began reporting moose in the 1940s and 1950s. The moose on the Arctic Refuge coastal plain are the northernmost moose in North America.

Opposite • Moose along Karen Creek; Mount Chamberlin, the second-highest peak in the Brooks Range (9,020 feet), dominates the background. Snow is rarely deep on the North Slope of the Arctic Refuge. Windblown ridges with exposed vegetation, combined with dwarf willows, provide food during harsh winter months for a wide variety of wildlife, including moose, muskox, ptarmigans, and porcupine.

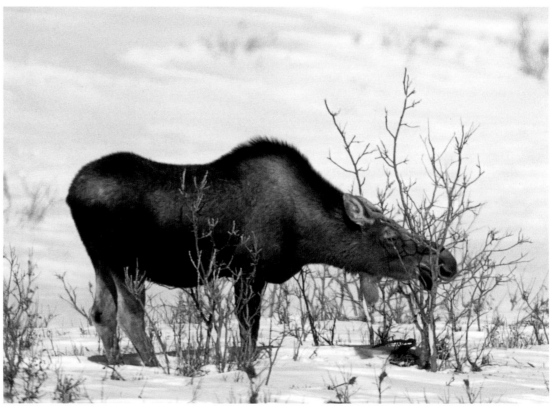

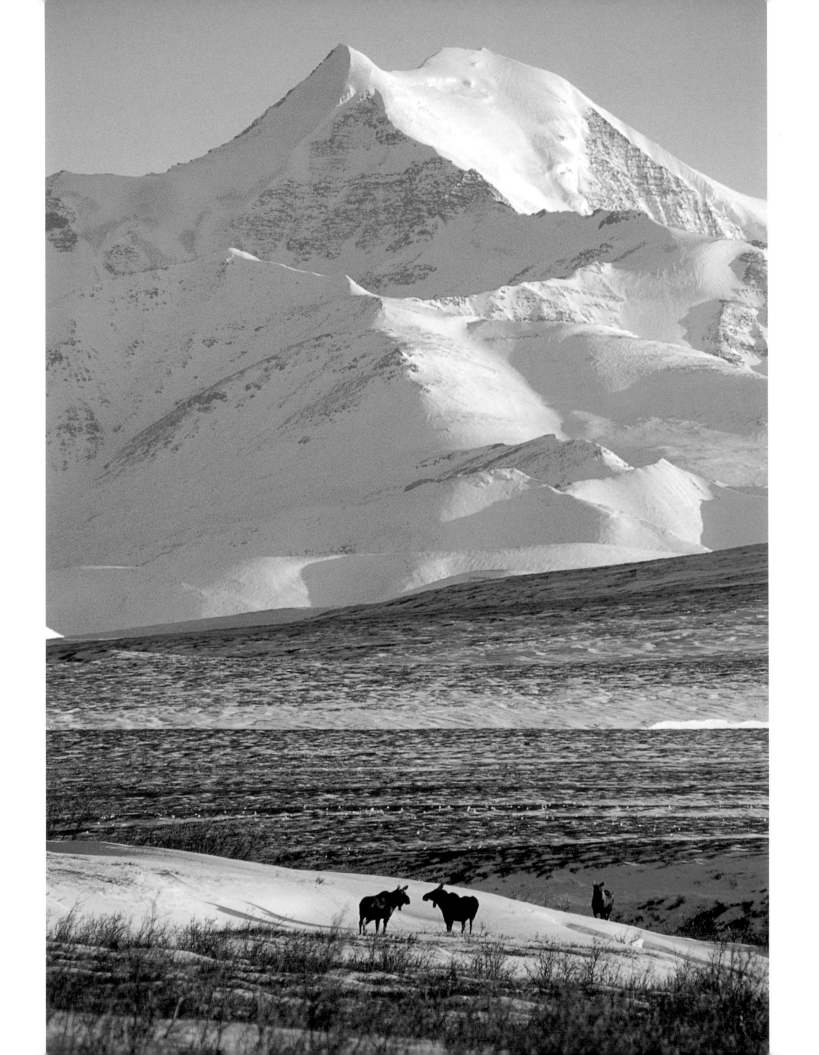

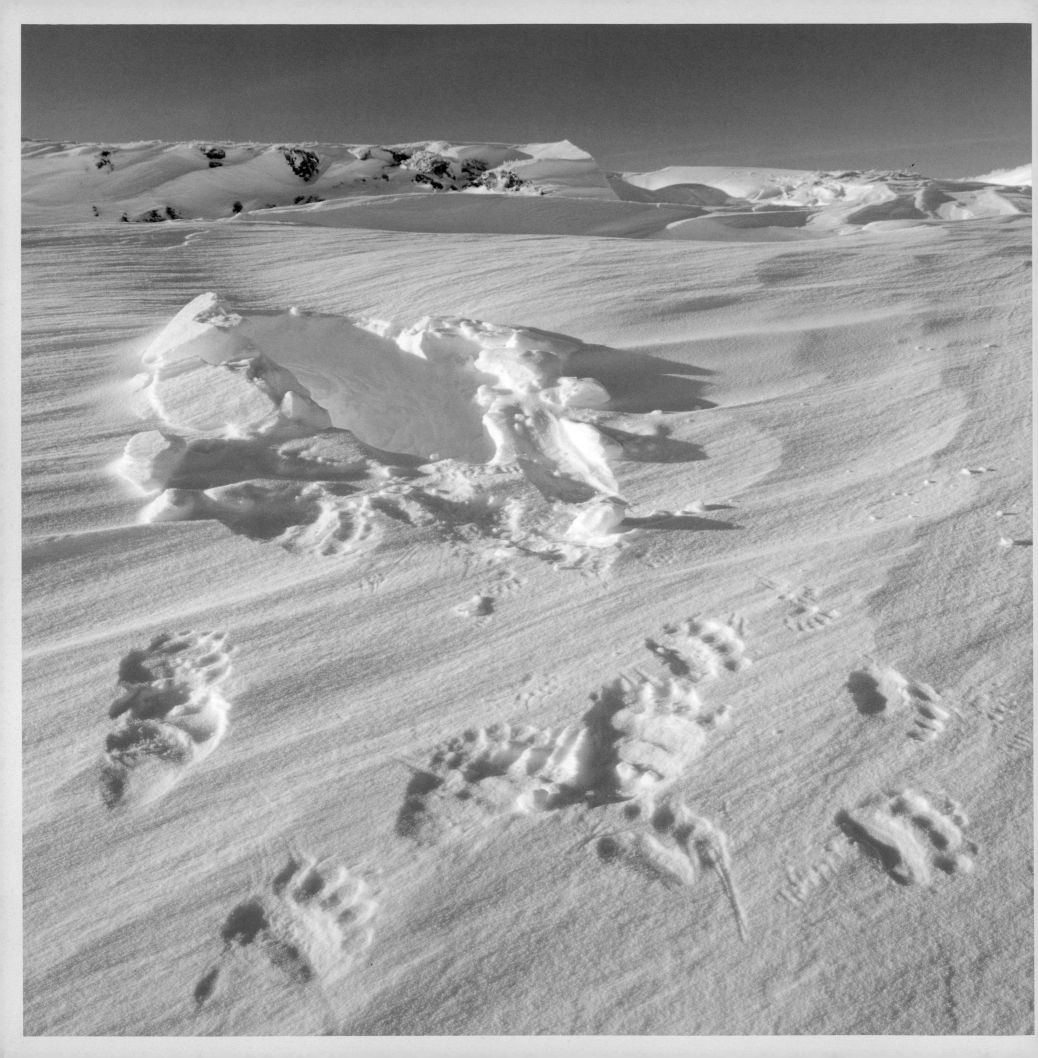

Coastal Plain: Home of the Ice Bear

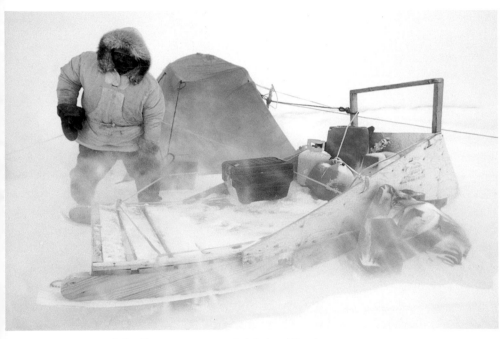

Robert Thompson secures our tent during a blizzard.

Opposite • Polar bear den with tracks of mother and cubs

March 23, 2002: Robert Thompson and I leave Kaktovik heading for the Canning River delta. It is not a particularly favorable day to travel. The temperature is minus thirty-five degrees F, with the wind blowing twenty-five miles an hour. We finally reach the delta after eight hours on snowmobiles in blizzard conditions. We struggle to set up our tent in the strong wind. Inside the tent we start our stove and I warm my feet. An hour later blood starts flowing in my veins and I realize I have just saved my toes from frostbite.

The next morning Robert and I walk to Brownlow Point, a bank on the Canning River that allows snowdrifts to form readily, providing suitable den locations for polar bears. It is a cold but calm day. Around ten thirty I spot a polar bear walking on the bank with two tiny cubs following right behind her. I am mesmerized at the sight: For the next half hour the bear and her cubs play on the bank—running, nuzzling, sharing moments of affection—before returning to their den.

That evening the blizzard picks up again, with strong winds blowing snow across the flat delta. The next day we find the den covered with snow, with no visible tracks to tell us whether the bears have already left the den for the sea ice.

For the next twenty-nine days, Robert and I camp out on the delta in the hope of seeing the bears again, with one break to resupply our food and fuel. In the nearly month-long excursion we have four calm days, the winds gusting to sixty miles an hour and temperatures sometimes dropping to nearly minus forty degrees F, at times driving the wind-chill below the bottom of the chart, at minus 100 degrees F. We wait and watch from behind a blind we have built of snow and ice so as to not disturb the bears during this sensitive time.

Much of our time is spent in our tent, waiting for the weather to change. Robert, an extremely thoughtful man, shares his stories of hunting, his views on the environment, his worries about global warming. There is always a certain level of anxiety and excitement as we wait: Is our tent going to cave in? If it does, what will we do? During a blizzard it is not possible to cook, and we subsist on ready-to-eat meals—so, of course, we spend a lot of time talking about gourmet food. The days pass quite wonderfully.

We never see the bears again. We do not know when they left the den; it was impossible to look for footprints in such strong blizzards. But that one day of viewing the bear and her cubs play on the snowbank of the Canning River delta made all those blizzardy days seem worthwhile. It was truly the wildest scene I witnessed during my stay at the refuge.

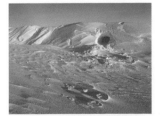

—S.B.

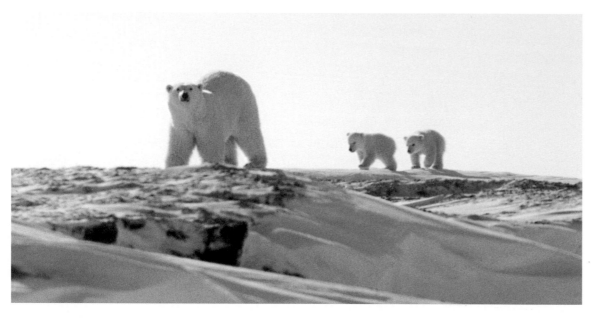

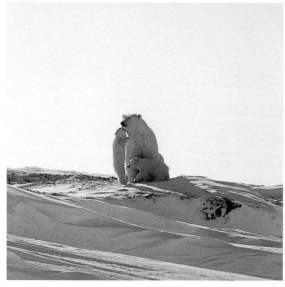 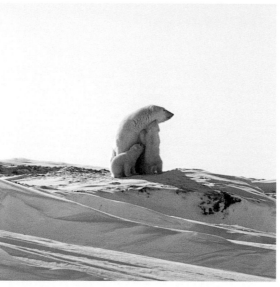 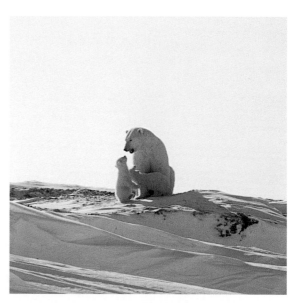

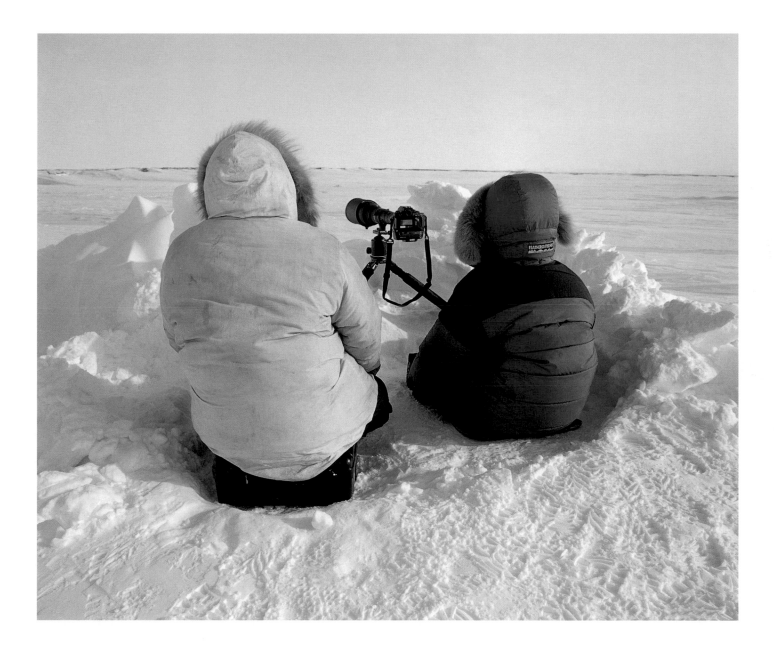

Subhankar Banerjee and Robert Thompson wait behind a snow blind, Canning River delta.

Opposite • Polar bear mother and cubs spend time outside the den before heading to the sea. The pregnant bears dig their dens in November, then give birth usually to one or two tiny cubs in December or January. The mothers nurse and care for the young at the den until March or early April.

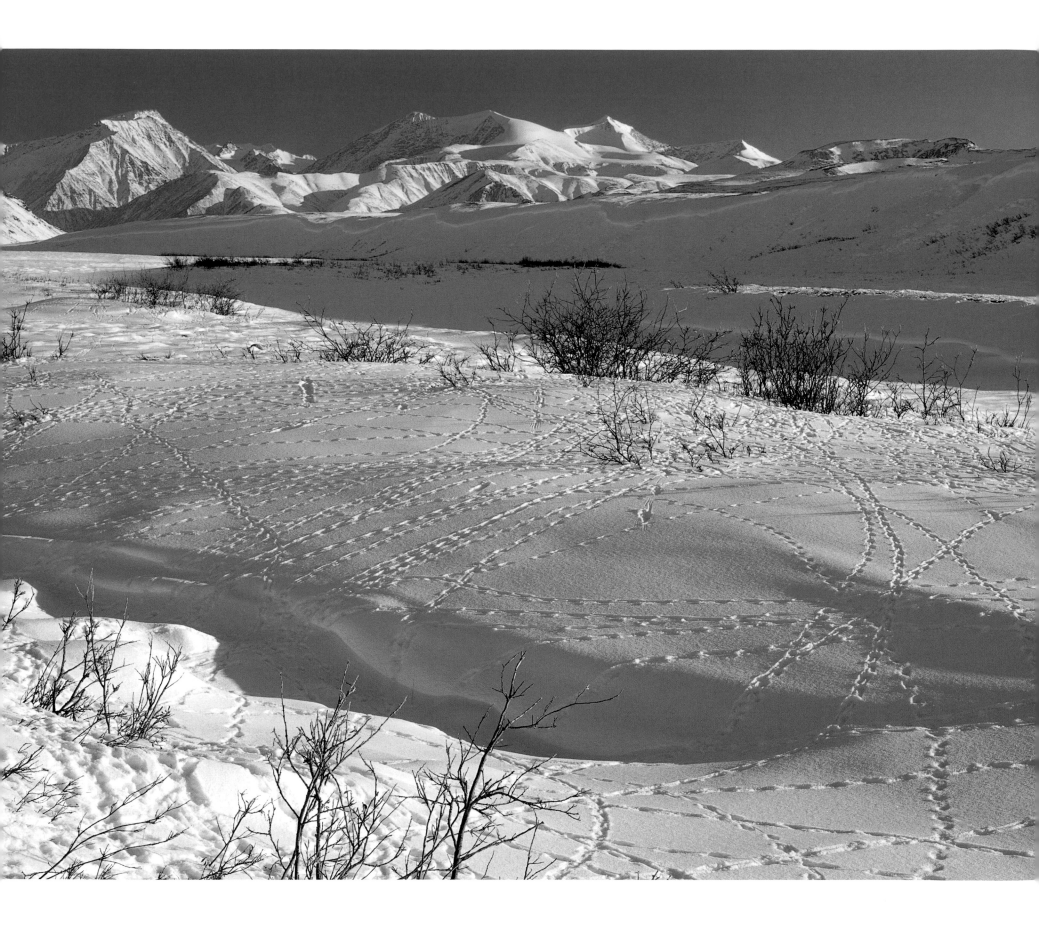

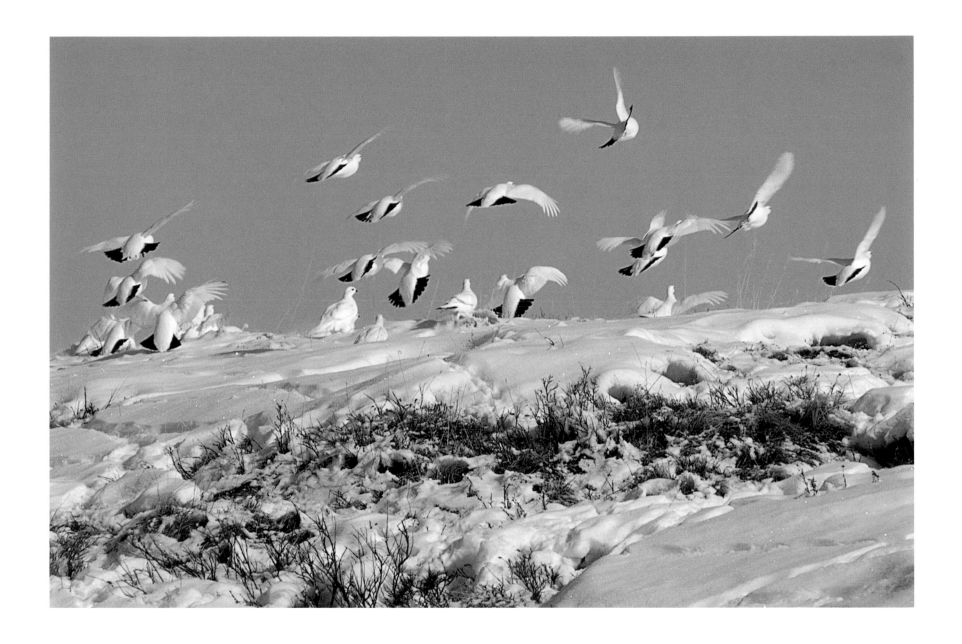

Willow ptarmigan along the Hulahula River valley

Opposite • Signs of life: Ptarmigan tracks in the Okpilak River valley, Mount Michelson and Romanzof Mountains in the background

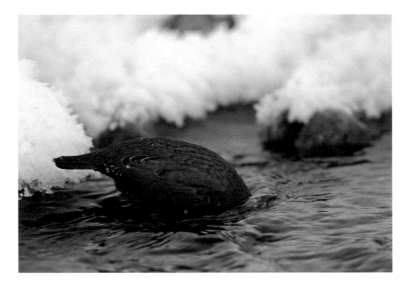

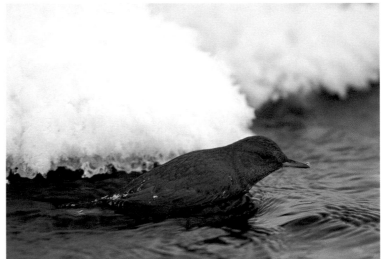

The greatest surprise I had in the Arctic Refuge was when I saw this tiny songbird, an American dipper, feed on the open waters of the Hulahula River on a very cold, early November morning. There was no direct light available; the sun would rise and skirt behind the Brooks Range, providing diffused, indirect lighting. Robert told me he had seen these small birds dip and feed on open waters during winter hunting trips. I was skeptical; how could such a thing happen in such unimaginable cold? But I soon found out that even when the air temperature drops to minus fifty degrees F, where there are deep underground sources the water temperature remains near forty degrees F, providing open water for feeding opportunities for this bird.

Big predator species such as the polar bear and wolf signify the biological health of an ecosystem. To me, in such a harsh environment, tiny life such as the dipper signifies a different kind of health of an ecosystem, the "spiritual health."

Opposite • Hulahula River valley and the Romanzof Mountains

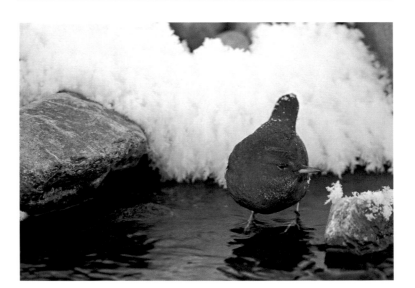

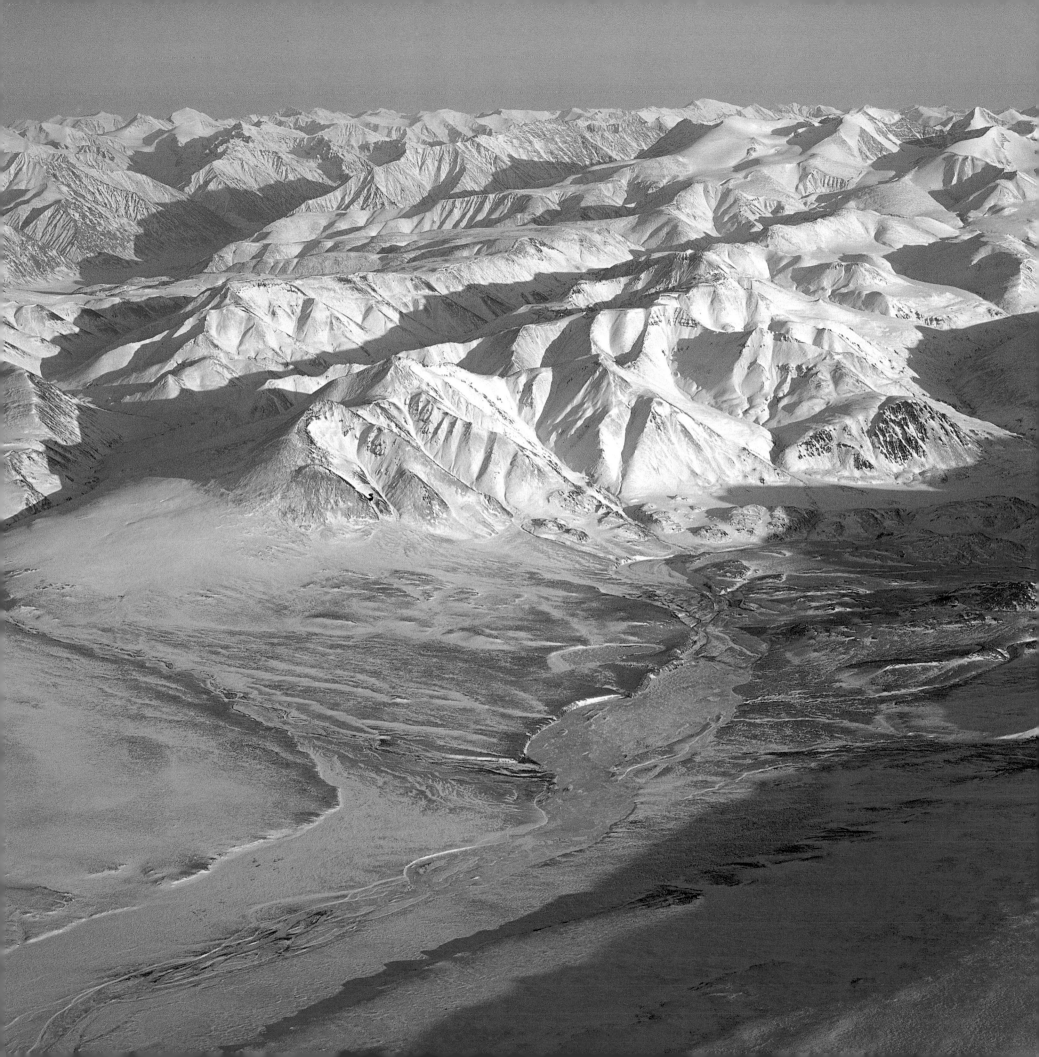

Muskox: Relics of the Pleistocene Era

May 5, 2001: We are traveling along the Canning River when Robert spots a track of a little animal alongside the track of a big one. I jump with joy as we conclude it is an adult muskoxen with a newborn calf. From the tracks we determine they are moving north, and within three miles the herd comes into view. There are fourteen adults and a baby that seems to be only a day or two old. We observed their "march to the coastal plain" for eight hours until the sun falls below the horizon, casting a deep golden glow across the overflow water of the Canning River.

The next day we find the remains of the afterbirth of a newborn muskox. We pick up some tracks heading eastward and follow them to where the track makes a sharp turn north. This track is joined by fresh grizzly tracks from the east. Soon we find small chunks of fresh meat and blood. I am sad, thinking that the grizzly has killed the baby muskox.

Robert examines the tracks carefully and concludes that it isn't our herd; there are only six animals in this bunch. I am skeptical, but we follow Robert's intuition and head west again, back toward the Canning River. Unfortunately, the wind picks up and soon we are right in the middle of a strong blizzard. We stop and struggle to set up a makeshift camp.

May 8: We stay inside our tent nearly sixteen hours, until the blizzard passes. When we finally come out, the sky is clear with a deep arctic-blue hue, and we are soon back on the trail again. Naturally, the blizzard has wiped out the animal tracks. After nearly eighteen miles Robert spots a herd of muskox in the far distance. We set up camp about two miles north of them. When we saw them two days earlier they were on a constant move, but here on the coastal plain they look at peace and in no rush to go anywhere. Through binoculars we can see the animals: The herd is intact, fourteen adults and one baby. The next morning as I sip hot coffee, the herd grazes peacefully in the distance. By the time we finish breakfast and leave camp to photograph them, they have gone to sleep. They are spread out nicely and sleeping in any old way. They sleep for about five hours, and we watch them from behind a mound of snow.

We return to camp that evening for supper, and a few hours later we go back and find them grazing. A thin ice fog moves in, shrouding the coastal plain. The sky is deep pink and the large yellow ball of the midnight sun looms over the herd. At this moment, I have the same feeling Aldo Leopold describes when he writes about flocks of sandhill cranes flying overhead in *A Sand County Almanac:* "We and they had found a common home in the remote vastness of space and time; we were both back in the Pleistocene."

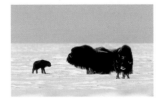

—S.B.

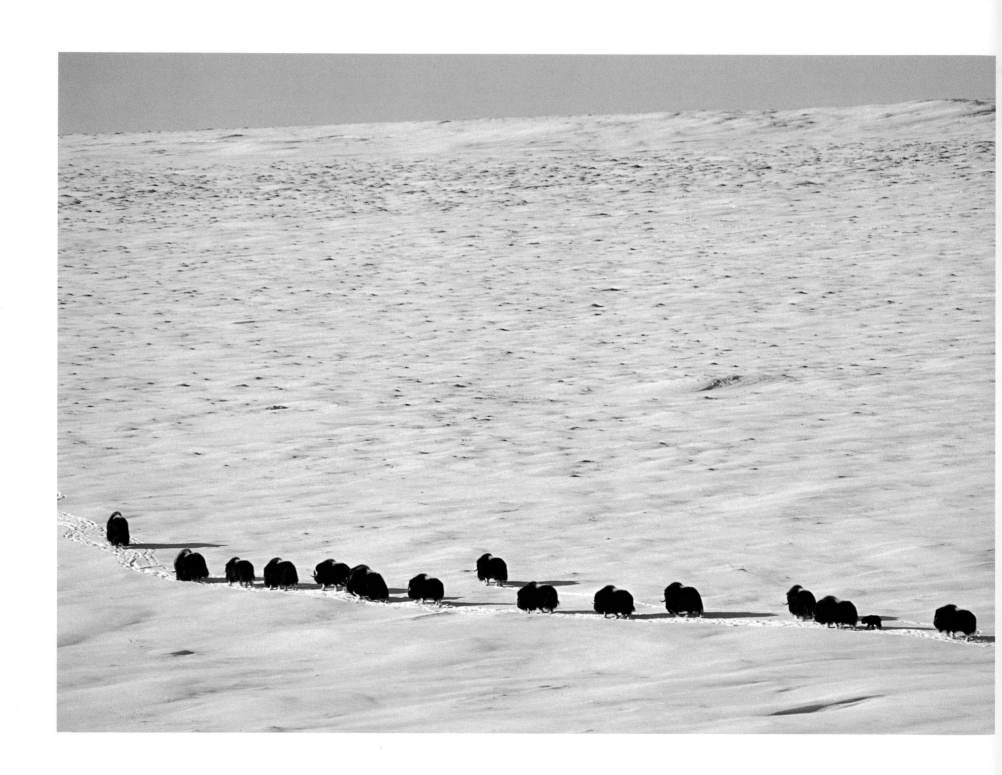

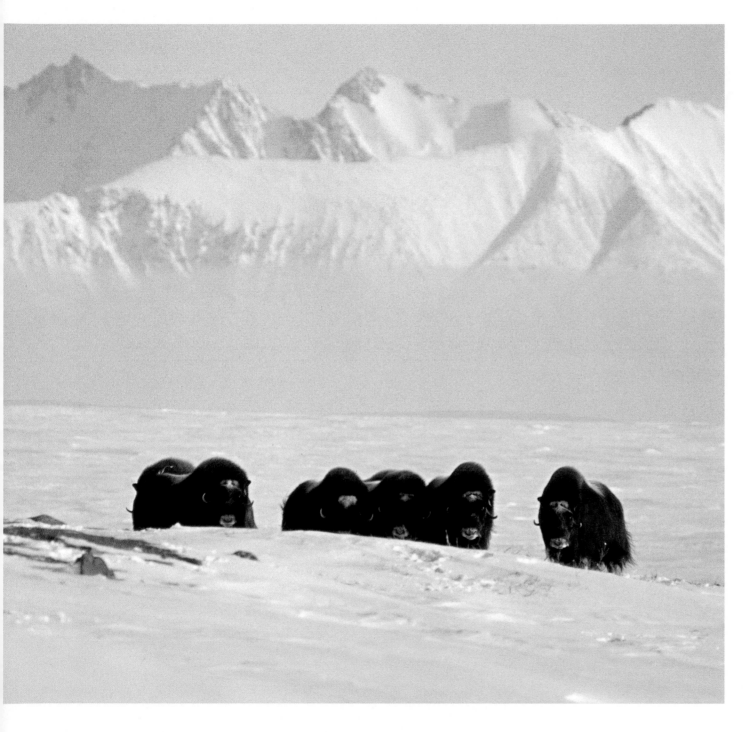

Muskox herd on foothills along the Hulahula River; Romanzof Mountains in the background. The muskox population is on a decline in the refuge, due to low calf production and grizzly predation. During the past several years, the coastal plain experienced deeper snow and a later spring thaw than usual, a phenomenon scientists believe is the result of the impact of climate change due to global warming. The deep snow has severely impacted several species at the refuge, of which the most notable are the caribou and the muskox. When the snow is deep on the coastal plain, muskox find it difficult to forage for food and move to the foothills, where they can feed on willow twigs and other growth on the windblown ridges. However, during calving time (mid-April to mid-May) they are more vulnerable to grizzly predation in the foothill areas and must go to the coastal plain to protect their calves.

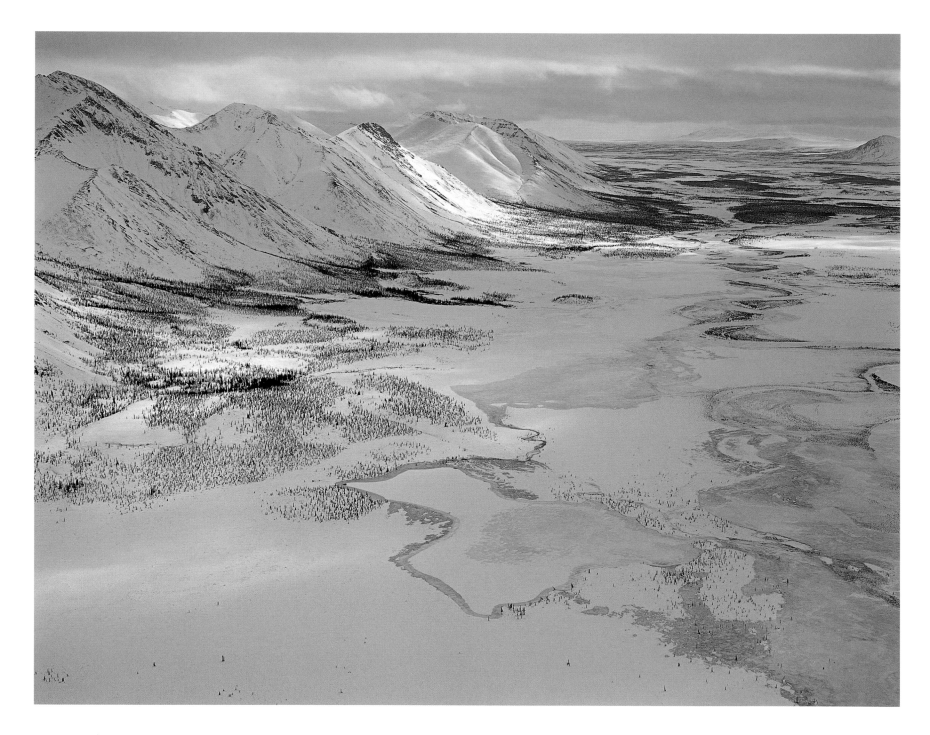

Sheenjek River valley: One of three designated Wild rivers in the Arctic Refuge. In 1956, Olaus and Mardy Murie led the first biological expedition in the refuge along the Sheenjek River.

Opposite • Double Mountain in the Sheenjek River valley: The blue ice in the foreground is *aufeis*, a unique phenomenon that occurs in winter in the Arctic when overflow water freezes again and again, forming layer upon layer of ice. These deep layers of ice are often the last to melt in summer.

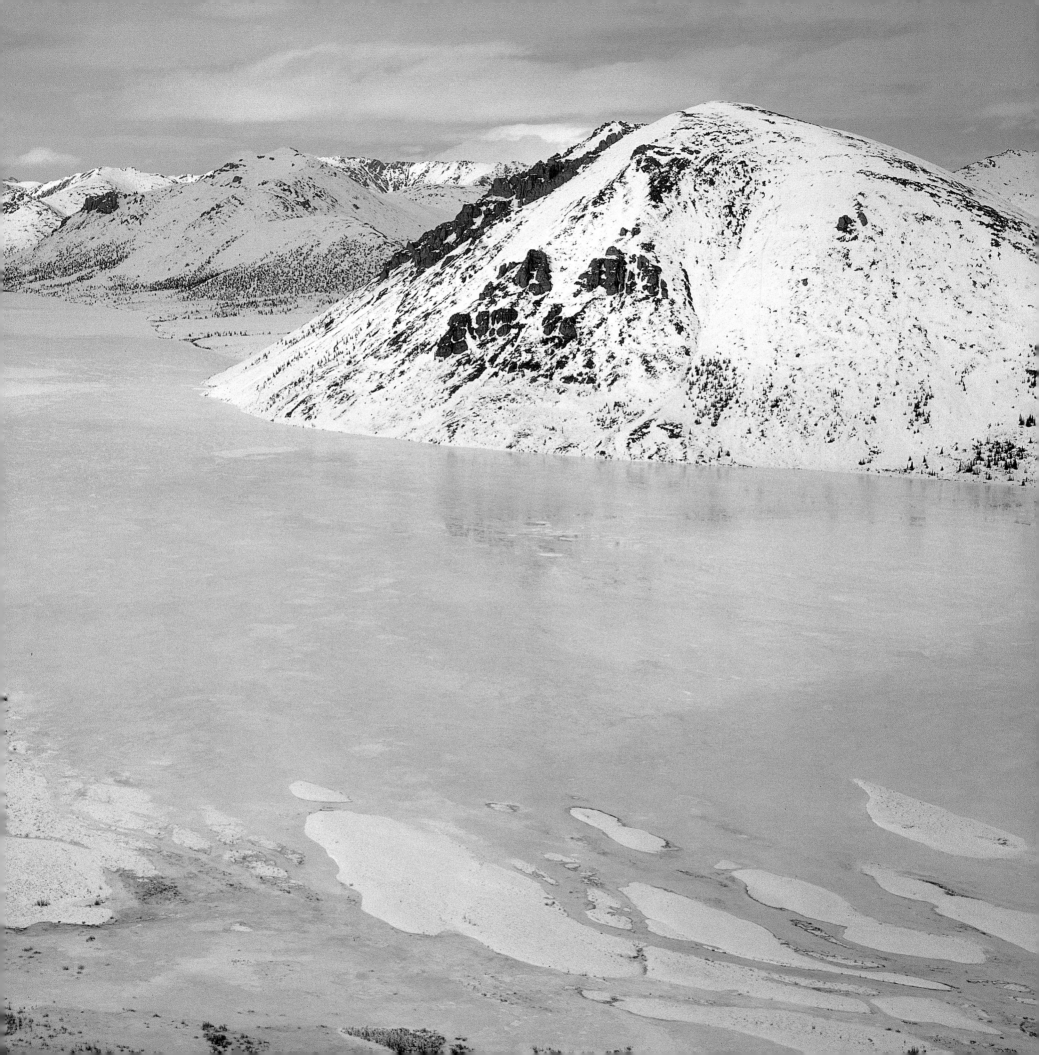

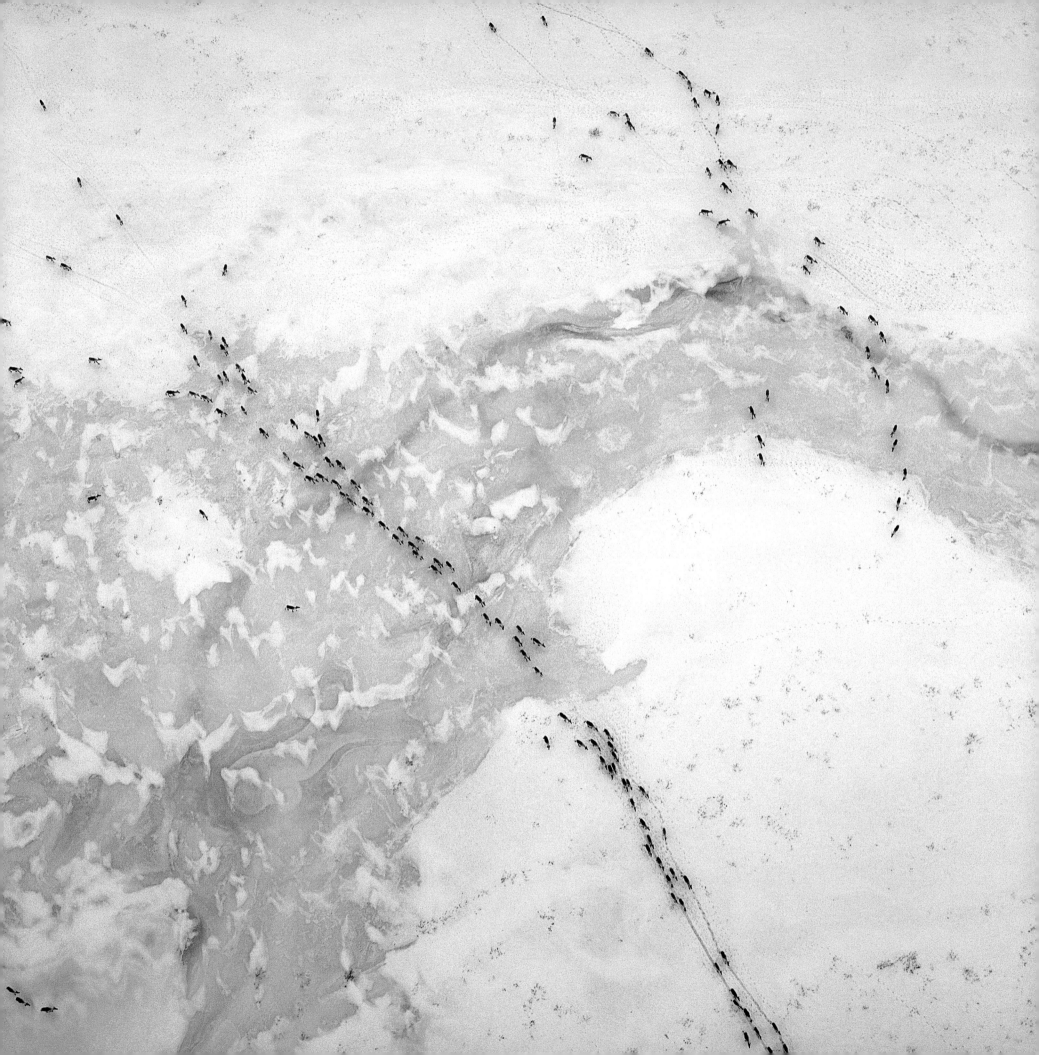

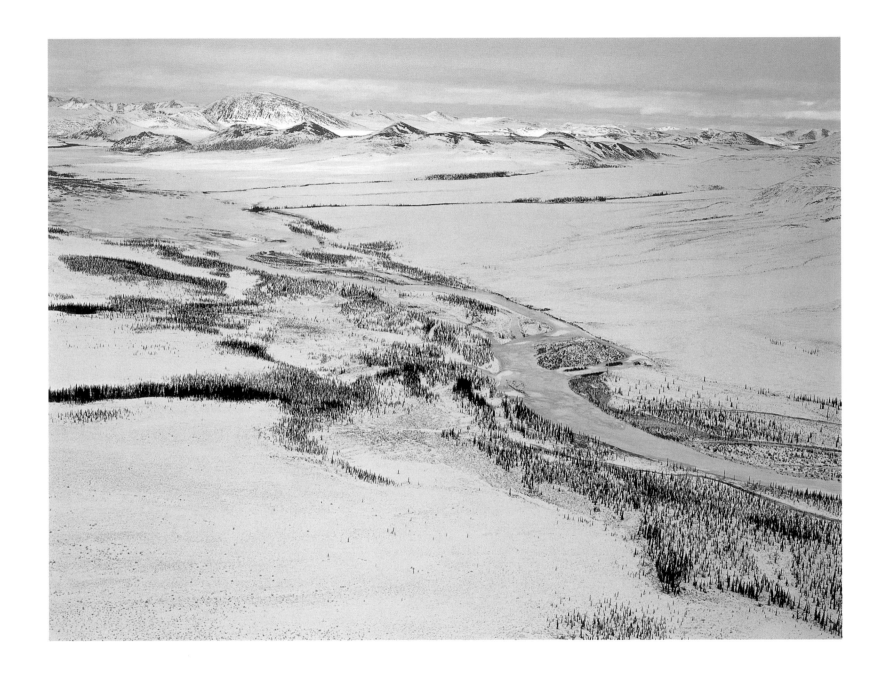

Coleen River valley and the Davidson Mountains

Opposite • Pregnant porcupine caribou migrate across frozen Coleen River. The caribou form long lines and move with a sense of purpose and determination to reach the coastal plain in time to calve.

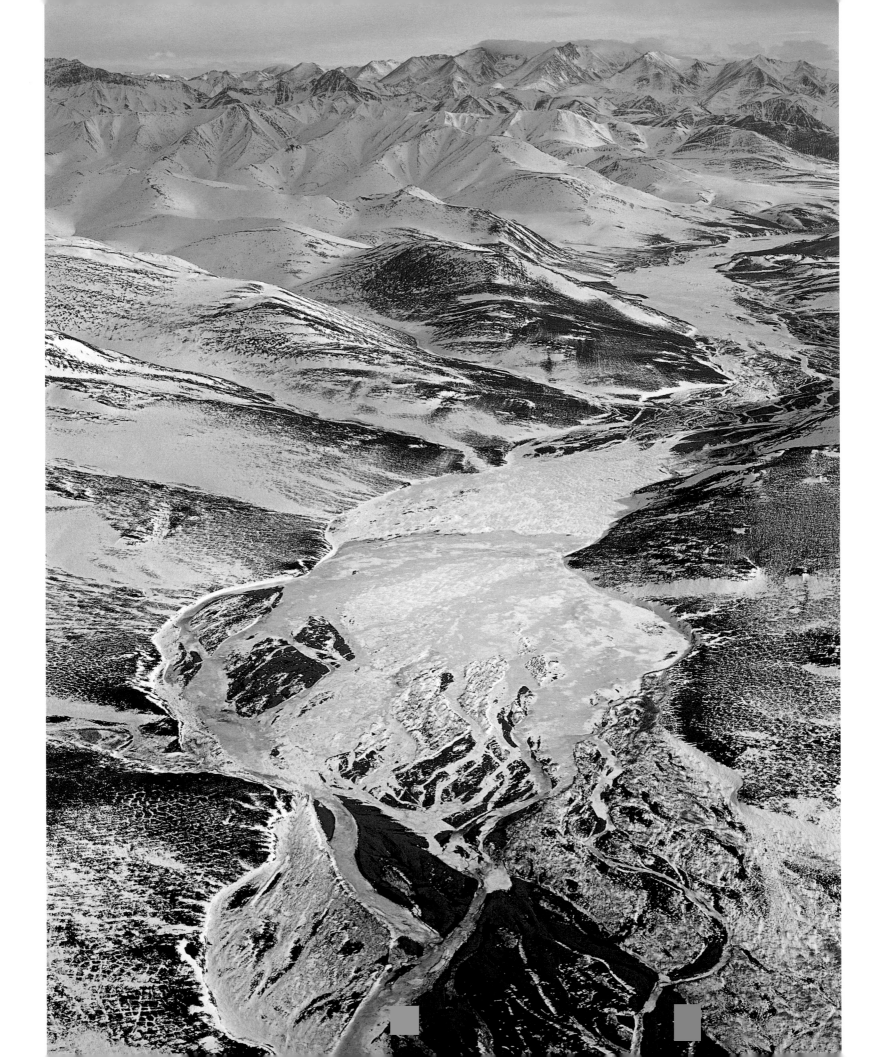

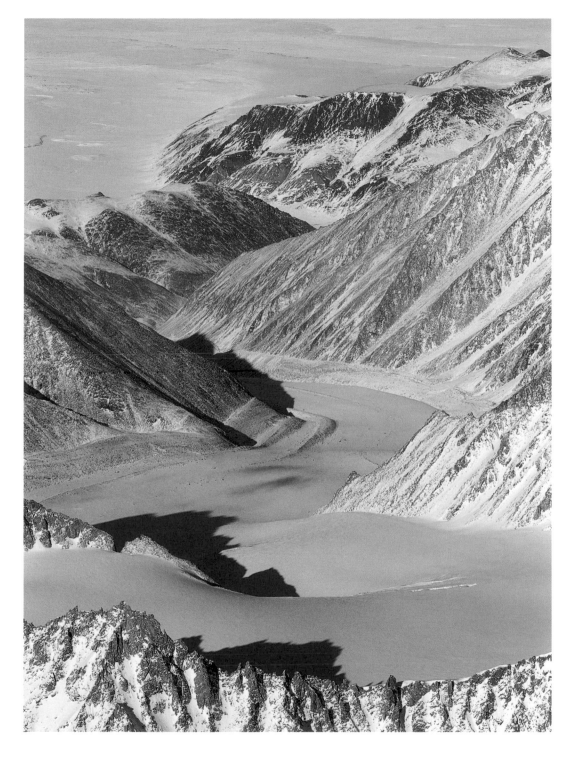

Romanzof Mountains

Opposite • Kongakut River valley and the British Mountains

peter matthiessen

IN THE GREAT COUNTRY

More important, to my mind, would be our having courage enough, in the face of all challenges, to protect this region for the sake of the land itself, and the wildlife it supports. . . . Will our society be wise enough to keep some of "The Great Country" empty of technology and full of life?

MARDY MURIE*

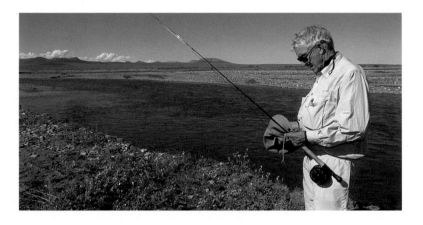

PETER MATTHIESSEN *is the acclaimed author of numerous works of fiction and nonfiction. His subjects include vanishing cultures, oppressed people, and endangered wildlife and landscapes, and his work is essentially based on his wilderness travels. His nonfiction books include* The Birds of Heaven: Travels With Cranes, Tigers in the Snow, The Tree Where Man Was Born, *which was nominated for the National Book Award, and* The Snow Leopard, *which won it. While writing* In the Spirit of Crazy Horse *and* Indian Country, *Matthiessen turned his attention toward the history, culture, and political plight of American Indians. In 1990, he was made a laureate of the Global Honor Roll of the United Nations Environmental Program (UNEP). In 1991, Matthiessen was honored with the John Steinbeck Award, which recognizes contributions to literature and humanity. He has also received lifetime achievement awards from the Heinz Foundation, the Lannan Foundation, and the Society of Conservation Biologists, and the Gold Medal in Natural History from the Philadelphia Academy of Sciences. Matthiessen is a member of the American Academy of Arts and Letters, and the American Academy of Arts and Sciences.*

On July 13, 2002, on the scheduled early morning flight from Fairbanks to Arctic Village, the airplane crosses the forested White Mountains to the Yukon drainage. Traversing the broad marshes of the Yukon Flats, it drops off two Gwich'in Indian boys at Fort Yukon, at the confluence of the Porcupine and Yukon Rivers, just north of the Arctic Circle. From there it flies north across the barrens of the Gwich'in reservation, dropping a Native passenger at Venetie (*Veena-tie,* as in shirt-and-tie), the Gwich'in village seventy miles to the north, before ascending the East Fork of the Chandalar and the caribou-tracked southern foothills of the Brooks Range. The boreal forest had already given way to the spruce-muskeg taiga of the far north, and traversing the huge roadless reservation, the plane crosses broad hills of alpine tundra and follows dark valleys of ranked conifers up toward the treeline.

Arctic Village, a scattered assembly of forty-odd log cabins built on granite ridges that overlook the serpentine bends, oxbows, and channels of the East Fork just south of the southwestern corner of the refuge, is one of the most remote settlements in this enormous state. High in the foothills of the Brooks Range, seventy-five miles north of the Arctic Circle and more than a hundred from the nearest road, it was chosen as a place to settle by the formerly nomadic Gwich'in because its sheltering forest provided timber for cabins and fuel and a variety of fur animals, and its river abundant fish. More important, in some years it is winter range for more than half of the Porcupine caribou herd, presently estimated at about 120,000 animals. Leaving smaller companies behind, the main herd drifts south and east into the Porcupine River drainage and Canada's Yukon Territory, where most of the animals will overwinter. The fifteen Gwich'in villages in northeast Alaska and northwestern Canada, consisting of about seven thousand people, are scattered along the caribou migration route, and all need stores of dried caribou meat—about twelve animals per family—to see them through

*From the foreword, *Midnight Wilderness: Journeys in Alaska's Arctic National Wildlife Refuge, *by Debbie S. Miller

the long hard winters. Indeed, they depend upon *vadzaih,* the caribou, as the Plains Indians once depended on the bison and the Pacific Northwest tribes on the salmon.

Back in 1971, Arctic Village and Venetie chose not to participate in the Alaska Native Claims Settlement Act (ANCSA), which was granting nearly $1 billion and 44 million acres of territory to the Native Americans and settling indigenous land claims for those tribes which accepted oil development and the construction of the pipeline. Refusing to accept the ANCSA terms, the two villages held out for their original tribal land claim of 1.8 million acres, in the full knowledge that this brave commitment to the integrity of their ancestral lands and their traditional ways would condemn them to a life of bare subsistence.

When our expedition into the Arctic National Wildlife Refuge passed through Arctic Village on the way north, the Gwich'in leaders were away at a tribal meeting in Old Crow, a Porcupine River village in the Yukon. Anxious to listen to the Indian point of view, I returned to Arctic Village a fortnight later, noticing even from the air the solid spruce-log cabins spaced well apart in clean, unlittered yards among the conifers—a strong sign, I reflect, of Gwich'in strength of spirit and morale. This strength is personified in the young village chief, Evon Peter, who meets the plane at the gravel airstrip located on high ground overlooking the river.

The real name of Arctic Village (plain "Arctic" to its 150-odd residents) is Vashraii K'oo, or "Steep Bank Creek," due to its location on rock ridges separated by sparkling river braids and creeks and ponds, in a beautiful mosaic of stone and water. Evon Peter gazes around him at his country as if seeing it for the first time. "Outsiders have called this place 'God's Country,' and that is how we see it, too," says this slight handsome man of twenty-five, a recent graduate of the University of Alaska. "We are certainly one of the poorest tribes, yet we are also rich, for we have our unspoiled original land, and we have our language and our traditional Way; we want to remain independent as far as possible." He is too polite to say, "independent of your white man's world." Indian Nations that have retained the spiritual strength of their traditional Way are now rare in North America, and plainly he feels the responsibility to maintain those traditions.

On Mr. Peter's all-terrain vehicle, which resembles a four-wheeled motorcycle, we return to the scattered village—an Episcopal logchurch, a water tank, a community hall and tribal office, forty log cabins, and a gigantic freezer for harvested caribou. Evon greets respectfully and introduces every person we come across that day, even young children.

At his modest desk against one wall of the main room in the small community building, the young chief discusses the many projects that

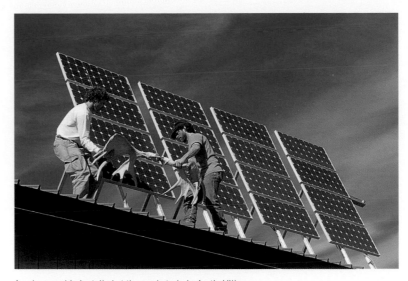

A solar panel is installed at the washateria in Arctic Village.

devour his time, not only in Vashraii K'oo but in all the other Gwich'in villages in Alaska and northwest Canada, and also in those matters that concern the Athabascan people of other Dineh tribes, including the Navajo and the Apache. In this village (which twenty years ago voted to ban alcohol), his projects include immersion-in-Gwich'in-language classes, mostly for those under thirty who formerly lived away or for some other reason cannot speak it. "We want to determine our own future, starting now. We want to cut way down on fossil fuel, we want sustainable energy. We hope to fully solarize this village and Venetie, too." The community laundry, which we visit later that day, is already under solar power; it can claim the only flush toilet in Vashraii K'oo. Asked if there was a spiritual reason for fighting further oil development on the Arctic Refuge in addition to the practical one of protecting the great calving ground, Evon nods and keeps on nodding for some time, not wishing to spit out some easy answer. "It is very difficult to speak of," he says finally. "The animals, the rivers—we're essentially a voice for things that cannot talk. We don't see ourselves as separate from those things. If the rivers and animals are poisoned, the poisons will work their way into us, too." But even this clear holistic view is more than this careful, measured man feels entitled to express. Recommending a visit to Trimble Gilbert, an elder and former village chief who serves here as spiritual leader, he heads his four-wheeler up the road past the small log church to a cabin perched on a high knoll where Mr. Gilbert soon arrives, lugging water from the creek, and welcomes us into his small cabin.

In Gwich'in mythology and creation stories, says Mr. Gilbert, a tall, long-haired elder with thick glasses and a big smile in a mouth with few front teeth, Caribou has a piece of Man's heart in its heart and Man

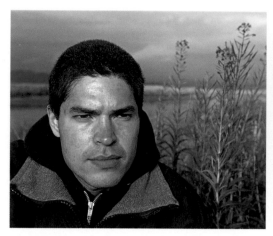 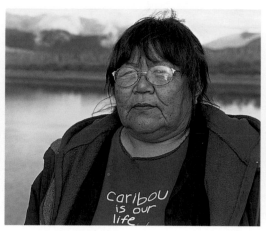 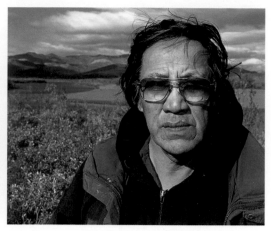

Evon Peter, first chief, Arctic Village   Sarah James, indigenous environmental leader, Arctic Village   Trimble Gilbert, traditional chief, Arctic Village

has a piece of Caribou's heart in his heart, so that each will always know what the other is doing. When hunters offer a prayer of thanks to the killed caribou, they sometimes eat a bit of raw heart at the kill site out of gratitude and respect.

"Those elders who followed Traditional Way knew a lot about animals," Mr. Gilbert says, "and they would know when our caribou were coming, they would dream that they would be here in a few days. Many caribou used to cross our river—not any more. When we went down to Fairbanks in winter with our dogsleds, we seen plenty of animals right there along the Chena River—not any more. In the last twenty, thirty years since the pipeline went there, things have changed. The birds don't come. We don't hear their singing. When I was growing up, I couldn't wait 'til spring, to see them, hear them! Every spring! No more, not even ptarmigan that used to sing on top of every bush—not any more. If we don't stop this oil development, everything will go. It might take twenty or thirty more years, then everything will be gone. Maybe our water, too. I went to L.A. once and drank that water. I got sick.

"I don't want to lose our animals. Those little birds that go round and round on the water (phalaropes), every pond: I haven't seen one in twenty years. And swallows! You'd see them all over, whirling up and down—it's fun! Now my wife Mary, she says, 'Where did the swallows go?'" He sighs, profoundly sad. "That is something taken from our lives that we can't put back.

"We try to keep our community together," he continues after a pause. "That is our Indian power. That is our Way. In the old days, hunting with bows and arrows, the hunters slowly surrounded the caribou," he spreads his arms, then slowly brings his fingertips together, "slowly, slowly closing in. Kill one, then another. Killed no more than they needed, just made sure everybody got enough to eat. Sometimes we go fifty miles north into the refuge, take a few white

sheep, not many. If we hunt caribou, hunt sheep, we go around, make sure everybody has enough. Did that for thousands of years, and it's still going on, just like the old days. I like it!" Trimble smiles. "We have the Good Spirit and we want to keep that. I come back, I see my father's fishing place, my grandfather's camp, then I am at peace again. We respect our land and the refuge is our land. This is our Home."

From Trimble's place, we cross the village and climb another hill to the house of Sarah James, whose son Mark is broiling salmon on a grill out in the yard. "King salmon from the Yukon—that's the best there is," says Mrs. James, a friendly, bespectacled person, well rounded out by a full life. She waves us through her door ahead of the mosquitoes and shuts the screen, bustling back to her small stove to put the last touches on a fine big feed of caribou stew, king salmon, potato, and canned vegetables, with her own delicious fry-bread dumplings on the side.

Sarah's cell phone, which is rarely still, is the one feverish symptom of the outside world (though many calls originate in the village). "What? Yes! We got plenty of good food here! Better come help eat it!"

From her modesty and simplicity of manner and appearance, not to mention that of her log house (which, like all houses at Vashraii K'oo, lacks running water), one would not know that Sarah James, aged fifty-six, was a co-winner of the prestigious Goldman Environmental Award (May, 2002) with two other Gwich'in elders (Jonathon Solomon, seventy, from Fort Yukon and Norma Kassi, forty-eight, from Old Crow, across the Yukon border) for their fight in defense of the Porcupine herd that has sustained Gwich'in culture for twenty thousand years.

For many years, Sarah James has spoken out against refuge development, and her efforts—which she deprecates—have received widespread and deserved recognition. "I only repeated what Indian people have always said about land and life, but this time we got heard because of the big fight over our caribou and their breeding ground; the leaders say this fight could be the rebirth of our Gwich'in Nation."

Like Trimble Gilbert, Sarah James laments that so many birds are missing now at Vashraii K'oo—a fact that even the most hardened apostle of material progress should consider, since Vashraii K'oo lies at the heart of the greatest montane wilderness left in North America, and if the birds are disappearing here, man had better find out why.

In Sarah's girlhood, the Gwich'in—the People—still had hunting camps on the braids of the Chandalar River, to harvest the caribou moving through, sometimes for four days at a time. "How to hunt and fish—that's all my people know. That's the only life we know and that's the only food we have," Sarah James said, "so we don't want to lose that." The annual coming of the big deer is so critical to Gwich'in economy and cultural well-being that the coastal plain where the caribou are born is revered as *Izhik Gwats'an Gwandaii Goodlit*—roughly "the Sacred Place Where Life Begins"—that is, Caribou Life and, by extension, the Life of the Caribou People—a mythic place that few Gwich'in have ever seen.

Such testimony is of little interest to Senator Ted Stevens (R-Alaska) who has suggested to his colleagues (Congressional Record, 4/17/02) that those pesky Indians who dare to fight oil drilling in the caribou calving grounds are actually "Canadian Indians . . . part of the Gwich'in tribe in Canada"—by implication not Americans at all, despite their presence here for thousands of years before the white men.

I first visited the Arctic in May of 1957, when I accompanied a Fish and Wildlife Service pilot on a polar bear survey east and west of Point Barrow while researching a book called *Wildlife in America*. Two years later, Alaska joined the Union as the forty-ninth state. The following year, almost 9 million acres of what was to become the Arctic National Wildlife Refuge were officially set aside by the Eisenhower administration; four years later, Congress would pass the Wilderness Act, which permitted certain federal lands to be permanently protected.

In 1961 I returned to the far north on a caribou research expedition to the Ross River region of the Yukon Territory, and in 1964 I traveled to Nunivak Island in the Bering Sea on an expedition to capture muskox calves for an experimental herd that might strengthen the Inuit economy. Passing through Anchorage that year, I took note of the saloons jammed with Indians and prospectors—no longer gold but oil. Sure enough, a major oil field with an estimated reserve of 9.6 billion barrels (and 26 trillion cubic feet of natural gas) was discovered a few years later (1968) just west of the Arctic National Wildlife Range at Prudhoe Bay,

where production would begin in the early 1970s.

The discovery alarmed the coastal Inupiat (Inuit) and also the Gwich'in Athabascans on the south slope of the Brooks Range, since both peoples, in different seasons, are hunters of the caribou that bred and birthed on the refuge coastal plain. The potential disruption of land and life posed by the oil wells, including the intrusion of roads and pipelines into the fragile tundra ecosystem, would precipitate the Native peoples into the struggle.

In January 1977, Representative Morris Udall (D-Arizona) introduced a prototype of what was to become the monumental Alaska National Interest Lands Conservation Act of 1980 (ANILCA), only to see it bog down in the Senate. As it happened, 1977 was the first year that oil flowed south down the 800-mile pipeline from Prudhoe Bay to the Port of Valdez on Prince William Sound, with billions of dollars in profits in the offing. Oil leases and public royalties and revenues were now a serious political consideration, and Udall's visionary legislation, actively endorsed by President Carter, was repeatedly forestalled by the oil industry's allies in Congress. Not until December 2, 1980, with a conservative Republican, Ronald Reagan, about to replace Carter, did the House leaders approve the Senate's weaker version of their bill.

The so-called Lands Act was a far-sighted triumph for conservation, extending protection to 103 million acres of new parks and wildlife refuges. In the process, the Arctic National Wildlife Refuge (ANWR) was virtually doubled in area to nearly 20 million acres, including an inviolable wilderness of 8.9 million acres, most of which lay in the barren mountains. The fine print in the Lands Act was Section 1002, which directed that a 1.5 million-acre coastal region be assessed not only for its biological significance but for its fossil fuel potential. The "Ten-Oh-Two," as it is called, was placed in an "undecided" category where it still languishes twenty-two years later, leaving the best caribou calving area on the refuge coastal plain entirely vulnerable.

The Lands Act would not have passed through Congress without this concession to Big Oil's lobbyists, a growing multitude that included every politician in Alaska, where 80 percent of the state budget soon derived from oil and where each citizen, exempt from state taxes, receives an oil royalty of nearly two thousand dollars every autumn. To nobody's surprise—and despite adverse testimony from its own Fish and Wildlife Service, which stated that the wilderness value of the 1002 would be "eliminated"—Reagan's Interior Department duly recommended that the entire area be opened to development. Beginning in 1987, the oil industry began an intense lobbying campaign in Congress to acquire leases and commence exploratory drilling. Despite passionate opposition by an environmental coalition that included the Gwich'in (but no longer the Inupiat, who had less at stake than the Gwich'in and finally accepted the oil payments), drilling in the 1002 seemed inevitable until the night of March 23, 1989, when the oil tanker *Exxon Valdez* went aground on an offshore reef in Prince William Sound, leaking 11 million gallons of oil and destroying the ecology of well over a thousand miles of Alaska's coast. By a great irony, North America's greatest ecological disaster, with the ensuing state and Congressional hearings and investigations of widespread oil contamination and pipeline leakage, was all that spared the 1002 from devastation.

Though Big Oil laid low after the *Exxon Valdez*, it had not changed its ambitions; Reagan's successor, a Greenwich, Connecticut oilman named George H. W. Bush, made drilling rights in the Arctic Refuge a plank of his energy policy. But his 1991 attempt to forward drilling stalled in Congress, and his successor, Bill Clinton, was to veto a draft of the national budget that contained a drilling provision. In this hopeful period, nuclear plants were shutting down, the Clean Air Act was being enforced by the EPA, the Superfund sites were being dealt with and the rivers cleaned, and renewable clean energy from wind and sun was being researched and encouraged, especially in Europe, as a long-overdue alternative to fossil fuels. Even the threat of "climate change" (the fossil fuelers' careful euphemism for greenhouse gases and global warming) was finally conceded by the industry itself, notably British Petroleum, which had started to emphasize solar energy research (and claims in its recent advertising that "BP" now signifies "Beyond Petroleum"). Yet wilderness status is still being withheld from the 1002 in what has become the longest and most critical environmental fight in our nation's history.

Ever since my first visit in May 1957, when the land was still under snow, I had longed to return to the Arctic coastal plain—and especially the Arctic Refuge—during the brief summer breeding season, but because the refuge has no roads or facilities—no real access, in fact, except by light aircraft—the journey to a region so remote that few have ever seen it had always seemed too difficult and expensive. Almost a half-century would pass before this opportunity arose, and it came from a most unlikely source. Subhankar Banerjee, a young Indian from Calcutta engaged in a photographic project on the refuge, telephoned to invite me on a ten-day river journey through the remote northeastern region of the refuge, from the Brooks Range foothills north across the tundra to the Arctic coast, making camp here and there along the way.

This exciting offer came in late 2001, when, like most environmentalists, I was seriously alarmed by the aggressive anti-environmental attitudes of the second Bush administration, which was plainly more concerned with huge tax cuts and subsidies for the large corporations than with the long-term interests of the nation. An energy bill that featured drilling in the refuge had been passed by the House a few months earlier and would soon have hearings in the Senate, whose approval seemed certain in the climate of terrorist scare talk and "patriotic" bullying after 9/11; these hearings would take place before our trip. But the battle for the 1002 had already lasted for twenty-two years, and however the Senate voted in this round, this bitter fight was far from over.

Mr. Banerjee backed up a series of letters and phone calls by turning up at readings I was giving at the Smithsonian in Washington and the American Museum of Natural History in New York. A tall, lean young man of thirty-four with an infectious smile and unbounded enthusiasm, he had no trouble persuading me that his exciting project was an immediate and effective way to help forward a cause I had first advocated forty years before, and again in that critical period in the late eighties, in a preface to the Natural Resources Defense Council (NRDC) publication called *Tracking the Oil*.

By then I had heard from the sponsor and leader of our expedition, a businessman from Everett, Washington, named Tom Campion, who dedicates a substantial percentage of his income to helping save the wilderness Arctic from despoliation. "I put my money where my mouth is, and I have a big mouth, and I'm pushy," says Mr. Campion, who generously offered to pay all expenses for me and my son Alex, an environmentalist who had worked with the Rain Forest Action Network and in Secretary Bruce Babbitt's office at the Department of the Interior. Alex, thirty-seven, was presently the Hudson Riverkeeper and head of the environmental organization of the same name. The group also included Campion's wife, Sonya, her niece, Andrea Maki, and his friends Mark Skatrud, Mike Matz, Jim Mankopf, and Jed and Joann Marshall, as well as our guides (the proprietors of Arctic Treks), Jim Campbell and Carol Kasza. We flew to Fairbanks on July 12, 2002, going on to Arctic Village the next morning and crossing the Brooks Range that same day.

From Arctic Village, two large chartered Cessnas shuttle the expedition across the Brooks Range to its northern foothills on the Kongakut River, taking three collapsible river rafts, two whitewater kayaks, and all food and gear. The planes follow the thinning line of spruce upriver almost to treeline before climbing northeast over alpine tundra meadows toward the bare ridges of the Arctic Divide; except for a few stunted conifers in one broad, deep valley in the mountains, these are the last trees that we shall see.

The Brooks Range is the northwest extension of the Rocky Mountains, rising to 9,000 feet and traversing Alaska for 600 miles, from the Yukon border to the Bering Sea. Its four tallest peaks and most of its cirque glaciers lie within the refuge, forming a dramatic badlands moonscape that extends a hundred miles or more from south to north. One of the earth's most remote wildernesses, the huge refuge encompasses all the sub-Arctic and Arctic ecosystems, from the boreal forest of the Porcupine River uplands to the dry Arctic tundra of the coastal plain

The mountain crossing is a long one in a light aircraft, heavily loaded, that is often less than a hundred feet above the tumult of black, snow-patched peaks, rock canyons, and steep inclines of gravel shale that fall away into deep ravines. A small band of white Dall sheep, poised on a thinly greened limestone "bald," are picked out of the landscape by the sharp eye of Mark Skatrud, a tracker and environmental activist who first met Campion back in the eighties during the campaign to conserve old-growth forest for the spotted owl. Beyond the Arctic Divide, the springs and ponds and narrow streams flow north down empty tundra valleys lost amidst stark ridges and rock towers. "Might take two weeks just to walk into one of these wild drainages," Tom says. "The first time I saw how many there were, it brought tears to my eyes. I swore to myself I would not permit those greedy bastards in Big Oil and its enablers in Congress to trash this wilderness for all other Americans, not on my dime." By bringing writers and politicians here to see for themselves, Campion hopes to summon support for his campaign to save the refuge for the nation's future.

Here and there move isolated rains. The Cessna passes in and out of rain clouds, traversing the dark and formidable Romanzof Mountains before starting a long gradual descent. Toward the end of the one-hour flight, as ravines widen into canyons and streams gather into torrents, the ocean light beyond the mountains comes in view. Soon the plane crosses the headwaters of the Kongakut, the easternmost of Alaska's North Slope rivers, drawn from deep glacier-carved tributary canyons that open out in alpine tundra at Caribou Pass, a thoroughfare for the great herd that flows north and west out of the Yukon, to judge from the spidery skeins of tracks across the mountain tundra and the hoof ruts along the willow banks at riverside. The torrent is braided by pale gray gravel bars shaped by the swift water into elegant pointed shapes like spearheads or long leaves or falcon feathers, and emerald water dances in the sun, arousing thoughts of the large Arctic char that are bound to take my fly.

On a broad bend where a gravel bench on the willow bank is wide enough to handle its small tires, the aircraft drops us near the river. Though the clouds thicken with hard rain in the mountains, night will not fall under the midnight sun, and the bush pilots Dirk Nickisch and

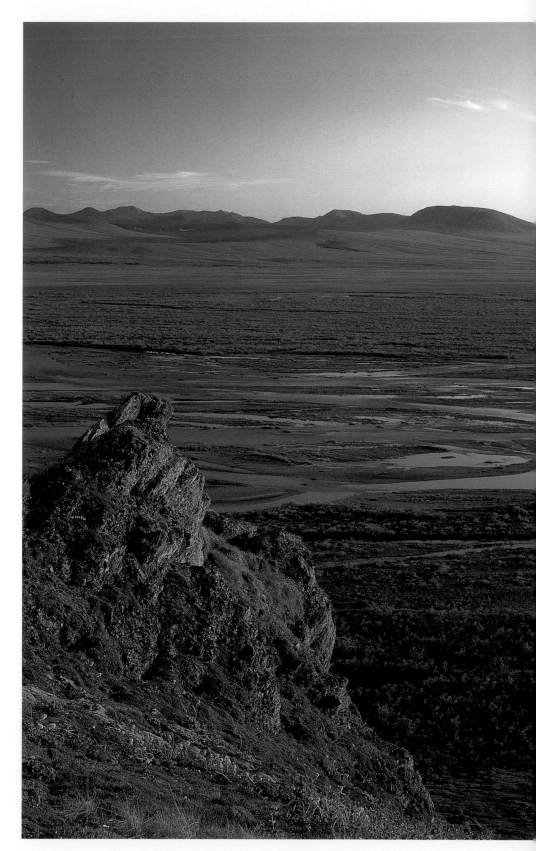

Summer midnight in the Kongakut River valley, Romanzof Mountains in the background

Kirk Sweetsir (whom Campion refers to as "the Irk brothers") have the expedition on the ground in time for a late supper. Mosquitoes rise in swirls around our heads as tents are pitched in a grassy meadow among willows; the cook tent goes up near the river's edge where the cool wind upriver from the sea holds them at bay. Proliferating in this fleeting season of unfrozen water, these pesky creatures are the living fuel that sustains the swarming bird life of the Arctic and thereby justifies their noisome existence.

Ravens, mew gulls, and the ice-white glaucous gulls inspect the camp, which is also inhabited by a chestnut-silver ground squirrel; later, a fox comes to inspect us. Downriver a ptarmigan wanders the willows, and hoary redpolls, whiter than willow catkins, blow through the thicket. Behind the meadow, a steep cutbank rises to a tundra slope, which rises in turn to a saddle between ridges and dark climbing peaks. As the raven flies, Caribou Pass is some twenty-five miles from the Beaufort Sea and less than fifteen from the Yukon border.

In the early evening the rain comes from the mountains, falling steadily and more or less heavily until after midnight and remaining as new snow next morning on high, dark Mount Greenough, which dominates the peaks to the south and west. Glacier rivers rise rapidly with rain, which has already turned the clear green current to thick-silted gray, ending my plan to go fly-fishing this morning. It is a day for the high country instead.

With Alex and Andrea Maki, a young artist, I walk upriver to where a ridge descends to a great bend, observing a mixed flock of redpolls and pine siskins in the willows. Where a tributary stream winds down out of the eastern ridges, joining the Kongakut a half-mile above camp, we climb the soft green moss and tussocks of wet tundra to the high rock outcrop on the ridge. Out of the wind, leaning back against soft lichens on the rocks, we breathe in a vast, beautiful, and stirring prospect. High snow-streaked peaks rise to the south and west, and to the north, the gray torrent, curving west under its cliffs, escapes the portals of the foothills and winds across the plain toward the hard white bar on the horizon—the dense wall of fog that hides the Beaufort Sea. This wild, free valley and the barren ground beyond is but a fragment of one of the last pristine regions left on earth, entirely unscarred by roads or signs, indifferent to mankind, utterly silent.

A rough-legged hawk—the only buteo that hovers—drifts across the face of the higher mountainside to the northeast; a pomarine jaeger, that marine pirate that leaves the open ocean to breed on the tundra, knifes overhead, the swift dark hunter of small birds and beasts. Spring flowers are everywhere in the July meadows: bluebells under sheltered banks and fresh blue lupine in the open; various peas, blue, purple, and magenta; lavender asters; yellow Icelandic poppies and wild

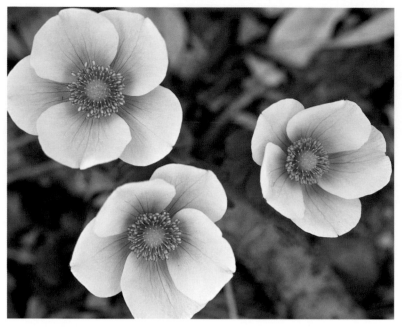

Anemone is one of the first flowers to bloom on the tundra after the snow melts.

primrose; ivory anemones, buttercups, the pink florets of moss campion, and a host of others. With the coming of the midnight sun and twenty-four-hour daylight, these plants grow rapidly, but their season is as fleeting as that of the nesting shorebirds, and their communities are fragile; even the light-browsing caribou, which drift like cloud shadows over this land, leave traces of their passage which take years to fade.

By midafternoon the river has cleared just at the interface of the tributary stream and the main current, and here we catch graylings and fine Arctic char, four to six pounds each, which we grill for supper.

About six o'clock on this beautiful clear evening, a cream-colored adult grizzly appears in the sunlit grassy saddle of the ridge and works its way downhill toward our tents, quartering the slope as it crops its favored greens but maintaining its general direction. Downwind of the camp, it must smell the cooking fish. At a certain point it stops and lifts its head, as if catching other scents, possibly ours; at this range, about 150 yards away, it can probably make out the dim shapes of the tents and the moving figures. Then it moves forward, shambling and browsing, close enough now so that we can admire the long-haired, shaggy belly dark with tundra mud, yet tending past us, angling along the tundra slope. It follows the descending ridge down a steep cutbank into the willow thickets by the water, just downstream of the confluence where we were fishing. Next morning, bear sign would be everywhere along that bank where the grizzly had worked back and forth trying to dig out ground squirrels.

After supper, before turning in, our excellent river guide Jim

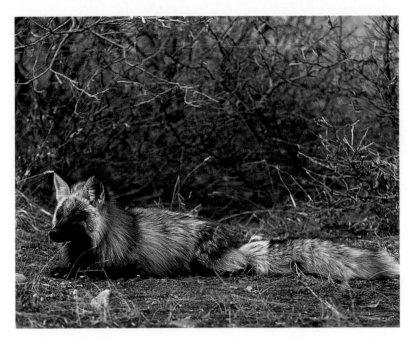

Cross fox at Caribou Pass

Campbell talks about the barren grounds grizzly, which earns a hard livelihood browsing greens and digging out roots, tubers, and ground squirrels when carrion or newborn caribou are unavailable. The grizzlies are smaller than their kinsmen south of the mountains, and though little hunted, are quite timid and will usually run away. However, they famously lie up in willow thickets and, having no predators, may sleep so hard that the unwary may walk right up on top of one, an especially dangerous occurrence when it involves a sow bear with her cubs. (Although all three North American bears—the grizzly, polar bear, and black bear—inhabit the Arctic Refuge, the black bear is a woodland animal that does not visit the North Slope, where there are no trees and few shrubs, only the willow thickets.)

The Arctic light in the long sunny evenings is so limpid and so lovely that one can scarcely bring oneself to go to bed. The camp is already on "Arctic time," which means no more than staying up well past the midnight sun. In the pallid dawn, Mark, Tom, and I are the only ones who rise more or less early out of long habit, and sit with our coffee by the cook tent on the square white food buckets that serve the camp as seats, scanning the landscape for wild creatures, talking softly so as not to wake the others.

By midmorning our companions emerge, and by noon we have launched the river rafts, twelve-foot inflatable crafts of tough, rubberized canvas, with mesh cargo platforms on the flotation tanks amidships and space for paddlers in the bow and stern. I travel with Mike Matz, a river veteran from Durango, Colorado, who is working with Jim and Carol as the third boat helmsman. Mike is a lifelong environmentalist and co-founder of the Alaska Wilderness League, which lobbies to protect the unspoiled wilderness, with special emphasis on the Arctic Refuge. Mike and Jim have two paddlers apiece and Carol three, with Alex and Mark manning two whitewater kayaks. On this shallow, braided river of broad gravel bars, which widens quickly to a half-mile across, dragging and portaging may give more trouble than the occasional rough channel, though in this stiff upriver wind, the cold water inevitably slops over the gunwales.

In the lead, the two kayaks are dived on by nesting glaucous gulls and the quick, forked-tailed Arctic terns; at its nest scrape on the gravel, a tern feeds its craning chick a silverling that glitters like tinsel, as its mate dips and lifts over the rapids, silver minnows bright in its crimson beak. In autumn, this species turns up in small numbers on my home coast on Long Island, New York, but the last place I'd seen it was on winter range in Tierra del Fuego and the Antarctic Peninsula. The Arctic tern has the longest migration of any bird on earth, an astonishing round-trip journey of twenty-four thousand miles each year.

Downriver, a cow moose with her big calf have come down to drink; wary, the enormous deer plunge like horses up the bank and disappear over the rise behind the blowing grasses. Ahead lies the coastal plain, flat, flat, flat, but this lower estuary is partially clogged by overflow ice, which forms where the river freezes to the bottom and the dammed-up current spreads over the ice, freezing hard in layer after layer and building platforms sometimes ten feet high that do not always melt away in summer. Even on this warm and sunny day, the wind off the sea, crossing the ice, has a hard edge. Mergansers hurtle up and down the river, the first loons and eider and a bufflehead appear, then a small dark duck, in all likelyhood a harlequin, heading up a tributary braid.

Tonight camp is made on soft, wet moss at the foot of the last river bluff before the plain. An hour before we came ashore, we had seen two figures waving from the high rim of the escarpment—Subhankar Banerjee and his partner, an Inupiat named Robert Thompson. Camped a half-mile upriver, they turn up at our camp in time for supper. Subhankar tells us that this very day, he and Robert have found gyrfalcons and peregrines nesting on rock towers close together; in recent days, they have seen muskox here as well as grizzlies.

We are still making camp when Tom Campion locates a large, dark grizzly in his spotting scope; it shambles across the plain east of the tents, as massive as an ambulating boulder. With his keen eye for bears, he soon locates another to the north, then two more off to the west under the low hills across the river; they roll along less than a hundred yards apart. It is exciting to observe four griz in the first hour of arrival, and Subhankar assures us that two others are close by. On the way to the falcon nests tomorrow, we are bound to run across them, and the muskox, too, he says, smiling broadly with his usual enthusiasm.

While working for Boeing in Seattle in mathematics and computer technology, this remarkable young scientist camped and trekked around the country. Eventually he went to Manitoba to observe the polar bears that convene in the early autumn at Cape Churchill, awaiting the advent of the ice. "I hated seeing them from behind plate glass in one of those huge tundra half-tracks," he says, "especially the dirty ones around the Churchill dump. I wanted to see them in a natural, wild setting, and grizzlies, too, and I was told that the Arctic Refuge was the place to go." Earnings made as a computer consultant financed the start of his new career as a photographer, and he did not wait for clement weather but set out in March of 2001 for Kaktovik, an Inupiat village on Barter Island just inside the refuge boundary. Arriving in minus forty-degree temperatures, he made contact with Robert Thompson, a professional guide with fifteen years' experience in the refuge and almost the only Inupiat left in Kaktovik who openly campaigned against oil development in the 1002, where the Inupiat themselves have a small inholding. In 2001, these two covered 1,700 miles, mostly on snowmobiles, and this past winter, photographing a polar bear den, they camped for four weeks on the Canning River, mostly in blizzard, with only four calm days.

From the start, Subhankar sought good wildlife photographs taken in winter, to show that the refuge was alive all year around, not a frozen wasteland nine months of the year, as alleged by Senator Frank Murkowski (R-Alaska), who sometimes demonstrates his perception of the refuge by waving a blank piece of white paper on the Senate floor. It's true that the coastal plain is mostly under snow from September through May, with snow flurries occurring even in summer, but the long-haired archaic *oomingmak,* or muskox, finds forage throughout the winter darkness. The male polar bear, too, hunts seals all year, digging temporary dens only in storm; though pregnant females go into hibernation in November, it is still full winter when, in March, they emerge with new cubs and returns to the drifting ice. Also, seven bird species remain active: the gyrfalcon, raven, snowy owl, the willow and rock ptarmigans, the hoary redpoll, and the dipper, or water ouzel, subsist in bitter cold down to fifty degrees below zero.

Setting off next morning for the falcon nests, I climb the steep tundra slope behind the camp, my eyes at the level of a sun-shimmered bed of fresh blue lupine and translucent yellow poppies whose airy petals, strewn like bright sundrops on green beds of grass and mosses, are mixed with white bear flowers, Arctic forget-me-not, pink Siberian

phlox, and the bog rosemary. I am soon overtaken by Subhankar and Robert, and Alex catches up with us on the crest of the plateau, from where we can see the opaque white horizon that marks the sea fog and the polar ice along the coast. These low hills west of the river— Robert points—are a favorite denning area of female polar bears; the refuge has the highest density of denning bears on the North Slope. Because the Brooks Range draws close to the coast here in far northeast Alaska, the rivers are steeper and swifter, with bluffs and cutbanks where the torrents have cut through. Since these valleys cross the prevailing winds, they accumulate snowdrifts much earlier in winter than occurs on the more gradual flat plains to the west, and these early drifts are sought by pregnant polar bears for digging out dens in which to hibernate and bear their young.

We head south along the escarpment, scanning the willow bottoms of the broad riverbed for the missing muskox. The endemic *Ovibos* of this region were eliminated by hunters over a century ago, in the 1890s; not until 1969–1970, after the original establishment of the refuge, were they reintroduced, with sixty-four animals brought from Nunivak Island. Though their numbers in the refuge rose as high as 450 (1985), the muskox have since declined to about 325 on the Alaskan North Slope, west of the refuge, with only 75 inside the refuge boundaries, apparently due to climate change and deeper winter snow, which has forced them to forage farther inland where their calves are much more vulnerable to predators.

If the theory of greenhouse gases is correct, the muskox may become an early casualty of global warming. Like the West Antarctic Ice Sheet (and most tropical coral reefs), Alaska is showing acute signs of stress. A *New York Times* editorial on July 8, the morning I left the East Coast, referred to "Alaska, where an astonishing 7-degree increase in average temperatures over thirty years has led to melting permafrost, sagging roads, dying forests, unexpected forest fires and disruption of marine life. Even Senator Stevens, a Republican who has little patience with environmentalists, is openly alarmed about global warming's potential cost to his home state, an amount that could run into the billions of dollars, and is privately even more alarmed by Washington's indifference."

With the changing climate, other animals such as the moose are moving north; once a rare sight on the North Slope, it is presently widespread, although not common. The upland sandpiper and other birds he now sees regularly were unheard of twenty years ago, Jim Campbell says, and the normal range of at least two breeding birds I've noted here—the pine siskin and Smith's longspur—is south of the Arctic Divide (the comprehensive report on refuge species issued in 1986 by the Fish and Wildlife Service lists both species as "rare visitants"). In early September, when his people hunt the bowhead

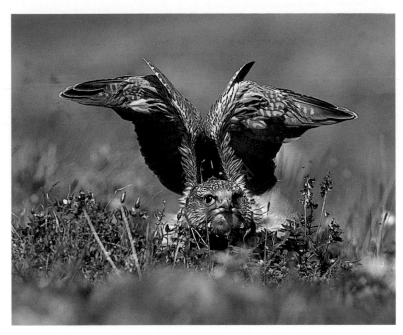

Fledgling gyrfalcon chick flexes its wings before taking its first flight.

whales that pass offshore, says Robert Thompson, there is much more open water than at anytime in memory, therefore bigger seas and increased risk to the hunters; in spring, the ice floes, thinner than before, are dangerous for travel. Polar bears may be seriously threatened by the retreat of the ice pack from the coasts, a phenomenon already recorded in Hudson's Bay. Should the permafrost continue melting, causing tundra collapse and flooding of this plain, the bird multitudes may also disappear.

A golden eagle flaps downriver, far below, and a gyrfalcon passes rapidly overhead. The tundra meadows are broken here and there by dolmenlike monoliths like giant headstones, and bountiful wildflowers watered by melting permafrost flourish in the soft carpet. Against the background of its rock towers and the farther mountains, this high plateau is mysterious and beautiful.

In early spring, the caribou herd in the Porcupine River drainage starts north toward Ivvavik—"a place for giving birth, a nursery"—a Canadian national park that includes the Yukon coastal plain. There part of the herd remains to calve while the rest tend westward into the Arctic Refuge. Two months ago during spring migration, this plateau was crossed by herds that appeared out of the Yukon Mountains to the east. With the longest migration of any terrestrial mammal—2,500 to 3,000 miles in its meanderings, or 800 miles in a straight line southeast to northwest—the big deer with its long legs and light body is also the most efficient walker; the broad hooves adapted to snow and swimming are seemingly analogous to the big, broad paws of polar bears and

wolves. When the snow here is still too deep for foraging, the caribou climb to the wind-scoured heights, where the snow cover is thinner. Near-vertical tracks stripe the alpine slopes, straight up to the point where bare rock replaces alpine tundra vegetation. These windswept plateaus on the river bluffs, where willow tips and the tussock growth form of the Arctic cotton grass may poke through the snow, are also a winter habitat for muskox.

Where the westering caribou descend into the willow bottoms and ford the river, we follow their tracks down to the foot of the escarpment, then continue southward up the valley to a group of rock towers high on the grassy inclines, where Subhankar points out the gyr nest on a rock ledge high above. Two big gray chicks are still hunched on the nest, and a half-fledged sibling flaps and flops on the rocks below. From a craggy outcrop that commands a view of the broad Kongakut Valley, the adult bird, a gray gyrfalcon, screeches a brief warning but otherwise sits still as stone, its pale buff breast and yellow talons shining in the sun.

On the next turret, on an open ledge, is the large crude nest of the rough-legged hawk that commands the rock above; from higher up, on a farther tower, comes the high screaming of peregrines, one of which darts into the sky over the valley and cuts back at once toward its hidden eyrie. To see the rough-leg, golden eagle, peregrine, and gyr in the same hour is a rare experience, and an unlikely one outside the Arctic Refuge.

Returning to camp, Alex and Subhankar walk the upland tussock underneath the cliffs, to avoid mosquitoes, while Robert and I choose the harder ground and better walking of the willow bottoms. In the maze of big deer prints—moose and caribou—we look for signs of muskox, finding wolf instead. Seeing fresh grizzly scat all along our path, I am content that my companion wears a .45 Long Colt six-shooter on his belt that is heavy enough to drag his pants down on that side as he rolls along. "I've never had to use it 'cause these North Slope bears mostly run off; the last guy who got mauled along this coast, back in '78, walked up on a bear here in the willows, which is how it happens."

Asked if his people have any name for this coastal plain that the Gwich'in refer to as "the Sacred Place Where Life Begins," Robert looks at the open landscape all around, bemused, as if he were thinking, 'This isn't Gwich'in country; those people never come here.' As elder Jonathon Solomon has said, "It is too fragile, so we stay away."

"It's just home," Robert says finally. "To us, it's home." That word, the way he uses it, has a capital H.

Next day the last foothills are left behind as the river descends into the flat coastal plain of the barren ground. The river has cleaned itself of the storm roil of a few days ago, brought down from the mountains by the rain; today it is clear jade over the stones, fresh turquoise in the channels. In the brilliant clarity of the pure light, the whites of the white birds seem to flash against the green-gray monotones of tundra. Perhaps ten miles due north (but a good deal farther on the serpentine braids of the spreading delta), where the river swings westward as if loath to meet the sea, a wall of ocean fog threatens to unroll across the plain.

Having made a late start, we make poor time, with only three or four miles gained by midafternoon. The heavy, round-bowed boats are buffeted by a stiff northeast wind, and the paddling is especially laborious where they threaten to ground on shallow bars or slide off into a side channel; with so many braids, the helmsman must choose quickly lest his craft go swirling past.

This morning, a hot sun drove us from the tents; this afternoon the sun feels cold, for the river is passing through overflow ice, which rises in walls up to five feet high on both banks of the channel, deepening the chill of the hard wind. The ice is interspersed with banks of thin topsoil over ice-filled gravel earth, laid bare where the bank has collapsed into the torrent and hung with dirt-filled icicles of perma-frost, presenting a grisly and primordial appearance, as if a mammoth tusk might protrude at any moment. At a small runnel in the melting ice, we go ashore to replenish the fresh water in our buckets, bags, and bottles, for we will cross the brackish lagoon and camp on a salt reef. "Any river this size, south of the mountains," as Mark says, filling his bottle, "you'd never consider drinking from, no matter how thirsty."

On a point of a high bank over a river bend sits a small turret of white ice that from a distance looks like a melted snowman, But in my binocu-lars, the snowman's head reveals a bright black eye. As it swivels, I holler, "Snowy owl!" In his kayak, Alex is waving his arm. He has seen it, too, a pure white owl that in the next instant flops down and away over the channel, alighting on the ice of the far bank. A stooping gull drives it aloft again, a frosty white bird chasing the bone white one, which preys on the young of gulls just as gulls might prey on the nests of owls. The white owl comes to rest on an ice plateau, in dignified solitude on the north sky.

The mew gulls inland have been replaced by the pale northern race of the herring gull called Thayer's gull. In the delta is the striking common merganser, another wanderer to the North Slope, and also two harbingers of outer coasts, the white-winged common eider and the elegant, silver-naped Pacific loon. Where the last ice banks and gravel bars fall behind, the bottom changes to the gray clay mud of the lagoon that separates the coastal plain from the barrier island a half-mile offshore. Because of the relentless sunlight the shallow lagoons are warm and full of foods, supporting great numbers of breeding birds such as the eider and brant geese, hurtling downwind, and the myriad shorebirds along the coast.

But on this tide, the lagoon is too shallow to float the boats; we jump out and drag them as the wind-driven water slops over our boots, hauling them all the way across to the barrier island.

Icy Reef is a gravel spit perhaps a hundred yards across and four feet above sea level that separates Siku (Ice) Lagoon from the polar seas. There we fortify the tents against the wind by pounding in heavy stakes culled from the silver driftwood stacked on the reef's spine; the line of driftwood travels the length of the narrow island, east and west for perhaps fifteen miles, disappearing into the mist in either direction. Astonishingly, the smooth silver stacks lack even one dark stump or rough-barked log, although a number, felled by beaver, have the butt end gnawed. Since there are no forests on Alaska's North Slope rivers, therefore no deadwood to float down to the sea, these burnished timbers can only have come from Canada's Mackenzie River delta, over one hundred miles away off to the east.

Buried in snow and ice most of the year, the silver wood deteriorates slowly on this arid coast; it is oddly light with age and desiccation, as if laid down very long ago in some late Ice Age, and we move whole tree trunks to weigh down tent stakes and ensure a stronger shelter. The only vegetation is a cushion plant and a coarse dune grass, so sparsely distributed that they might be overlooked entirely; no mosquitoes breed here since, on this sandbar, on this arid coast, there is no moisture.

Crowding the reef's outer beach are the sculpted forms of stranded icebergs, whose delicate pinnacles and arches, tilted mushrooms, and cantilevered shelves are marvelously balanced and supported. They extend offshore a quarter-mile to a half-mile, like floating sculptures brilliantly reflected in the still black water that the white masses shelter from the wind. The Arctic ice pack, at this time of year, is perhaps five miles farther out to sea, in the realm of the bowhead whale, ringed seal, and polar bear, whose carnivore's dense scat and big prints in the sand, perhaps months old, are still well preserved in this arid place.

The wind off the ice bites through the light fabric of my summer tent. After good hot soup, I am happy to turn in, wearing all my high-tech layers—an early evening on this expedition, although well past midnight.

At morning, the reef is deep within the banks of ocean fog. Walking the beach, what one hears in the near mist are hushed groans and grunts and sometimes a soft rushing sound like the puff of a large mammal. Last evening, seals were hunting char in the black water between icebergs, but these are not seal noises; whales make such sounds, but the ghostly sculptures, as Mark and I discover on a kayak foray, are all but touching underwater, leaving no channels suitable for beluga. A disgruntled polar bear floated inshore on a floe was what came to mind when I first heard this whispering of hidden ice, rolling over or collapsing into the sea.

When the fog clears at midmorning, we can see across the water the soaring prospect of the northernmost mountains of the New World, rising from the sunny mists to 9,000 feet; the peaks appear impregnable, majestic. Because the mountains here come close to the sea, the coastal plain is scarcely twenty miles across, but in this clear air the distance looks like six miles at the most. From the mainland shore comes thunder, cannonades, for the river ice in the Kongakut is restless.

The remote plain has few visitors, and most of these few—unaware, perhaps, of its astonishing biodiversity—find it bleak and barren. But in the endless sunshine of the Arctic summer, in this rare light, the soft greens of the tundra and the shadows of the mountains seem deeply harmonious. The very cleanliness is beautiful, if only because man has sullied most of the New World south of those mountains and will do the same for this continental edge, if the oil industry is permitted to exploit it.

After one day on the reef, we travel east down the Siku Lagoon toward Demarcation Bay, near the Yukon border. In a kayak, I set out ahead into the glassy stillness, the great silence. Where the sea has broken through the barrier island, a large pale grayish seal—the bearded seal, I think—parts the surface in the cutway and slides beneath again, but another is so taken aback by its sudden confrontation with a big black gliding thing that it somersaults backward in a great thrash as it disappears.

An owl-like stump on a silver log turns out to be a snowy owl, pale silver gray; with deceptive speed it crosses the lagoon to the tundra rim, where it resumes its existence as a stump. On that low cliff where the barren ground touches the sea walk the misted silhouettes of caribou, and near the caribou a pair of sandhill cranes is calling—the little brown crane, or Canadian crane, as the smallest race of this far-flung species is known. The two that answer from far off are probably not a separate pair: At this time of year it seems more likely that the parent birds, out foraging, are each accompanied by one of their two young, maintaining the family unity with rolling cries.

A white owl swings out over the ice before heading back down the seacoast toward the west. On the beach crest, upright and heraldic on a silver limb, a magnificent peregrine, gray-blue above and lightly barred ivory on the breast and belly, watches the half-man in the black craft without the smallest shift or twitch of wing. I drift for a long time in the light of endless day, wondering why two adult owls and an adult peregrine are drawn to the bony reef, where there is no water nor good habitat for vole or lemming.

Across the lagoon is an old hunting and fishing camp on a grassy headland known to the Inupiat as Pingokraluk. On the mud where we

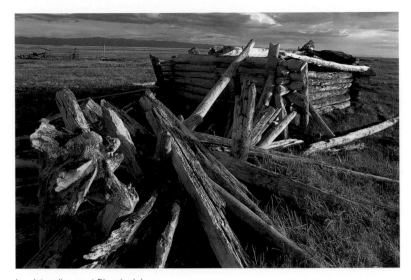

Inupiat sodhouse at Pingokraluk

go ashore under the point are bold tracks of both grizzly and polar bear, and Mark uses up most of his plaster making a fine cast of a polar bear print, which lacks the grizzly's long digging claws, although it is larger, with wider spaces between the toes and a broad pad adapted for ice travel and swimming. The measured track is ten inches long by seven inches across the toe prints (compared to an average five to five-and-a-half inches for the barren ground grizzly). "Seeing tracks like these," says Mark, " is almost as exciting as seeing the animal itself."

Because the white bear, unlike the brown one, will stalk and kill a human being with intent to feed, one imagines the big animal that made these tracks shambling along under the grassy point, swinging its small head on its long neck, raising its black nose to test the air. Incongruous beside its track is the small print of the Arctic fox that perhaps attended it, but the fox was too light to make much impression on the cold tough mud; only the twin pinholes made by its foreclaws betray its passing.

Near the bear prints are tracks of the tundra swan, whose central toe is about six inches long. These traces of ancient mighty creatures evoke the interglacial days of the Pleistocene era of eleven thousand years ago, when lions and saber-toothed cats, camels and ponies wandered this unglaciated plain with the muskox, caribou, and wolf before falling to the spears of ancestral Asians.

I am interested in exploring this headland where the Inupiat have come and gone away again—probably for good, according to Robert Thompson. His Kaktovik people, now accustomed by oil royalties to motor snow sleds and outboard boats, use the camps that are far from home less frequently than before. In the quarter-century since the first oil left the Arctic slope in the trans-Alaska pipeline, the dogsled and the dogs themselves have largely vanished.

I stake my tent in the lee of a sod-roofed cabin, whose seaward end has tilted over the eroded bank and down to the shore mud. Here a huge stump from the Mackenzie, wedged in tight by wind and weather, blocks the door. The rough-hewn side timbers are massive, fitted closely to cross timbers at the ends without a nail, and on the roof, a wild garden of grass and moss and flowers is alight with sun and wind.

A second cabin on the headland is mostly fallen down. Not far away are a small graveyard and some grassy platforms with assembled stones, where tents were erected and large hides pegged out to be scraped and dried. Behind the point is a small lake where we draw fresh water, and north of the lake is a high knoll from which we can scan the plain all the way to Canada. Between the old huts and this knoll, two compound oil drums, perhaps ten feet long, lie rusting, an offense to the eye. Jim Campbell says they were supposed to be removed but nobody has gotten around to it, a story which will become familiar when the oil fields give out and the public is told that the industry cannot afford the cleanup of the colossal mess at Prudhoe Bay, which includes some fifty-five contaminated sites and hundreds of polluting waste pits—another environmental disaster to be billed, not to the corporate polluters who support political campaigns, but to the taxpayers.

This morning we travel to the eastern end of Icy Reef, where the chartered planes will pick us up day after tomorrow. A strong wind is coming from the east, with massed dark columns of heavy weather over the Yukon peaks, but soon the wind shifts into the west, speeding our passage down Siku Lagoon. By the time camp is made, the sun appears across the border on the white peaks of Canada's British Mountains.

Only three miles from Demarcation Bay and less than a mile offshore, our final camp lies not far from an old hunting camp at the eastern end of Icy Reef, where drift timbers buried upright in the sand once framed hide shelters. With wind-smoothed roots knobbing the pole tops like grotesque heads, the lonely company, seen from a distance in the mist, look like survivors or perhaps gaunt, giant birds.

All afternoon the wind dies down and the clouds over the Yukon vanish, but thin rain sheets work their slow way west across the foothills of the Brooks Range, skirting the arid plain; the rain turns pink, then gold in the far west where the curved wisps cross the ever-setting sun. By ten in the evening the water on the seaward side is still, reflecting the exquisite shapes of the small icebergs, and loons and long-tailed duck and golden-eye pitch in and skid across the glassy surface. Here and there the mirror dimples, for the char are rising. These two-pound fish, much smaller and paler than those caught upriver, are icy white and icy

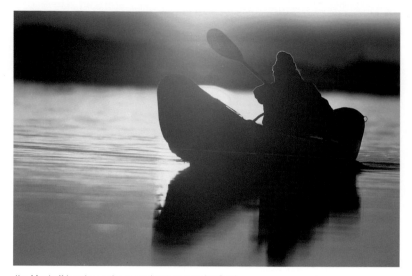

Jim Mankoff kayaks on the coastal waters near Icy Reef.

cold in the bare hand, and their stomachs are packed with small shrimplike copepods (which may feed in turn on the diatoms released by the melting ice). Around midnight a ringed seal appears among the ice shapes, hunting the fishes that move along the beach hunting the krill, but like other seals seen along the reef, this one is wary, peering across the black mirror of the surface with its large dark eyes.

For another day and another night the fog bank stays offshore. By nine in the morning on July 23, when Kirk Sweetsir lands his Cessna on the gravel bench that crests the reef, the day is clear. With Robert and Subhankar, who caught up with us last evening after two days at the raptor nests upriver, I go out on the first flight west over the 1002, which we will cross on our way to Kaktovik.

Looking for muskox, the plane flies low along the coast, which is sprinkled white by a hundred pairs of tundra swans. Two cow moose with well-grown calves are perhaps a mile apart, throwing big shadows in the morning light. Farther on, under a steep cutbank, Kirk Sweetsir spots muskox tracks but of *Ovibos* itself there is no sign. He cannot recall another flight over the refuge when he has not seen one.

Crossing the Aichilik delta, the plane enters the 1002—what the oilmen refer to as "the *An*-War." In its olive monotones and grassy ponds, this disputed area is indistinguishable from the Kongakut tundra except that as the plane flies west, the Brooks Range recedes into the southern mist and the coastal plain widens, until finally the mountains disappear entirely. This wider plain, far from the mountains, is the heart of the Porcupine herd's 740-square-mile calving ground.

In June 2001, at the behest of Senator Frank Murkowski (R-Alaska) in his ongoing campaign to deliver the 1002 to the oil industry, Interior Secretary Gail Norton visited the area under the expert guidance of the refuge's retired senior biologist Fran Mauer, who told me in Fairbanks that Norton was uninterested in any fact that did not fit her plan to play down the 1002's biological importance. She "never asked one substantive question in five hours," Fran Mauer said. "Didn't want to hear the truth, I guess."

Even so, Mauer informed Norton that the Porcupine herd had concentrated its calving in the 1002 in twenty-seven out of the last thirty years. Yet the Secretary advised the grateful Senator that in more years than not (eleven out of eighteen) the caribou assembled *outside* of the 1002, suggesting that its biological importance had been much exaggerated. ("That's the way this administration does things," Mauer said ruefully.) Until the truth was exposed, Murkowski trumpeted these false figures on the Senate floor, together with Norton's claim that "Every day the U.S. imports 700,000 barrels of oil from Saddam Hussein. . . . It's time to start producing that energy in the U.S." The inspired Murkowski saw fit to almost double that figure, asserting that "Government figures show we imported 1.2 million barrels of oil from Iraq every day in September (2001), the most since 1990." In fact, only 3.18 percent of total U.S. consumption comes from Iraq, one of sixty different countries that enable our gluttonous oil habit, and, as it happens, the most strenuous advocates of *An*-War drilling—Exxon-Mobil, Chevron, Phillips—were all selling that Iraqi oil at a hefty profit.

It is now late July, and the Porcupine herd, with its new young, has already returned inland; on the myriad trails that web the odd, polygonal surface of the tundra, a lone deer plods southward, head low under its great antlers. The huge herd, packed close to protect itself against botflies and mosquitoes, is already returning through the mountains, and some will arrive in the Gwich'in country in late summer and early autumn.

Kaktovik is located on Barter Island, so-called because Inupiat bands scattered up and down the coast met here to trade. A traditional fishing place (Kaktovik means "Place for Seining") with a large pond of good freshwater on the high ground, the site has been occupied for thousands of years, says Robert Thompson. Not until it was built up as a Distant Early Warning (DEW Line) system site back in the fifties were the outlying Inupiat brought together to benefit from the new clinic and school; the advent of oil royalties in the late seventies and the need for a bureaucracy to dispense the money has given a kind of semipermanence to what is now a village of 280 people.

At the airstrip I am introduced to Walt Audi, a legendary bush pilot who rattles up in an old blue truck, a little late for his shuttle flight to pick up our companions on Icy Reef. A trim man with a white moustache and gray-white hair tied back in a thin ponytail, Walt wears a lavender sateen jacket inscribed "Nunamiut Trading Co. Anaktuvuk Pass"; he came here thirty-eight years ago with the DEW Line crews and stayed on to found a charter air service and a small inn, the Waldo Arms. Mr. Audi is renowned for his philosophical attitude toward the thick coastal fogs that all prudent pilots abhor. Fran Mauer describes flying with Walt "in fog so thick that any other pilot would be sitting forward, nose to the plexiglass, peering out for any sign or clue as to where he was, and here's Walt lounged back in his seat, munching his sandwich."

"I've heard a lot about you," I told Mr. Audi. "Uh-oh," said Walt shortly, going on about his business. He had come to the airstrip to fly to Icy Reef only to discover that his battery was dead. I didn't mention that nobody at Icy Reef expected him to show up before noon.

At his small blue house up in the village, Robert stares at the litter that overflows his yard, looking vaguely astonished and a bit sheepish. "All the things I meant to clean up here before I left, and they're still here," he says, waving regretfully at a collection that includes heaped fishnets, a kayak, oil cans, boots, and many other objects that would identify this yard all across the world as that of a commercial fisherman. What is different is an abandoned dogsled and some long, black strips of baleen from the great jaws of a bowhead whale. Robert says that the bowhead population, considered endangered only a few years ago, has now increased to an estimated ten thousand animals; Kaktovik is allowed a quota of three whales each year. As a crewman in the whaleboat, Robert receives a share of the baleen, which he uses in his spare time to fashion the little sailing craft and baleen-fiber baskets that adorn his shelves and walls.

Robert moves some stuff around to make room at the kitchen table, then digs out a few plates and pans and cooks up an eggs-and-bacon breakfast in which we are joined by his spirited wife Jane, who notifies Robert that just yesterday, on the first day of the hunting season, her brothers Bert and Joseph killed seven caribou, ensuring a fresh meat supply for everybody. Robert was describing the new military construction that was starting up in Alaska: The appallingly expensive system being rushed into place to defend the greatest superpower in all history against unimaginable enemies was the largest military build-up since the Vietnam War.

"Looks like big new dollars for *somebody,* I guess. You think us American people are getting brainwashed?" Robert smiles, but as an intelligent and thoughtful citizen, he is not joking. Unlike most of today's flag-wavers, he was a Vietnam volunteer, and would rather not be cynical about the brand of patriotism stemming from Congress and the White House. "Got to have a brain to get brainwashed, so that counts me out," he adds ruefully. "They got to have something to work with." We all laugh, more than a bit unhappy about the scary and undemocratic turn our great nation has taken.

Thirty years after oil production commenced at Prudhoe Bay, Kaktovik

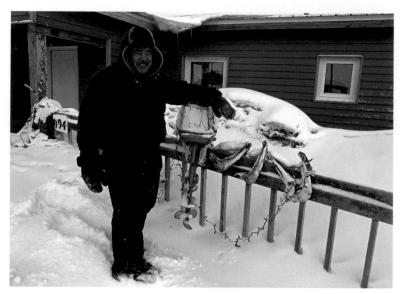
Robert Thompson outside his house at Kaktovik

still lacks running water, but $60 million dollars has now been allotted to installing a water and sewage system for the seventy-odd families in the village; at nearly a million dollars per household, Robert said with mock astonishment, this will certainly provide adequate plumbing, not to speak of the benefits to the politicians and contractors. ("That's why most of 'em will always vote for oil," as Tom Campion says. "So we have to fight this fight and win this fight outside of Alaska, because with all that money the politicians have to play with, there's no hope we're going to win it here.")

Though Robert was raised at Lake Minchumina, seventy miles northwest of Mount Denali, his wife, born Jane Akootchook, was raised in a leading family in Kaktovik. "Our people never had no rights," Jane says, "from the very start. Who gave the Russians the right to sell Alaska to the Americans? Sold my people to America right along with it. We were nobody, no more than the bugs—they got sold, too." Although she strongly favors the protection of the Arctic Refuge, she points out that the environmentalists and others involved in the early negotiations neglected the rights of the Inupiat when they dealt away their Native allotments, denying them the right to acquire land that was granted them almost a century ago, in 1906.

"When the Air Force came here in 1947, all our coast people were moved into Kaktovik, clear the way for Big Oil, I imagine. We never had no say about it even though this coastal plain out here—" she waves toward the south to indicate the inholding across the water in the 1002, where her people have surface rights to about 96,000 acres, "is our land, not theirs. We call it Home—this is *It*," she emphasizes, to make sure we understand. "And our people were put here to take care of it."

Years ago, in the late eighties, when public hearings about the 1002

were held here at Kaktovik, one of the officials demanded to hear the opinion of an ordinary person rather than another politician, who would clearly favor development—a housewife, say. For a long while, nobody dared speak, but finally someone piped up in a quavering voice, "Back home in the Lower 48, you people all have gardens in your yard. We can't have gardens in the Arctic. This place you call the North Slope, that is our garden. It is all we have, so we don't want to lose it."

"That was the most powerful speech given that day," Robert says proudly. "You could have heard a pin drop. But the mayor's wife, she was all shined up, she spoke out for development. She just repeated what they all say, how people like Jane and Robert Thompson are against progress, don't want good schools for our kids, want to keep the Inupiat back in the Stone Age. I guess some of 'em believed that. I guess they still do. All the same, there's other people in this village who are against development of the 1002," he says, as his wife nods. "They just don't dare say so."

The Inupiat at Kaktovik supported the Gwich'in against oil development as late as 1979, enjoining the federal government to enlarge the refuge and award permanent protection to the calving area. Though they were persuaded to cease their resistance and accept oil royalties, they still oppose the leases issued to BP and others for offshore drilling, since the sea and its creatures are sacred to their life in the way that the caribou are sacred to the Gwich'in. "Our people accepted oil development because they have always been very poor and need the money, so they are unhappy when others say that they are greedy. This is their chance to live like other Americans, maybe own some of the things they see on the TV—well, you can't blame 'em."

The Thompsons have paid dearly for their courage in standing fast against popular opinion. At one point, for about eight months, Robert and Jane found no jobs open to them in Kaktovik's oil-fuelled economy. When he finally got a job, Robert found himself repeatedly passed over for advancement by those less qualified. (He is modest and also bluntly honest, so one knows this must be true.) "Guess they didn't realize that I never cared for work," he says, his round face opening in a strong white-toothed smile as his wife laughs.

Though they regret the loss of those old ways that followed the coerced collection of traditional hunting and fishing communities into one big village, the Thompsons appreciate the benefits represented by a good clinic and a good school with good teachers. "But what happens when the oil runs out and the land is ruined and the people have forgotten how to live in our old way?"

Arriving toward midday, Alex wants to look for birds around Kaktovik and Robert is kind enough to guide us. Retrieving my son from the

Waldo Arms, a makeshift, rather windowless frontier hostel with a pool table, kitchen, and dining room-lounge, we set off along the dusty frozen streets—the only roads in all the Arctic Refuge. Robert points out with pride the new school, clinic, and firehouse, the new water tank used in winter (when Kaktovik's pond will freeze right to the bottom), and the new housing fitted with modern insulation, with dramatic savings in heating oil and expense—conservation which, if practiced country-wide, would obviate any perceived need to trash the refuge.

From a promontory, we scan the immense, ragged remains of a bowhead whale that had rotted beyond use by the time it was hauled out after a storm, but the rare gulls we seek are nowhere to be seen. Returning, we encounter Jane's sister Susie, accompanied by her young son. Ms. Akootchook is a pretty woman who welcomes us warmly to Kaktovik and tactfully parries my question about her views on oil development in the 1002 by pretending she has not made up her mind. At the airstrip, a white woman, Merilyn Trayner, advises me that although her companion, Walt Audi, is against oil development, she herself is "on the fence." However, she says that she's been told by Kaktovik's oldest resident, Nora Agiak, ninety-two, that her family, which had always hunted in the Prudhoe Bay region, had had their hunting camp bulldozed right out from under them by the oil people back in the 1970s. She says folks are wondering what would happen in the 1002 if those people get control.

Robert's concern is that wilderness designation for the 1002 might ignore Inupiat interests. "Nobody is consulting us," he says. "People are scared they can't hunt or fish on the refuge any more, which isn't true, but there's no education about it. You people say, 'Oh, that's all taken care of, that's fine'—well, we've heard that before. We want to see it written down on paper."

A larger plane will fly us west to Prudhoe Bay, to refuel at Deadhorse before returning south to Fairbanks. By the time we leave Kaktovik in late afternoon, the coast weather has turned colder. The sky is dark, with wind gusts and light rain, and a heavy sea fog sweeps in over the Inupiat land in the western region of the 1002, which is said to be highly promising for oil exploration. Back in the mid-1980s, the Chevron Corporation dug test holes within a few miles of its boundaries, raising the suspicion that the oil industry might be scouting the area with the encouragement of willing Inupiat politicians.

Some sixty miles west of Kaktovik near the Canning River, which separates the 1002 from the oil fields, the low-flying aircraft approaches a caribou herd of 150 to 200 animals; not far away is another of about 30 or 40. These caribou west of the 1002 belong to the so-called Central

Arctic herd, which is often photographed against a pipeline background to demonstrate the industry's beneficent effects on the wild creatures. But the coastal plain in the Prudhoe region is anywhere from 100 to 200 miles wide, whereas in the refuge it is but 24 to 40, and therefore this Central Arctic population, one fifth the size of the Porcupine herd, has a calving area five times as large in which to escape the sound and sight and smell of man's activities. Furthermore, the wolves and bears—though not the foxes, gulls, and ravens drawn to the dumps—have been largely eliminated by human proximity. Even so, according to Ken Whitten, a caribou biologist we spoke with in Fairbanks, the female caribou avoid bearing their calves in the pipeline area and are less likely to graze nearby thereafter; this herd has shown a marked decline as drilling activities spread into their calving areas. One can assume that the great Porcupine herd would also shift its calving area should the disruption spread into the refuge. But unlike the Central Arctic herd, there is no suitable alternate place for the Porcupine herd to go. The consequence of this may be a significant decline of the Porcupine herd.

Soon the first drilling pad takes shape in the blowing fog, its twelve ghostly wells lined up in two neat rows. Behind the well pumps lie several huge rectangular reserve pits for the highly toxic drilling fluids used for cooling and lubrication. Thirty years of oil field operations have produced millions of tons of toxic "drilling muds," which nobody has figured out how to get rid of—a great pity, since the permafrost resists a great amount of heavy metal hydrocarbons, which overflow and leak into the tundra. The migratory birds that try to breed here are directly affected, with unknown consequences up and down the food chains. (Injecting the poisoned muds beneath the permafrost has been attempted as an improvised solution, but unfortunately, as Alaska's mean temperature has risen due to global warming, the permafrost seems to be melting.)

Beyond the first wells, roads and land scars gouged by tracked vehicles begin accumulating; more drilling pads loom dimly through the fog, which mercifully shrouds the huge industrial site, one of the largest in the world. Prudhoe has almost four thousand wells and 500 miles of gravel roads, not to speak of proliferating feeder lines and the twelve enormous flow stations that separate the oil from the gas and water.

For a time, its deposits of high-quality crude oil, readily "recovered" from permeable rock, were immensely profitable, delivering as many as 2 million barrels a day into the trans-Alaska pipeline. Also delivered was an annual toxic burden of 56,000 tons of nitrogen oxides (which contribute to smog and acid rain), up to 11 metric tons of carbon dioxide, and some 24,000 to 114,000 metric tons of methane. The oil fields and pipeline average about one spill daily; there were 1,600 recorded spills from 1996 to 1999, most of them involving diesel fuel, which is highly toxic to plant life.

In support of its claim that future drilling will only affect a small area of the refuge, the industry offers more precise mapping of oil deposits, multilateral drilling from smaller pads up to four miles from the wells, and other new technology which it claims will reduce the size of its "footprint" to an area no larger than one medium-size airport. Much of the damage, it is claimed, might be offset by confining explorations to the frozen winter, using ice roads instead of digging gravel. If implemented, these steps would certainly improve matters, but to drill a new oil field efficiently would still require, besides the wells themselves, an estimated 280 miles of new roads and hundreds of miles of pipelines, whether built on ice roads or the usual foundation of millions of cubic yards of gravel scraped off every riverbed and lake bottom across the tundra—an awful devastation of such bare terrain, made all the more intrusive by airstrips and production facilities, service buildings and sewage plants, and housing for thousands of workers.

In effect, the "footprint" is a public relations euphemism, even more misleading than "recovering" the oil (which tends to suggest that instead of being violently sucked out, along with drilling muds, chemicals, and poisoned water, the raw petroleum had somehow been lost and now was found, not by some Amazing Grace but thanks to the bountiful public spirit of Exxon or Enron or whatever). The footprint implies the visible infrastructure of the whole oil field operation could be mushed together on that one unimaginable airport. By that gauge, as Tom Campion points out, the footprint of a tripod—the space actually taken up by the opened tripod—would be confined to the three small spots where its leg tips touch the ground.

Instead of phantom footprints, one might consider that over 96 percent of the North Slope of Alaska is already open to leasing and drilling; that the National Petroleum Reserve, a substantially larger area adjoining the Prudhoe oil fields to the west, lies undeveloped seventy-five years after it was designated a reserve; that realistic estimates of economically exploitable oil potential in the 1002, based on U.S. Geological Survey studies in 1998, work out to about 3.2 billion barrels, or less than a six-month supply for the wasteful fossil fuel economy of the U.S., which consumes 25 percent of the world's oil production while possessing only 3 percent of its known reserves. Even were the refuge to produce double the estimates, supplying enough oil for a year, five or ten years of heavy footprinting would pass before the first drop entered the economy.

Consider, too, that the same corporations that holler about "dependence on foreign oil" and fight to exploit the refuge also fought to lift the ban against the export of Alaska oil, which until recently was marketed in China and Japan. Consider next that due to the high cost of extraction in the remote far north, the dwindling reserves scarcely justify so much investment (and so much bad publicity), and many

companies are cutting back on production in the region, even though, after twenty-two years, they want this "victory" so badly that they still harass Congress for the 1002.

The abandonment of the Kyoto Protocol by the Bush administration laid the groundwork for the disastrous "national energy initiative" led by Vice President Richard Cheney. In May 2001, after months of consultations with his Big Oil associates, Cheney produced a National Energy Policy that included an astonishing $27 billion worth of corporate welfare in the form of public subsidies and tax cuts for the already opulent oil, coal, and nuclear power industries, a giveaway as shocking as the top-heavy Bush tax cut, and positively grotesque when contrasted with the less than $1 billion for research and development of the clean wind and solar alternatives, which were tossed a poor scrap amounting to less than 1 percent of the amount lavished on the big polluters. Not surprisingly, the resulting energy bill passed by the House (H.R. 4) featured provisions for industrial oil drilling in the Arctic Refuge.

Europe is already far ahead of the U.S. in sustainable energy development (especially wind and solar power), with predictable future consequences for America's diehard fossil fuel economy. In this era of worldwide climate disruption, these archaic industries continue to work against the national interest, dispensing an insupportable burden of filth and poisons and transgressing the rights and welfare of all other beings, other creatures, who must suffer their toxic wastes.

Consider, finally, that the entire 1002 production could easily be made up by the less wasteful oil use already under way in Arctic Village and Kaktovik. In addition, the EPA has projected that increasing fuel consumption standards by just three miles per gallon would save more than a million barrels a day, or five times what the 1002 could possibly supply, reducing the dread "dependence on foreign oil" far faster and more reliably than problematic drilling in a beautiful and precious wilderness that is sacred to our Native peoples. The Arctic Refuge belongs not to the multinational corporations and their minions in public office but in public trust for our inheritors—indeed, for all mankind around the world.

Leaving Deadhorse at Prudhoe Bay, the pilot follows the silver tube of the trans-Alaska pipeline and its service road—the so-called Dalton Highway, or Haul Road—which follows the braided Sagavanirktok upriver toward the mountains. Built in 1974, the Haul Road was restricted to transporting workers and supplies, but in 1995, the state opened it up to all and sundry. Seeing no guard stations, no guards, no dust nor sign of vehicles along the Haul Road, I realize how simple it would be to sabotage this artery, rupture it or blow it up, splashing a toxic gusher onto the frozen ground. (Already the Sagavanirktok delta is so poisoned that the 117 snow goose nests that were monitored in 2000 produced only three goslings.)

A few miles inland, the sea mist dissipates and sunlight glints on the river's steep ochre cliffs and the steel pipe that winds its dragon way over the tundra. From here it is 400 miles to Fairbanks and about twice that distance to the great tankers at Valdez. To the west lies Service City, a defunct camp where the oil gave out; there will be many Service Cities in this landscape once the coastal plain has been looted and befouled and the oil is gone. Service City and the Sacred Place Where Life Begins —the names tell us more than we might care to confront about our materialist culture, our ever-increasing alienation from what the traditional people know as Land and Life.

The day is clearing as immensities of empty land fade into the mists in all directions. The airplane has left the pipeline, tending southwest, and once again, almost a half-century after that flight north to Point Barrow, I peer down into the emptiness and silence of the National Petroleum Reserve (NPR)-Alaska. What lies beneath the wing is the largest block of undeveloped wilderness in the United States, 23.5 million acres, from the polar seas all the way south to the mountains. Set aside by President Harding in 1923, NPR-Alaska was never drilled during World War II nor even in the oil crisis of the 1970s. In 1997, President Clinton's Department of the Interior, under pressure from Alaska's politicians, began the process of leasing 3.9 million acres for exploratory drilling in this northeastern region of the NPR that adjoins the existing oil fields, yet the NPR has yet to deliver its first drop of oil to the trans-Alaska pipeline— a point to keep in mind, perhaps, when considering what the fossil fuelers seem so bent on perpetrating in the adjoining 1002.

The younger Bush, like his father before him, made drilling in the Arctic Refuge the emblem of his energy policy—indeed, it was the solitary environmental issue he campaigned on—but despite the heavy effluvium of Big Oil that accompanied both Bushes into the White House, the idea of marginal drilling in this last pristine area was resisted by the Senate in April 2002. Despite this setback, Alaska's senators and this oil-steeped administration are still gunning for the "An-War," and meanwhile the Bush administration has rushed ahead with plans to lease an additional 10 million acres in the NPR, even while fighting all attempts to increase fuel efficiency and develop the sustainable clean alternatives.

How truly sad it seems to me, after fifty years as an environmentalist, that so many years of progress in conservation and sustainable energies, together with the world's great hopes for control of carbon dioxide emissions from the burning of fossil fuels that might defer the coming cataclysm of global warming, are being blocked, stalled,

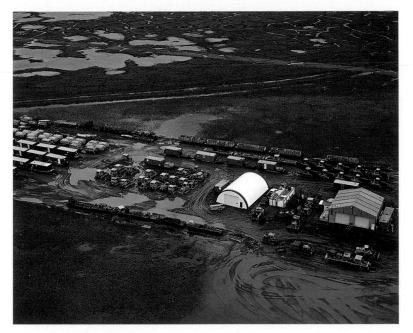

Prudhoe Bay industrial complex

derailed, and turned back toward the past by the oil and automotive industries and their team in Washington. Indeed, I am outraged that the last pristine places on our looted earth are being sullied without mercy, vision, or good sense by greedy people who are robbing their fellow citizens of the last natural bounty and profusion that Americans once took for granted. Many years will be lost trying to undo some of the recent reckless damage to clean air and water, old-growth forest, biodiversity, and many other crucial aspects of our environment that is being committed for the profit of a few by this administration. No one can say that in his first two years, the younger Bush has not made his mark in regard to the environment (the great impending crisis of the new century even before this backward turn by the conservatives)— an indelible mark that is fast becoming an ugly, spreading stain.

Perhaps as soon as the end of this decade, the bright and boundless energy of sun and wind will have largely supplanted fossil fuels, removing its greatest toxic burden from our strangled planet and putting an end to the foremost cause of global warming. By that time, however—failing our demand that America's last great wilderness be protected—the magnificent Arctic Refuge may be fatally disrupted to no worthy purpose.

"If we fail to save the land, God may forgive us," as a Togiak elder has said, "but our children won't."

Peter Matthiessen

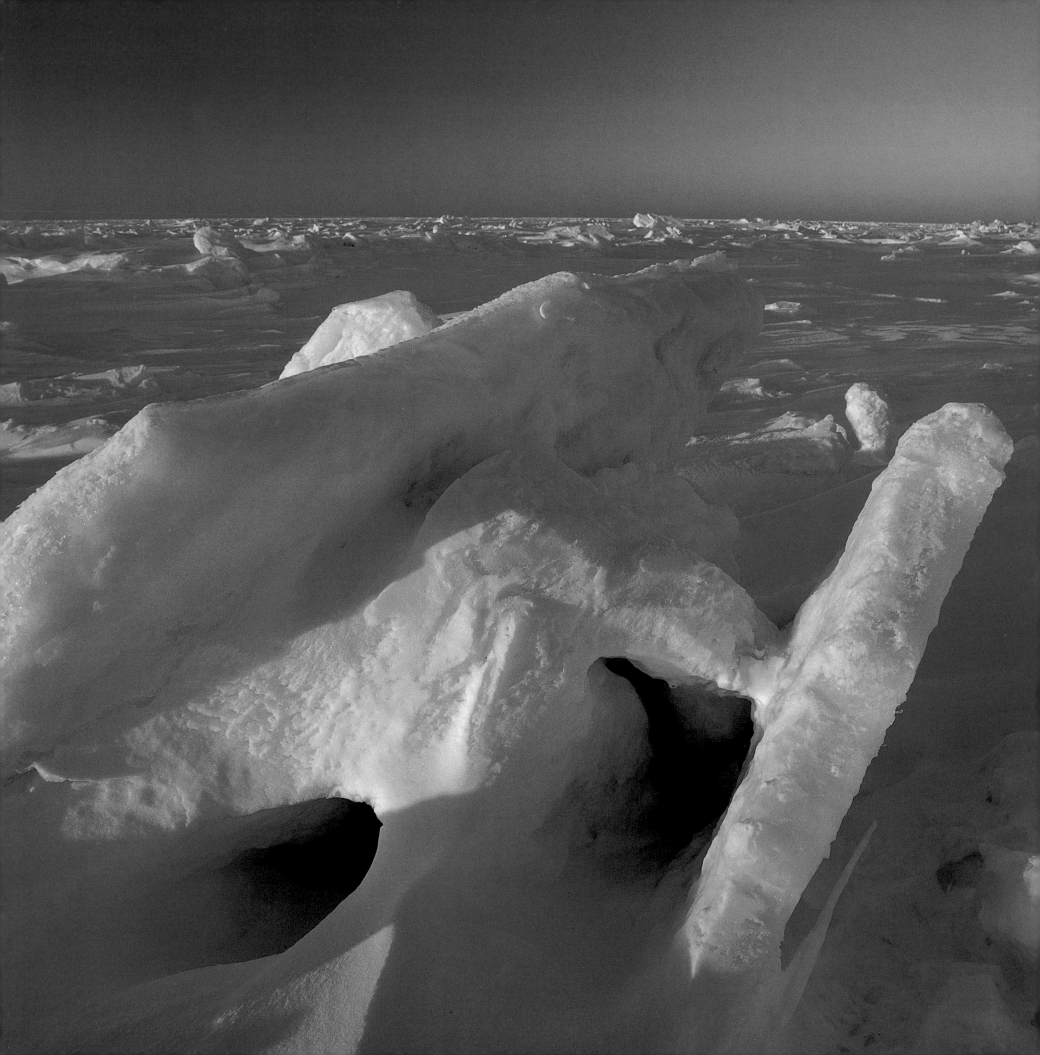

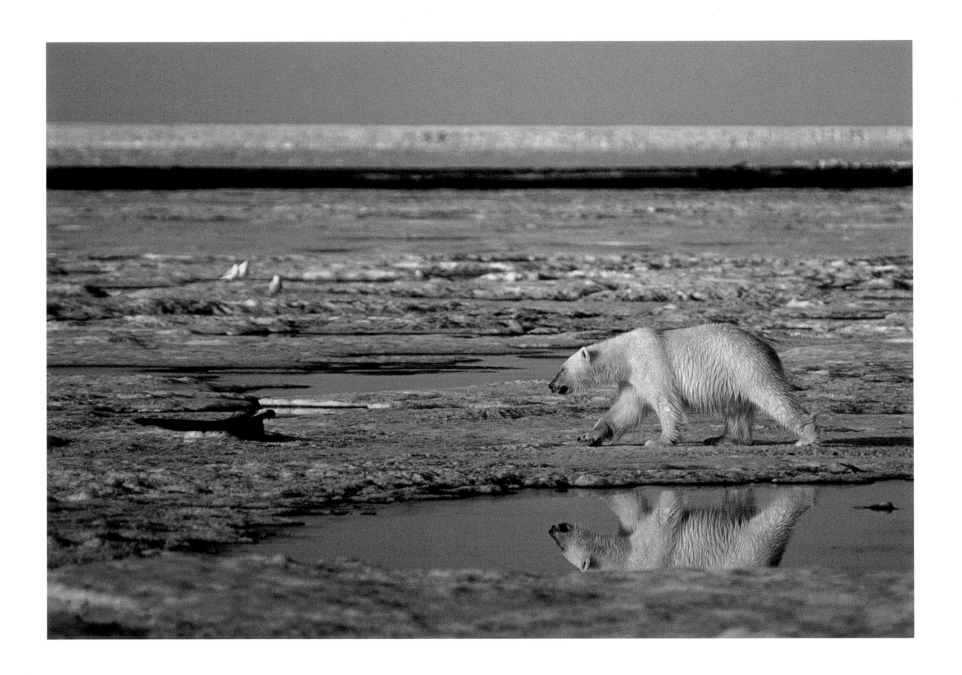

Polar bear approaches whale bones from the previous years' hunt on frozen Bernard Harbor in early June.
The whale remains are left on the ice to be consumed by polar bears, grizzly bears, Arctic foxes, and gulls.

Opposite • Frozen sea on the coast of the refuge: Wave action during fall freeze-up causes jumbled patterns of ice.

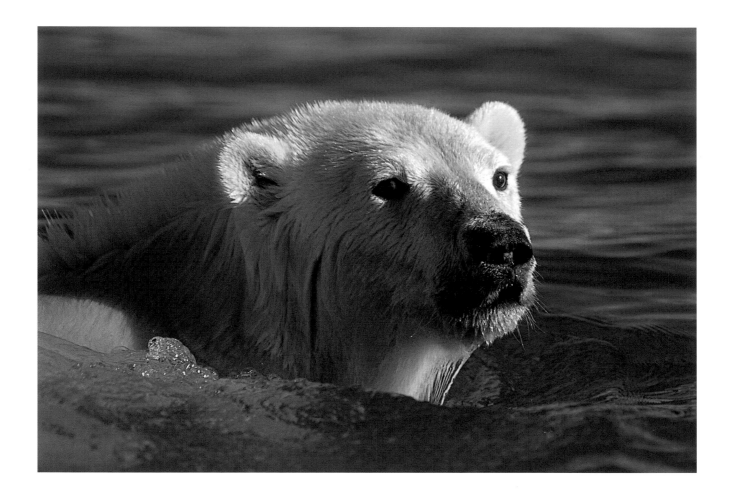

Polar bear in Bernard Harbor

Opposite • Icebergs along the coastal waters of Icy Reef

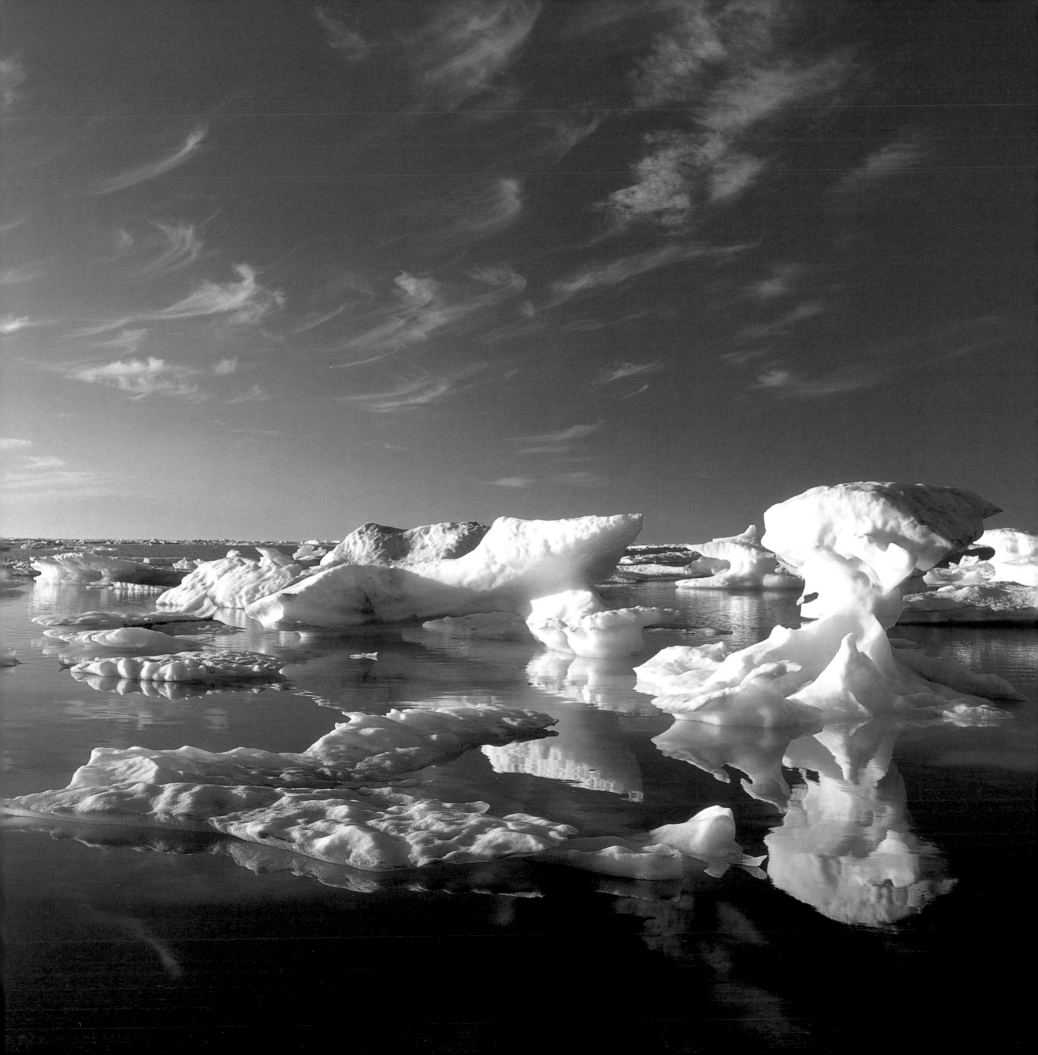

george b. schaller

ARCTIC LEGACY

Conservationists have to win again and again and again; the enemy only has to win once.

DAVID BROWER
Founder, Friends of the Earth
and Earth Island Institute

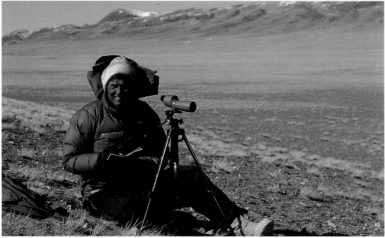

Photo by George B. Schaller

GEORGE B. SCHALLER *is a field biologist and since 1998 has served as Director for Science at the Wildlife Conservation Society in New York. He was born in 1933 and went to the Universities of Alaska and Wisconsin. He was a member of the 1956 Murie expedition to Alaska, which resulted in the establishment of the Arctic National Wildlife Refuge. Schaller has spent most of his time during the past fifty years in the wilds of Asia, Africa, and South America, and has studied and helped protect species as diverse as the mountain gorilla, lion, jaguar, tiger, giant panda, and wild sheep and goats of the Himalaya. These studies have been the basis for his scientific and popular writings, including fifteen books, among them* The Year of the Gorilla; The Last Panda; *and* The Serengeti Lion: A Study of Predator–Prey Relations, *which won the National Book Award in 1972. For the past decade he has studied wildlife in Laos, Mongolia, and the Tibetan Plateau of China. His work helped persuade the Chinese government to set aside a portion of Tibet for nature preserves. His awards include the International Cosmos Prize (Japan) and the Tyler Prize for Environmental Achievement (USA).*

June 1, 1956: Bush pilot Keith Harrington banks his Cessna 180 over a lake in the Sheenjek River valley in northeastern Alaska and lands on the frozen surface. Bob Krear and I, both graduate students in wildlife ecology, quickly unload the plane, which then returns south to Fort Yukon. We cut poles and erect tents on a knoll among stunted spruce. Beyond the lake Table Mountain is still capped with snow, but here in the valley, at an elevation of 2,000 feet, spring is near, with the first purple saxifrages in bloom and a willow ptarmigan on her clutch of six eggs beneath a rhododendron shrub. Sanderlings, black-bellied plovers, and other shorebirds wheel over the lake, migrants traveling north across the Brooks Range to the Arctic tundra. A muskrat splashes and a pair of old squaw ducks paddles in a lead between ice and shore. The valley is resurgent with life after a long, harsh winter.

The following day brings Olaus and Margaret (Mardy) Murie, as well as Brina Kessel, an ornithologist at the University of Alaska. Olaus is president of The Wilderness Society and a renowned mammalogist who, with Mardy, has done research on Alaska's wildlife since the 1920s. After our summer's work they will become leaders in the four-year struggle to protect this region. As we settle into camp we immediately begin to absorb the wild beauty around us. We have come to study not only the natural history but also to gather impressions of the "precious intangible values," as Olaus phrased it, with the hope that this knowledge will lead to protection of the area.

In this land of the midnight sun the jubilant singing of juncos, myrtle warblers, tree sparrows, and gray-cheeked thrushes can be heard twenty-four hours a day. From our tents we see occasional bands of caribou crossing the lake ice in single file and hear the sound of their clicking hooves. They are part of what is known as the Porcupine herd, and they, too, are heading to the tundra of the coastal plain, where they will gather by the tens of thousands to calve. One day two massive grizzlies the color of winter grass trace the shoreline eating tender green sedges. And once a gray wolf trots past our tents; we name the lake by our camp Lobo Lake in his honor.

On first hearing about this proposed expedition, I wrote a letter to

Olaus offering my services as assistant for free, my reward being the chance to learn from him. Olaus replied graciously that he would "be very glad to have you with me." And he further explained why he wanted to visit the Brooks Range: "I simply had the urge to get into that mountain country, to see what animal life is there, to photograph and to sketch, and to somehow get the feel of the country. . . . You might be glad to explore the country out from camp, to gather what information you can, and gain an understanding of the ecology of the region that may be useful to you in your future work." What aspiring naturalist could resist such an invitation and the quiet passion, enthusiasm, and spirit of adventure of the person extending it!

We roam daily from camp, alone or in twos and threes, observing, recording, photographing. Our plant collection grows rapidly as we examine different habitats, including the riverbank with its occasional stands of cottonwood trees and the lowland meadows with their tussocks of cotton grass. I scrape different kinds of lichens off the bark of white spruce and seek others hidden close to the ground among the crowberries and cranberries. Tree borings show that a spruce twenty feet tall is about one hundred years old. Leaving the valley, I climb among the stark, gray limestone cliffs bordering it up to the alpine tundra, where I note the first gentian and delphinium of the season and add wheatear, horned lark, and Lapland longspur to our bird list. I collect invertebrates too, preserving them in vials of alcohol, from fleet wolf spiders to ants, beetles, and even mosquitoes, three species of which have become our intrusive companions. It is warm now, daytime temperatures into the sixties.

Evenings at camp we gather to share our experiences: a beaver track in the mud of a river bar, a cow moose with calf, a red fox hunting meadow voles, a gyrfalcon eyrie high in a rock niche with three young. "I watched a female ptarmigan chase a ground squirrel when it came too close to the nest," relates Mardy. Olaus shows us his vibrant field sketches, perhaps of an Arctic loon or a cast caribou antler. Occasionally Bob returns with a string of grayling he has caught with a fly rod. Before enjoying them for dinner we measure them—most are eight to fourteen inches long—and detach a scale by which they can be aged. Later analysis shows that they generally are six to eight years old.

During our wanderings we also collect the droppings, or scats, of fox, wolf, lynx, and grizzly. Olaus shows us how to identify what these predators have eaten by the color, thickness, and length of the hair and the fragments of bone. At this season, grizzlies dig mainly for roots and graze on sedges, but they also consume whatever meat they can obtain, from grayling to ground squirrel and caribou. I remember with what delight Olaus knelt on the tundra to lift a soggy pile of grizzly scat to

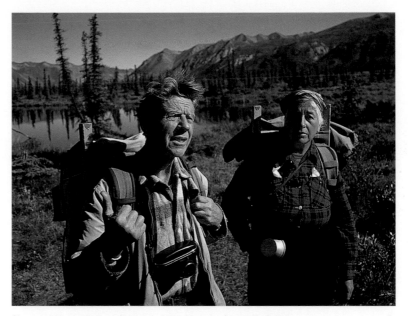

Olaus and Mardy Murie at Sheenjek, 1956 *Photo by George B. Schaller*

inspect its contents closely. Wolves hunt mainly caribou and lynx at this season and often catch ground squirrels, probably because their favored snowshoe hares are at the low point of a population cycle. The red fox lives on lemmings, voles, ptarmigan, ground squirrel, and caribou, the last no doubt scavenged from wolf kills.

All these facts may seem trivial, but they add to our knowledge of the natural history of the region. Our evening discussions also have a deeper dimension. Olaus emphasizes that we must keep this region "in its natural state so the people from all over the world may visit it for hunting, fishing, and photography, or just to get away from it all." And Mardy speaks of "the gift of personal satisfaction, the personal well-being purchased by striving, by lifting and setting down legs over and over through muskeg, up the slopes, gaining the summit."

This procession of perfect days, of sharing observations and knowledge and companionship, has a great influence on me. My admiration of Olaus and Mardy grows as with warmth and modesty they lead our expedition and set an outstanding example of how to study and enjoy the life around them. Olaus is in his late sixties, a lean man with unruly hair and an infectious, broad smile, yet he approaches each day with curiosity, a responsive heart, and an undimmed capacity for wonder.

He is teaching me the value of good fieldwork, but, more important, he conveys the spiritual values of wilderness. Within days of our arrival in the Sheenjek valley we are held captive by its splendor. Here one can recapture the rhythm of life and the feeling of belonging to the natural world. We all know that it must be preserved as an original fragment of our past, a last opportunity to protect part of this continent as it once was.

In late June we move camp upvalley to the shore of Last Lake, as we name it. I set off one day on a lone week-long walk "to explore the country," as Olaus had urged me, around the headwaters of the Sheenjek. My pack is heavy with enough food for ten days, a pot, a sleeping bag, an air mattress, and a tarp beneath which to crawl if it rains or snows at night. Trudging along, I scan ahead for wildlife, especially for grizzlies, hoping yet not hoping to encounter one of these potentially dangerous creatures. A few days before I left, Brina, Bob, and I were moving through a stand of dense spruce, our tread muted by sphagnum moss, when suddenly a grizzly charged furiously from the shadows, the hair on its back raised. Bob yelled and jumped forward, Brina and I leaped back, and the bear landed between us, turned, and vanished. We had carelessly disturbed the grizzly's midday rest.

After hiking about forty miles toward the crest of the Brooks Range, I skirt a cirque glacier at 7,000 feet and stand on a knoll near the divide, a passing snow squall swirling around me. Twelve Dall sheep rams are nearby, their white coats bright against leaden scree. It is July 15. From here the Sheenjek River drains south and the Hulahula River drains north to the sea, the latter named for Hawaiian whalers who overwintered at its mouth in the early 1900s. Standing among sharp-edged peaks, at the convergence of mountain and sky, I am alone at a place without roads or people, not even trails except those trodden by wild sheep and caribou; there is nothing to violate the peace, with mountains still unaffected by humankind. Here one can recapture the rhythm of life and the feeling of belonging to the natural world. I also have the atavistic pleasure of seemingly being an explorer. Back in 1894, Frederick Funston of the Department of Agriculture sledded up the Sheenjek and down the Kongakut to the coast. And in 1926 and 1927, the geologist J. B. Mertie traversed the area on foot. To my knowledge, with few exceptions, only Native peoples have known these mountains intimately until now.

Looking at the rivulets that would join to become the Hulahula River, I wish that I could follow the valley down to the coastal plain. These plains, which extend only about thirty miles between mountains and sea, are the biological heart of the region. Polar bears den there in snowdrifts in November, give birth to cubs in December or January, and finally emerge in March or early April. More polar bears make dens in the refuge than anywhere else along Alaska's coast, and it is the only conservation area in the nation where polar bears den regularly. Well over 100,000 caribou of the Porcupine herd gather on the plains to calve, often packed together for protection against the

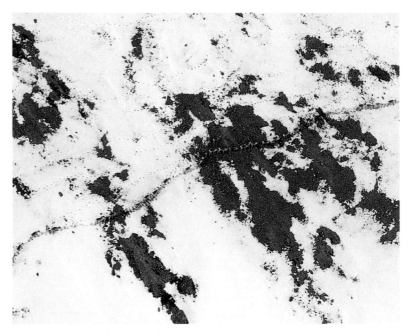

Porcupine caribou moving north during spring migration

hordes of mosquitoes and botflies. The bird life there is extraordinary, with many species not found in the Sheenjek valley: Tundra swans, various species of ducks and geese, and shorebirds share the ponds and ocean flats. Flocks of king eiders trace the edge of the Arctic Ocean in flight. I had marveled at this bird life farther west during the summer of 1952 on a trip made along the Colville River, when we recorded sixty-two species of birds, but I have yet to see the white blizzard of snow geese that use the plain to forage on white-plumed cotton grass and other foods before their long autumn migration south.

Bob would no doubt enjoy fishing for Dolly Varden trout in the Hulahula River. But our task is to survey a sample area, not the whole region. Perhaps I can visit the coastal plain another year.

I cross a divide toward the west and descend to the headwaters of the East Fork of the Chandalar River, where I unroll my sleeping bag on a river bar. Dinner consists of crackers, raisins, and a cup of cold water. I am too weary to make a fire and cook, but am filled with the contentment that comes from achievement and exhaustion.

A noise awakens me at five o'clock the following morning, a cacophony of grunts, churning gravel, and rushing water. I sit up. Caribou! They flow down the shadowed valley toward me, some in single file, others in a compact mass. I recline and wait motionless. The animals pass, ignoring me a mere sixty feet away, of no more relevance than a stray log of driftwood. Bulls with heads bent under the weight of antlers and weary cows with still wearier calves at heel

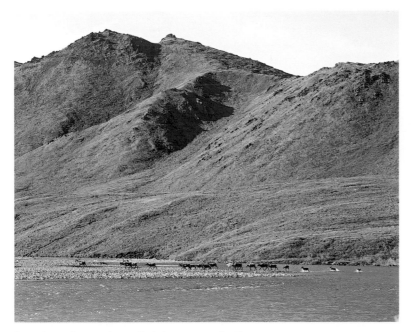 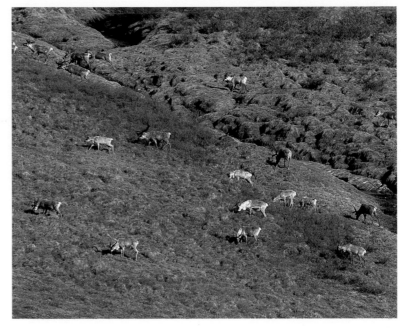

Porcupine caribou moving south during summer migration

surge down the valley at a hectic pace. Wave after wave washes by me, a total of some two thousand, before the clatter of hooves recedes. The return migration has begun.

The Porcupine herd, estimated to number between 170,000 and 200,000 at the time, generally heads eastward from the plains and into the mountains after calving, up and down valleys and over alpine passes toward Canada. In some years the animals will winter in the forested lowlands of the Yukon Territory, having migrated some three hundred to four hundred miles from the calving grounds, and in other years a part of the population remains in what is now the Arctic Refuge. The animals dominate the landscape wherever they are, a river of life, always moving, moving toward the ridge beyond, not only defining this Arctic ecosystem but also symbolizing the freedom of its wilderness.

Days later, back at camp, I find a piece of gray chert with a serrated edge on a knoll. It is a hide scraper made by a hunter long ago, perhaps as he scanned the valley for prey. Further searching reveals other stone tools and waste flakes. An archaeologist later tells us that these artifacts may be as much as eight thousand years old. One morning we spot a white tent across the valley. I wade the braided Sheenjek to investigate and find three Gwich'in Indians from Arctic Village, south of the Brooks Range, close to what is now the Arctic Refuge. Ambrose William, the eldest, gnaws on a porcupine leg while David Peter fries dough in deep grease over hot coals. Peter Tritt watches, awaiting his breakfast. Pack dogs are chained to nearby spruce. A wolf hide is stretched out to dry.

"Wolf hunting?" I ask, continuing a conversation. "Hunting wolf and prospecting some," replies Ambrose William. At that time the Territory of Alaska paid a bounty of fifty dollars for every dead wolf. The hunters later visit our camp and give us useful information about the region. The Gwich'in in Alaska and Canada depend on caribou hunting for survival and cultural identity, the destinies of caribou and humans intertwined. Olaus assures them that if an Arctic reserve is established, they will still be able to continue their ancestral ways.

By late July, the brief Arctic summer grades into autumn as blueberries ripen and willow leaves turn gold. Every rainstorm in the valley brings snow to the peaks. On August 1, the family of resident short-billed gulls suddenly leaves Last Lake. Two months have passed since our arrival and we have collected much information. We have recorded 85 bird species and 18 mammal species in this valley. My plant press holds 40 species of lichen and 138 species of flowering plants. And my vials contain 23 spider species, to give just one example of the invertebrates. Our tallies represent only a small fraction of the totals in the region. Years later the Fish and Wildlife Service would list 180 bird species for the Arctic Refuge as a whole, and also 36 land mammals, 9 marine mammals including ringed seal and bowhead whale, and 40 fish species. Such figures illustrate the remarkable diversity of life in a region that many consider an empty wasteland, or "a barren desert," as Senator Ted Stevens (R-Alaska) phrased it just a few years ago.

Invited by Olaus, Supreme Court Justice William O. Douglas,

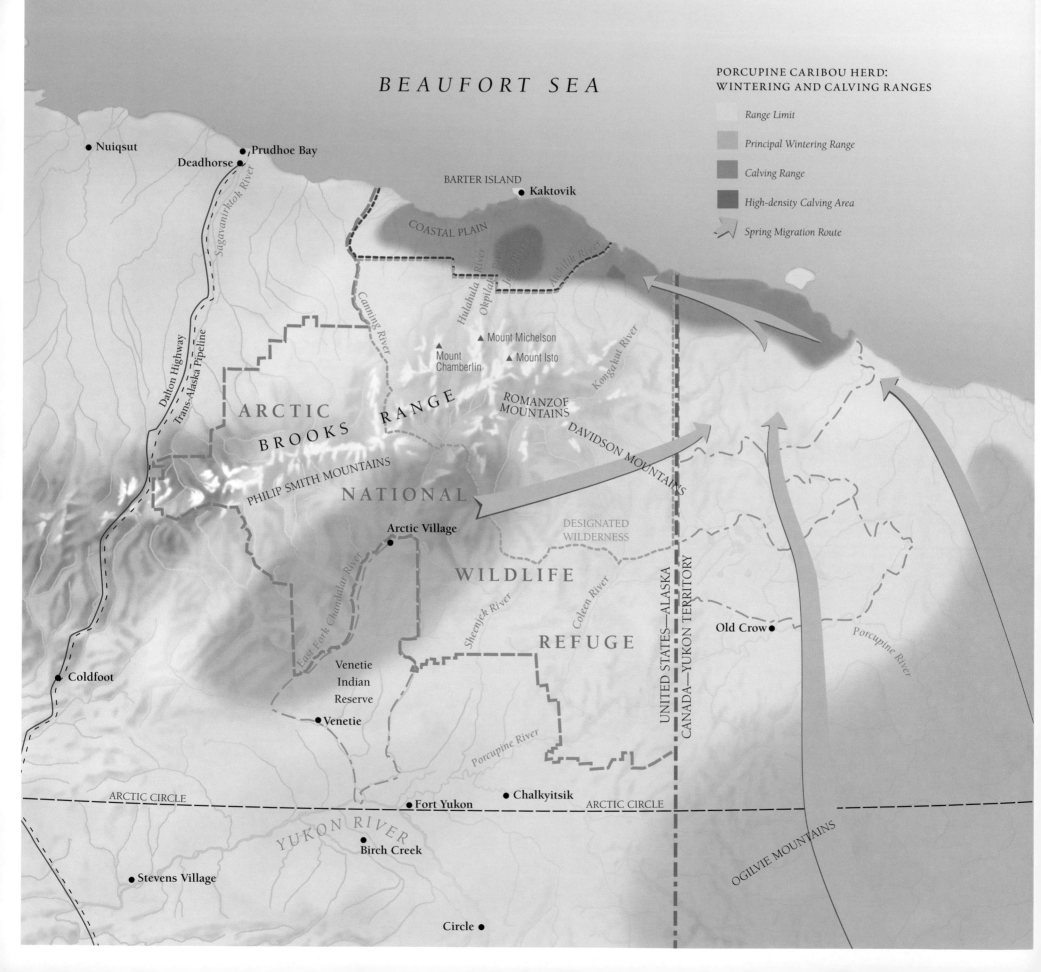

BEAUFORT SEA

PORCUPINE CARIBOU HERD:
WINTERING AND CALVING RANGES

Range Limit

Principal Wintering Range

Calving Range

High-density Calving Area

Spring Migration Route

Nuiqsut

Prudhoe Bay

Deadhorse

BARTER ISLAND

Kaktovik

COASTAL PLAIN

Sagavanirktok River

Canning River

Hulahula River

Okpilak River

Jago River

Aichilik River

Kongakut River

Mount Michelson

Mount Chamberlin

Mount Isto

Dalton Highway

Trans-Alaska Pipeline

ARCTIC

BROOKS   RANGE

ROMANZOF
MOUNTAINS

DAVIDSON MOUNTAINS

PHILIP SMITH MOUNTAINS

NATIONAL

Arctic Village

DESIGNATED
WILDERNESS

WILDLIFE

East Fork Chandalar River

Sheenjek River

Coleen River

REFUGE

Old Crow

Porcupine River

Coldfoot

Venetie
Indian
Reserve

UNITED STATES—ALASKA

CANADA—YUKON TERRITORY

Venetie

Porcupine River

ARCTIC CIRCLE

Fort Yukon

Chalkyitsik

ARCTIC CIRCLE

YUKON RIVER

Birch Creek

OGILVIE MOUNTAINS

Stevens Village

Circle

an ardent proponent of wilderness, visited our camp with his wife Mercedes. In discussions about the future of this region, he helped to make me aware that conservation is basically politics, that powerful voices in Washington will ultimately determine the course of events. Later he reflected our feelings when he wrote, "This last American living wilderness must remain sacrosanct."

On August 5 we leave the Sheenjek with the early migrant birds.

Upon our return from the 1956 expedition, Olaus began a campaign to arouse interest in protecting northeastern Alaska. As a result of his efforts and those of others, public support for a reserve became widespread. But C. L. Anderson, a former commissioner of the Alaska Fish and Game Department, grumbled in 1959, "The Arctic is probably in little more danger of being trampled in future years than is the moon."

My summer in the Sheenjek valley bequeathed to me a legacy of memory and desire. So naturally I was elated when, on December 6, 1960, a year after Alaska became a state and just before the Eisenhower administration ended, Secretary of the Interior Fred Seaton issued a Public Land Order officially establishing the 8.9 million-acre Arctic National Wildlife Range. It was the culmination of many years of effort to protect America's last great wilderness. Robert Marshall, a forester and founding member of The Wilderness Society, had first urged wilderness protection for the Brooks Range in the 1930s. And in 1952 and 1953, two National Park Service biologists, George Collins and Lowell Sumner, had surveyed the mountains and coastal plain and envisioned a park there. Then in 1956, the New York Zoological Society (now renamed the Wildlife Conservation Society) and the Conservation Foundation had sponsored Olaus and Mardy "to push a movement to establish a large permanent reserve in the Brooks Range region extending perhaps across the border into Canada." And our expedition had finally led to success.

With the discovery of oil at Prudhoe Bay in 1968, the tranquil outlook for the reserve vanished. Beginning in 1987, the oil companies, especially British Petroleum (BP), lobbied Congress intensively for drilling rights in the Arctic Refuge. President Bush the Elder made drilling there the centerpiece of his national energy policy. The Department of the Interior released a resource assessment that recommended oil and gas leasing in the refuge, a rather predictable political conclusion from a department that had three different heads during the 1980s, each with a pro-development agenda.

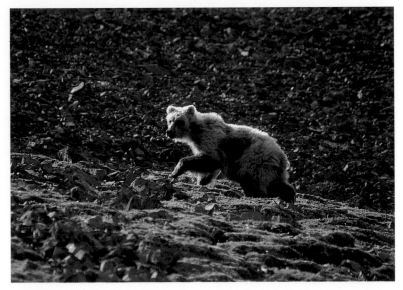

Grizzly bear

Then on March 23, 1989, the *Exxon Valdez* tanker ran aground in Prince William Sound, spilling over 10 million gallons of oil. The oil companies, complacent and unprepared, had assured legislators in Alaska and Washington that a large spill was "highly unlikely." The effort to invade the Arctic Refuge became a political casualty, temporarily, because the public became so well aware of the potential damage from oil spills that legislators felt it advisable to lie low for a while.

For over two decades the same arguments have been recycled for and against drilling in the reserve by politicians, oil companies, and conservationists. The United States still lacks a coherent energy policy, one that encourages conservation of resources at least as much as it does oil and gas extraction. We cannot drill ourselves to energy independence. The United States depends on over 50 percent of its oil from imports and the figure will rise even if the Arctic Refuge adds its oil—which would total less than 5 percent of annual U.S. consumption. We need motivation to save energy. But if we cannot reduce the insatiable urge to consume, then legislation must force us. Yet, pandering to business interests, the Senate voted on March 13, 2002, to delay any increase in the gas mileage standards for vehicles.

In an op-ed piece in *The New York Times* in October 2000, Senator Frank Murkowski (R-Alaska) offered the view that "energy production and environmental protection can coexist." But take a look at Prudhoe Bay. This industrial oil complex sprawls over eight hundred square miles. It consists of gravel pits, drilling rigs, airstrips, massive buildings, and over a thousand miles of pipeline. According to various sources, there are an average of nearly five hundred large and small oil spills each year. Some 64 million gallons of toxic metals and chemicals were

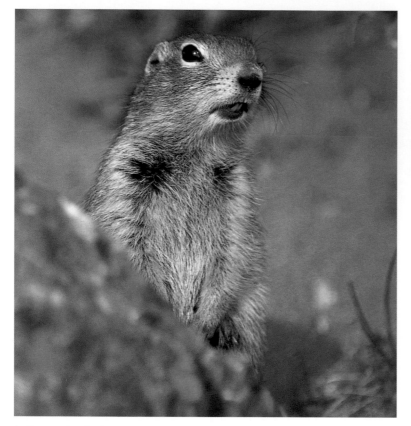

Arctic ground squirrel

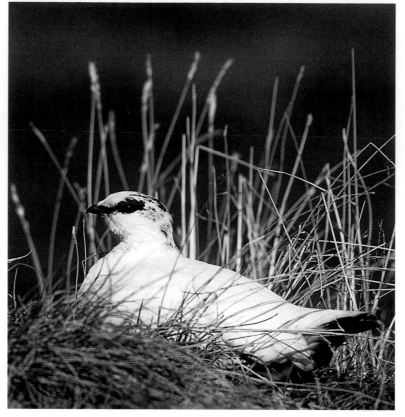

Male rock ptarmigan in winter plumage: The males change to summer plumage later than the females. Their brilliant white feathers against the rich brown foothills distract predators while the camouflaged females attend the nest.

discharged onto the tundra in 1986 alone. Up to a third of the safety cutoff valves on the pipelines did not work during the winter of 2000–2001. Emissions from the industrial complex at Prudhoe Bay of nitrogen oxide and sulfur dioxide, both compounds of acid rain, are said to rival those of some large cities. Oil companies have a legal mandate to restore any damaged habitat, but still lack the knowledge, technology, and willpower to do so. There is as yet no "environmentally sensitive" way to extract oil. Those who find splendor in industrial sprawl and pollution can now seek spiritual solace at Prudhoe Bay.

Wilderness has given North America its vision and identity. The Arctic Refuge remains a place where one can return to this continent's cultural beginnings two centuries ago when Europeans first penetrated the unknown. What will future generations have if we destroy this last true wilderness, sacrificing the eternal for the expedient? Oil companies already have rights to 96.5 percent of Alaska's coastal plain. The last 3.5 percent can certainly be preserved solely for its own sake, unaffected by greed, where people can regain a feeling of solitude, seek spiritual values, and enjoy a world unaffected by humankind.

The Arctic Refuge retains its ecological integrity, something increasingly uncommon in a world of consumption. It contains the full range of Arctic habitats with all its varied animals and plants, from grizzly bears and caribou to wolves and gyrfalcons, and from tundra and high mountains to boreal forest. Given the increasing exploitation of natural resources in the Arctic, we need an undamaged ecosystem to provide a baseline from which to compare, measure, and record climate-induced and other environmental changes.

The Arctic Refuge is a place of living grandeur, one throbbing with life, an Arctic legacy of world importance that we must treat with respect and restraint. Its presence honors the past, assures the Native peoples, especially the Gwich'in of Alaska and Canada, their subsistence and cultural identity, and makes a bequest to the future. Few people will ever visit this remote place. But one need not see a grizzly or a throng of caribou or fog-shrouded peaks rising above nameless valleys to benefit from their presence. Wilderness values are too precious to permit them to succumb to special interests. One must question what is ethically and esthetically correct, and not just

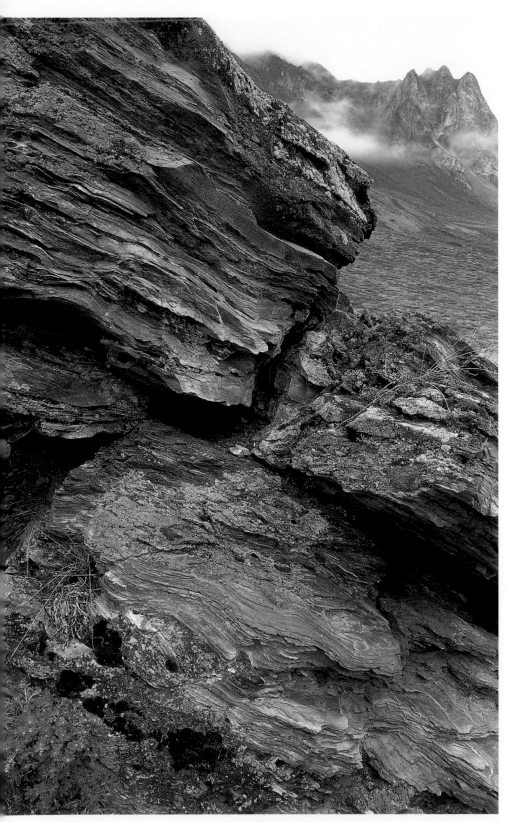

Rock lichens and the Romanzof Mountains, Hulahula River valley

what is economically and politically expedient. As the past four decades have shown, conservationists may win some battles but never a final victory, unless the whole Arctic Refuge is given permanent protection by Congress. Only constant vigilance, clarity of purpose, compassion, scientific fact, eloquence, and commitment, lasting not decades but centuries, will prevent this natural treasure from becoming a vanished reality.

Olaus and Mardy revisited Lobo Lake in 1961, where, as Olaus wrote, "we had the midnight sun and were in the midst of natural unmodified scenery that had been there through the centuries. How can one describe what all this meant for us?"

Above the fireplace in the Murie home in Moose, Wyoming, is a plaque with words taken from an old headstone:

"THE WONDER OF THE WORLD,

THE BEAUTY AND THE POWER;

THE SHAPES OF THINGS,

THEIR COLOURS, LIGHTS AND SHADES.

THESE I SAW.

LOOK YE ALSO WHILE LIFE LASTS."

Olaus and Mardy truly looked and saw. . . .

Olaus died in 1963. Mardy continued the fight on behalf of the Arctic Refuge, writing, lecturing, and lobbying. Brina, Bob, Mardy, and I had a reunion of the Sheenjek team in 1991 at her home, with the memory of Olaus a strong presence. And in 2002, Mardy celebrated her one-hundredth birthday. She gave us this statement of hope:

"I hope the United States of America is not so rich that she can let these wildernesses pass by—or so poor she cannot afford to keep them."

I retain my dreams from the summer of 1956.

George B. Schaller

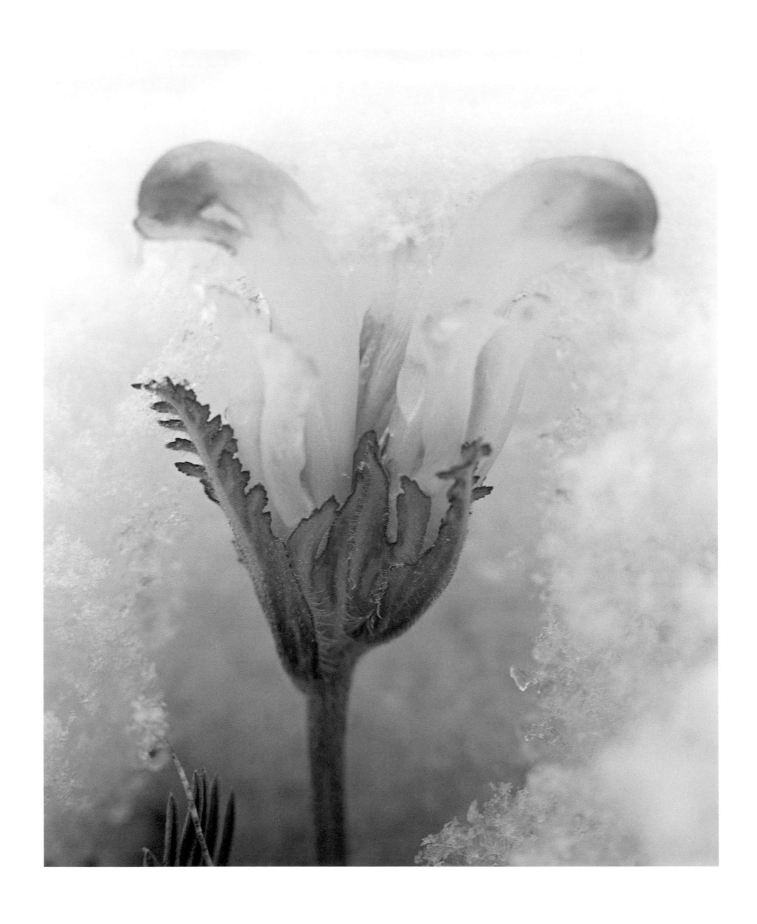

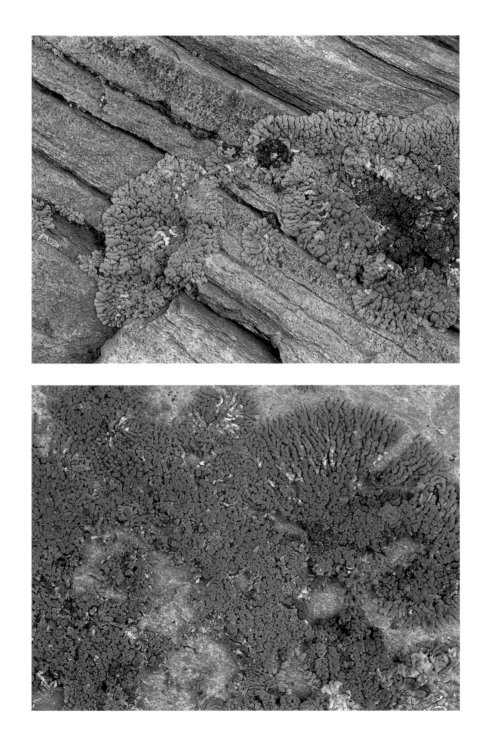

Rock lichens in the Hulahula River valley

Opposite • Capitate lousewort pushes through snow after a summer storm

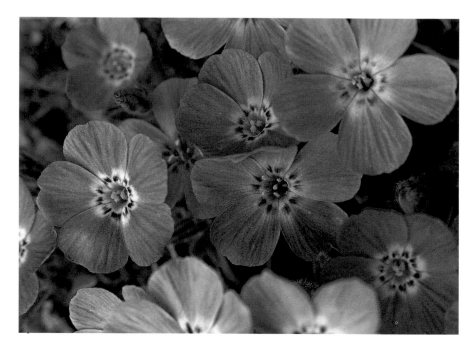

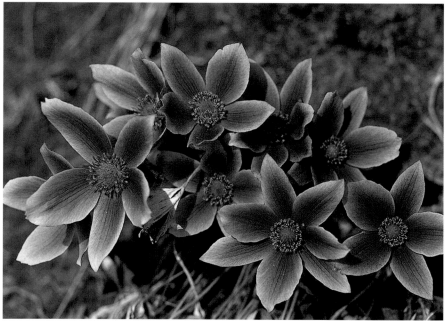

Rare wildflowers in the Arctic Refuge: Siberian phlox and purple anemone

Opposite • Two fog systems collide above the Hulahula River.

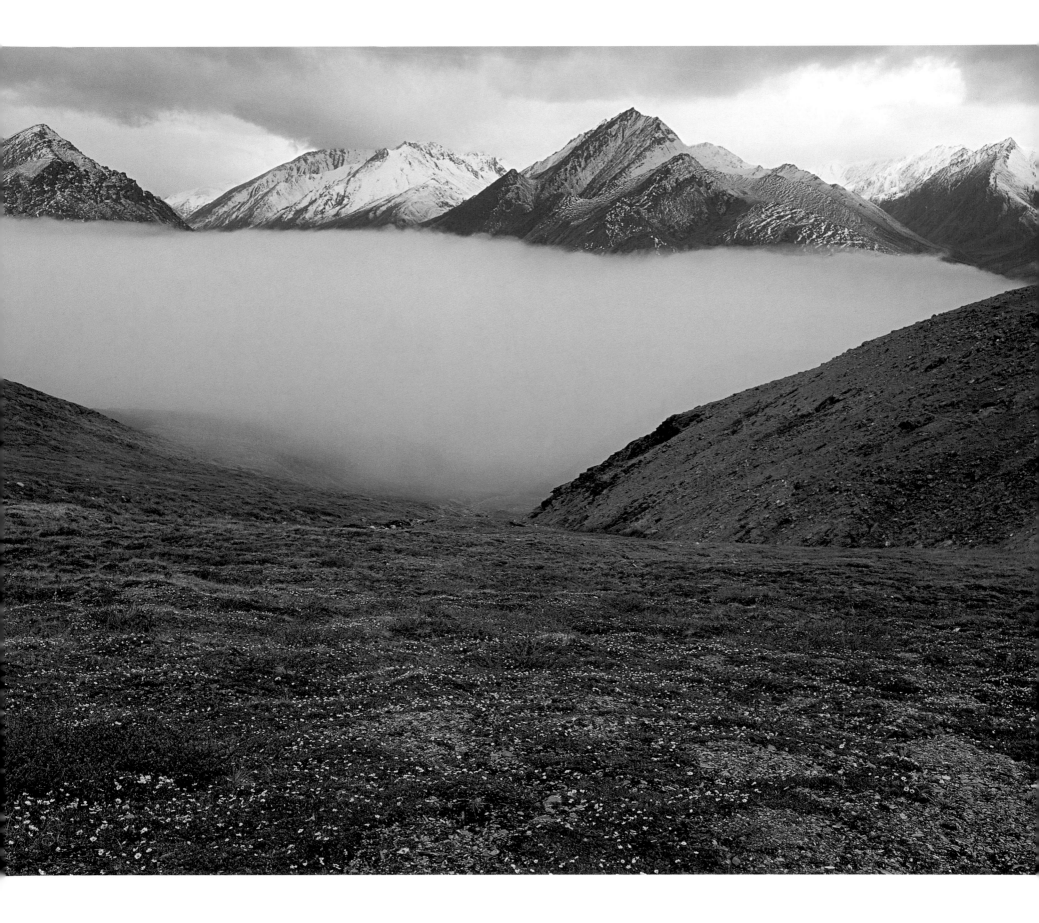

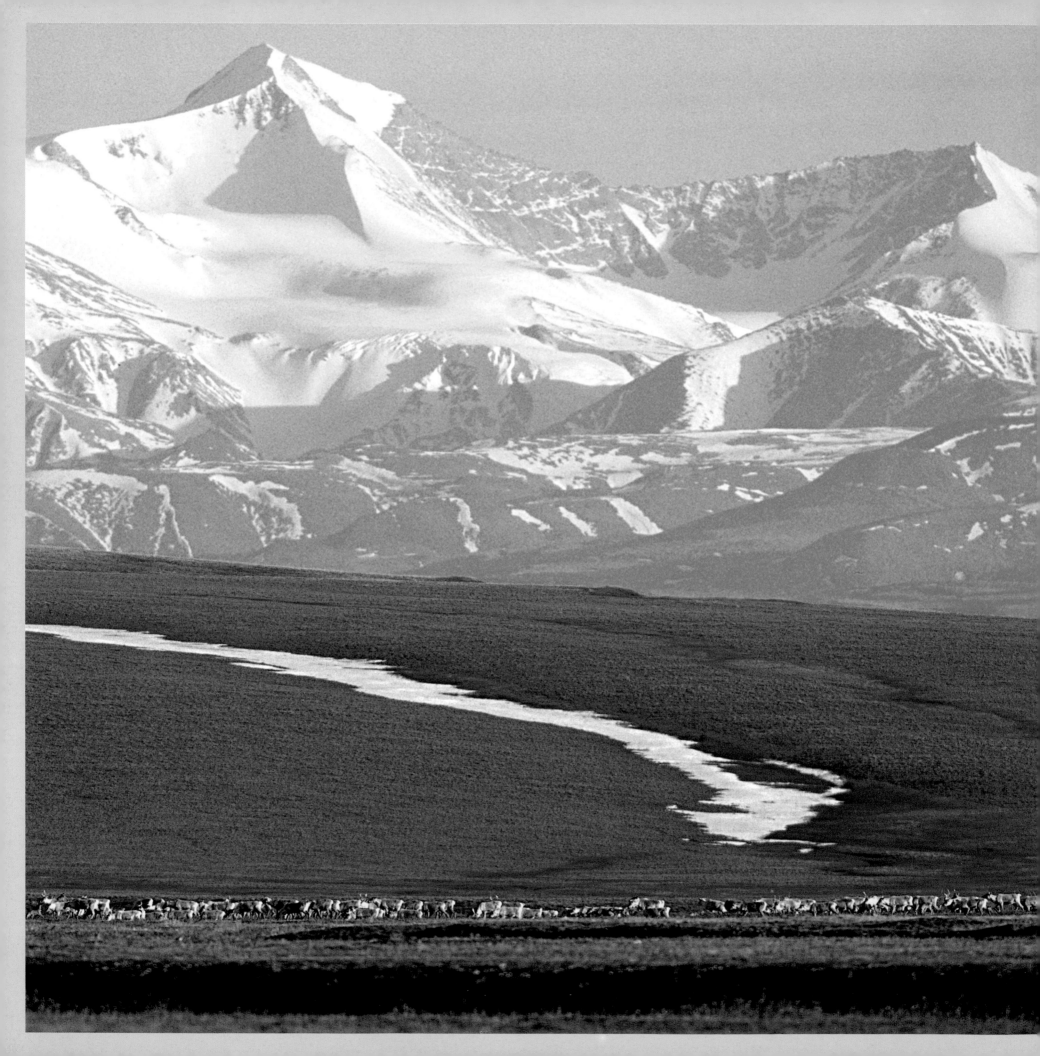

Porcupine Caribou: Nomads of the Arctic Refuge

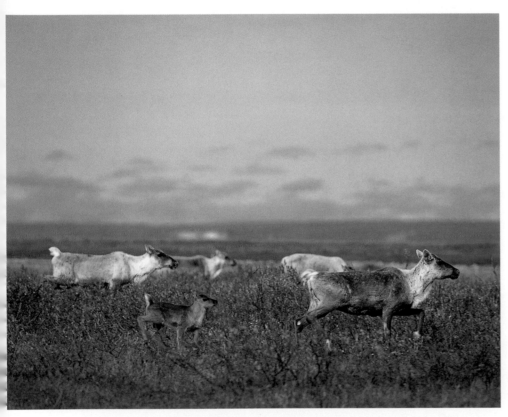

Opposite • Porcupine caribou on the coastal plain, Mount Michelson in the background

June 3, 2002: Walt drops Robert and me off at a little island on the Jago River. The snow has just melted and fresh spring vegetation is bursting out on the tundra. The coastal plain of the Jago River is considered to be one of the most consistently used areas for caribou calving. There are a couple hundred caribou scattered across the island when we arrive. From my initial observation with binoculars and spotting scope, I can see that the calving has just begun, with very few calves born so far.

That night we wait in the willow bushes. It is cold, and heavy fog has rolled in from the north. Around three in the morning a small band of caribou with a few calves approaches from the east channel of the river. They come within a hundred yards of us and begin grazing. We are motionless, savoring every minute, observing them through the thick fog. They graze for an hour or more and then move on, just as they always have: constantly moving, stopping briefly only to graze, the majestic wanderer of the Arctic.

Over the next few days, new life is born at a steady pace. Every day we see more and more caribou with calves. While the magical calving of the caribou is unfolding in front of us, we see multitudes of birds busy with their courtship displays, preparing to build nests. Among them are rare buff-breasted sandpipers, American golden plovers, Lapland longspurs, Savannah sparrows, and the opportunistic jaegers, always waiting for a chance to feed on bird eggs or chicks.

One evening a caribou comes very close to us and then runs swiftly away; she seems distressed, as if she is looking for something. She crosses the east channel of the Jago River and walks along the far bank, making noise.

With my binoculars I spot, far in the distance, a calf without a cow, and the next fifteen minutes are amazing. The cow and the calf are about a mile apart and are not aware of one another, but both start making noise. Suddenly something happens: It must be that they recognize each other's voice, because they begin loping toward one another. They reunite with a quick nuzzle, the calf bounding happily around its mother as they move to rejoin the herd.

June 9: We are leaving the island today. This morning I look around and see that almost every cow has a calf with her, and I begin to realize why the Gwich'in people call the coastal plain "the Sacred Place Where Life Begins."

—S.B.

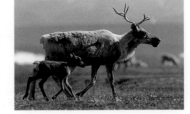

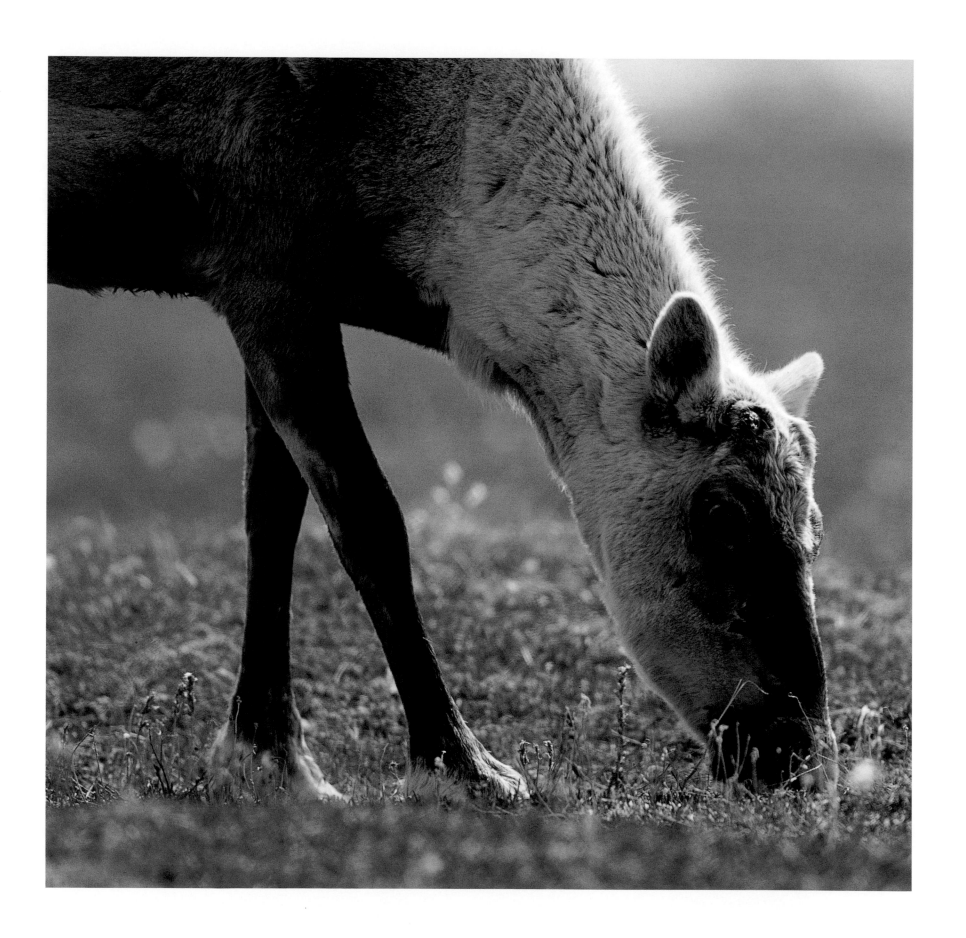

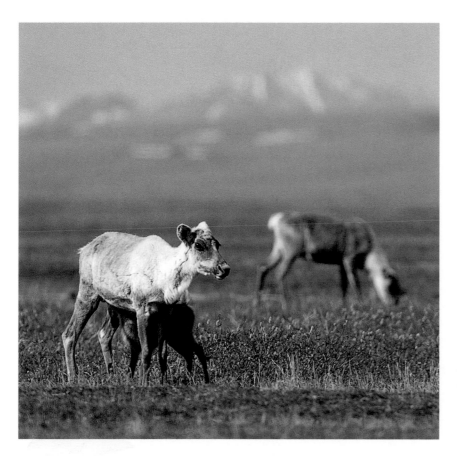 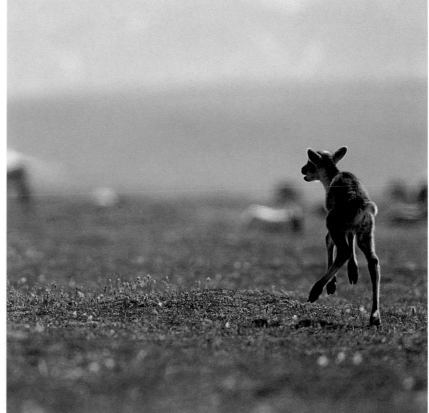

Opposite • Pregnant caribou grazes on fresh spring vegetation. The nutrient-rich spring vegetation of the coastal plain is essential for caribou, to rebuild energy after migrating and giving birth and to produce milk for nursing their calves. The calves must grow quickly so they can join the herd for the southward migration.

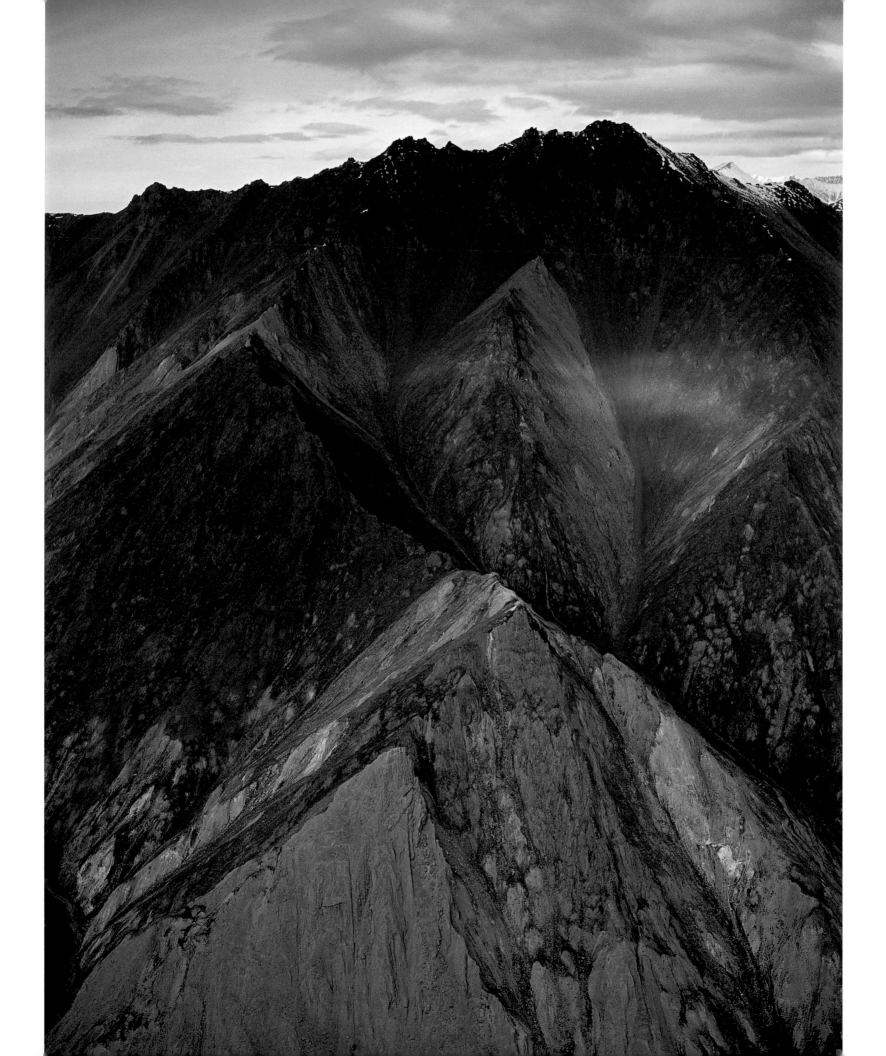

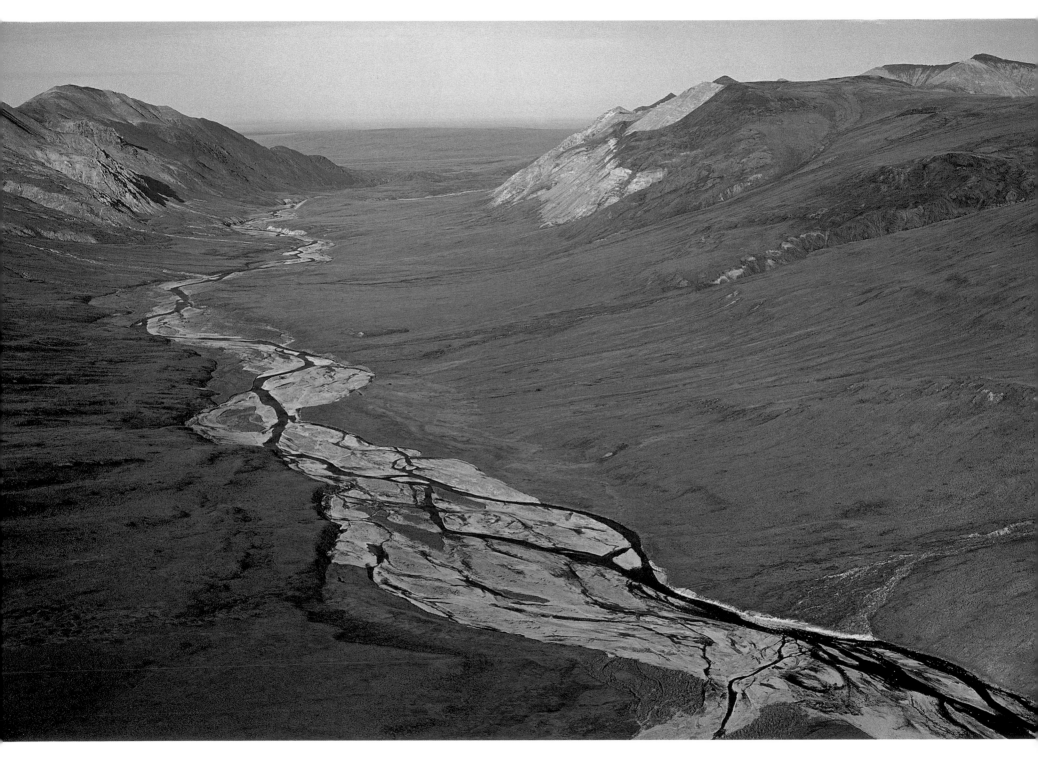

Hulahula River valley looking north to the coastal plain

Opposite • Romanzof Mountains

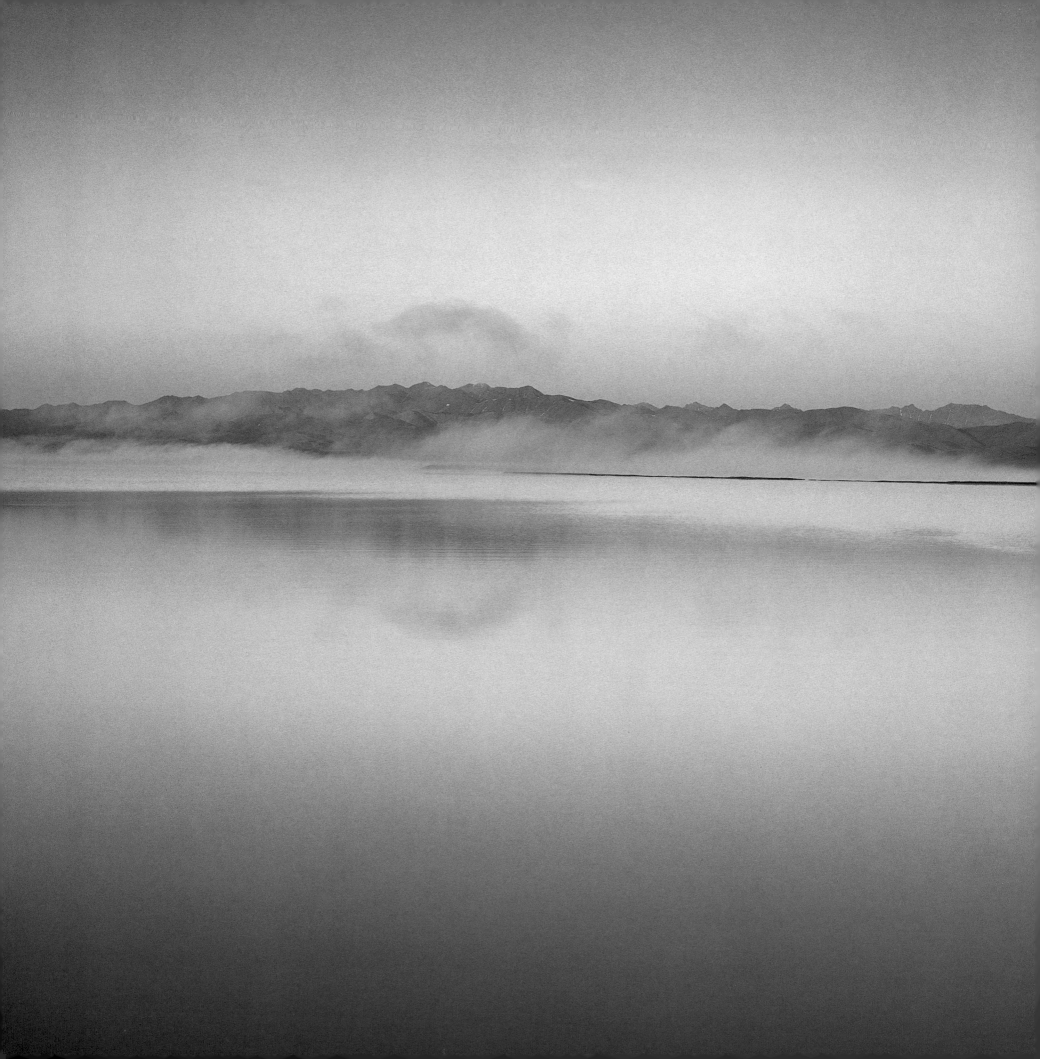

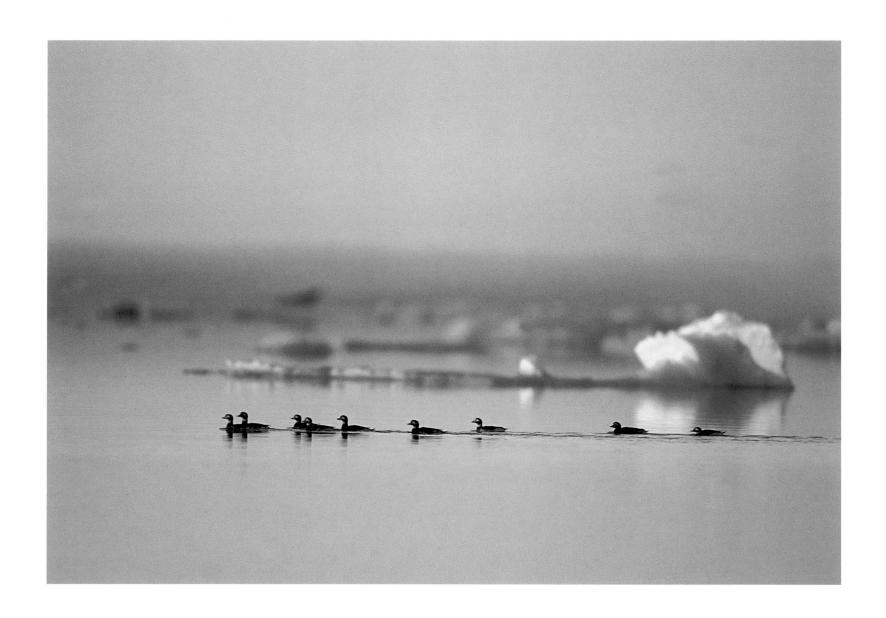

Long-tailed ducks on the coastal waters near Icy Reef

Opposite • Early morning on a coastal lagoon

fran mauer

OUR GEOGRAPHY OF HOPE

So far, no pages of this long history of interaction between environment and life have been torn out or re-written by mankind for fame or profit. Here there still survives one of Planet Earth's own works of art, and this one, too, symbolizes freedom: . . . freedom to continue, unhindered and forever if we are willing, the particular story of Planet Earth's unfolding here. . . .

LOWELL SUMNER
National Park Service Wildlife Biologist, in a 1985 letter to conservationists celebrating the twenty-fifth anniversary of the refuge

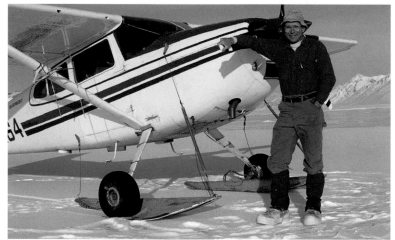

Photo by Roger Kaye

FRAN MAUER *moved to Alaska more than thirty years ago to attend graduate school at the University of Alaska at Fairbanks, where he earned a master of science degree in zoology in 1974. He began his career with the U.S. Fish and Wildlife Service as an entry-level wildlife biologist, and from 1976 to 1980 worked as staff biologist with the proposed Alaska National Interest Lands Conservation Act. For the past twenty-one years he was wildlife biologist on staff of the Arctic National Wildlife Refuge, until his retirement in 2002. Mauer's fieldwork in the Arctic Refuge focused on study and management of the Porcupine caribou herd, Dall sheep, moose, wolverines, golden eagles, and peregrine falcons. He has provided information to numerous media sources on the issue of proposed oil development in the Arctic Refuge, and has frequently spoken to the irreplaceable values that are at stake.*

The black wolf is stalking something in the willow thicket. From my vantage point across the narrow valley, I can see the wolf move carefully into the willows, scenting the air. Suddenly, a ptarmigan bursts up from the bushes as the wolf lunges and snaps its jaws at the flapping bird. Just as the ptarmigan escapes the wolf and rises above the willow tops, there is an explosion of feathers. The lightning comes in the form of a swiftly diving golden eagle as it snatches the ptarmigan in its talons and glides away, leaving the wolf looking up, rather astonished.

This event, which took place nearly twenty years ago in the northern part of the Arctic National Wildlife Refuge, illustrates the fine-tuning of the refuge's ecological systems. The timing of the dive was in response to cues the eagle perceived from the interaction between wolf and ptarmigan. But what precision! And to think that while soaring overhead, eagles using their acute vision will watch the hunting behavior of their terrestrial counterparts to take advantage of distracted prey. This and other experiences over the years have enriched my appreciation of the Arctic National Wildlife Refuge, which stands today among a dwindling number of wild places where creatures still exist in their natural relationships as they have from the beginning of life on Earth.

What are some of the features of this part of the planet that make it so special? How do the physical and biological components manifest them- selves here in such splendid interaction? Nearly every year, a small number of adventurous visitors hike across the refuge, starting from either the north or south ends. In this essay, we'll go on such a trek (without the physical exertion) to experience the refuge's great diversity and begin to find explanations to these and other questions. During our journey, keep in mind that there remains much we do not know about this vast landscape, for here there still remain elements

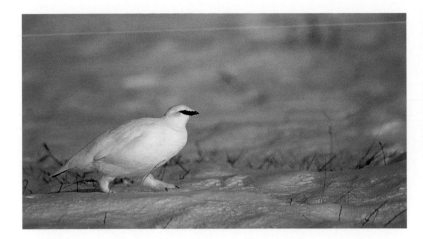

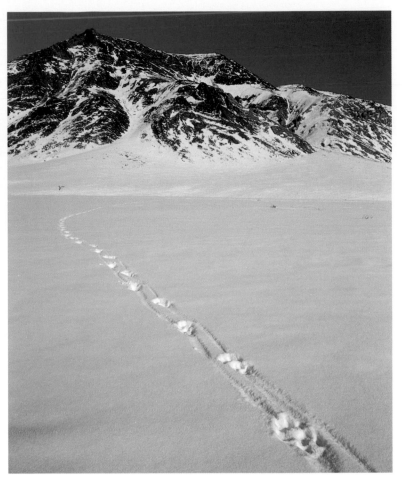

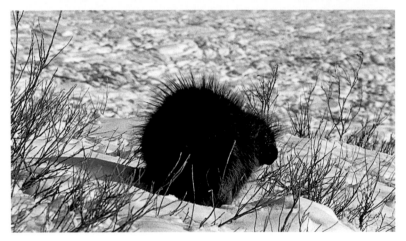

Willow ptarmigan in winter plumage; porcupine; wolf tracks

of mystery and the unknown, which in themselves have great value in the human perception of wilderness.

A Diversity of Landscapes

If we hike up any of the mountain valleys of the Arctic Refuge, we will find numerous cobbles of coral and other fossils of marine life on the river's gravel bars. Some 300 million years ago, many of the rock layers of these mountains were sediments on the bottom of a warm, shallow sea. Mountain building events beginning more than 100 million years ago ultimately lifted the sea bottom to their present heights. This process began first in the western Brooks Range and most recently in the eastern portion, which is now the Arctic Refuge. Northward movement of the Pacific Plate in the eastern area of uplift created the current curvature of the mountains in the refuge, which arch northeastward, close to the Arctic Ocean. The result of this sequence of events is a compression of ecological zones in the refuge

that is unmatched in the remainder of the Alaskan Arctic.

Here in the Arctic Refuge, a relatively short traverse of 120 miles southward takes us from the polar ice pack past barrier islands and rich coastal lagoons, across Arctic tundra plains and foothills, over the Arctic mountains to the tundra-forest transition (taiga), and finally to the boreal forest. This entire north-to-south transect, with its many subtle transitions between ecozones, is essentially unaltered by modern humans. The diversity of topography, soil, water, and weather found in this compact area sets the stage for unique animal and plant interactions. Let's walk the transect and see what we find along the way.

Coastal Lands

We begin our trek at the northernmost point of the refuge, the shore of the Arctic Ocean. Looking south, flat land rises gradually up to high, rugged mountains on the southern horizon ranging from five to thirty-five miles distant. Gravel and silt, washed down from the

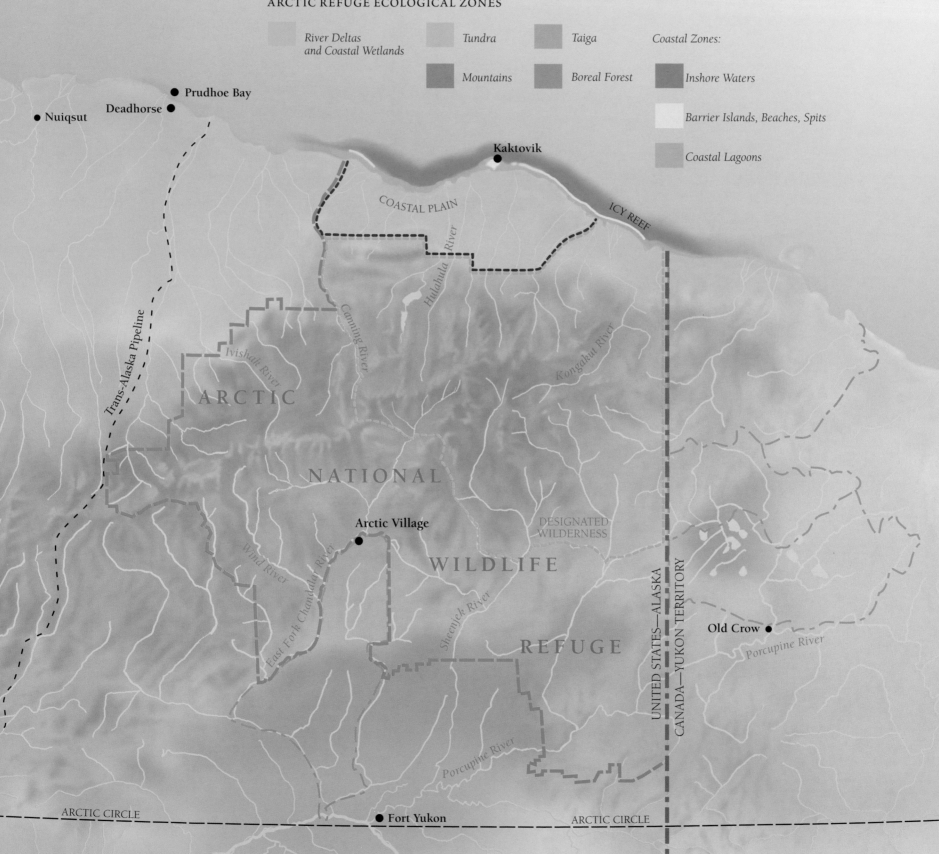

ARCTIC REFUGE ECOLOGICAL ZONES

River Deltas
and Coastal Wetlands

Tundra

Taiga

Coastal Zones:

Mountains

Boreal Forest

Inshore Waters

Barrier Islands, Beaches, Spits

Coastal Lagoons

Nuiqsut

Deadhorse

Prudhoe Bay

Kaktovik

COASTAL PLAIN

ICY REEF

Hulahula River

Canning River

Ivishak River

Kongakut River

Trans-Alaska Pipeline

ARCTIC

NATIONAL

DESIGNATED
WILDERNESS

Arctic Village

WILDLIFE

Wind River

East Fork Chandalar River

Sheenjek River

REFUGE

Old Crow

Porcupine River

UNITED STATES—ALASKA

CANADA—YUKON TERRITORY

Porcupine River

ARCTIC CIRCLE

Fort Yukon

ARCTIC CIRCLE

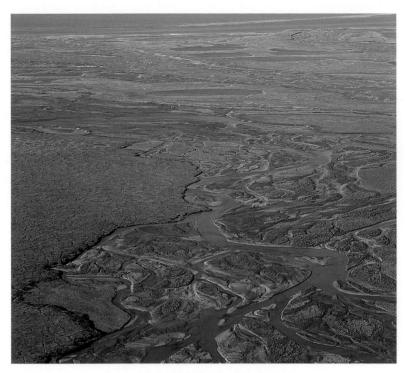

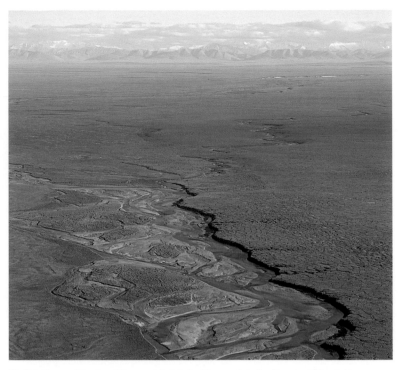

The Hulahula River meets Arey Island and the Arctic coast to the north

Okpilak River and tundra of the coastal plain looking south to the Romanzof Mountains

interior of these mountains by the swift, north-flowing rivers, have interacted with coastal currents to build a system of barrier islands and shallow, brackish lagoons along the northern edge of the refuge. The lagoons collect nutrients that have been flushed from the land, and when their waters are warmed by the perpetual summer sun, they become centers of biological productivity. The river deltas, barrier islands, and coastal lagoons of the Arctic Refuge provide habitat for a host of migratory shorebirds and waterfowl, including northern phalaropes, red-throated loons, common eiders, and long-tailed ducks. Arctic char, which spawn and overwinter in rivers, spend the summer foraging in these rich coastal waters. The relatively warm, near-shore waters are critical for coastal fish migration. A large population of Arctic cisco (a whitefish species), which spawn in the large Mackenzie River system in Canada, migrate as juveniles along the Arctic Refuge shore to and from the Colville River west of the refuge, where they grow to adulthood. Just beyond the barrier islands, bowhead and beluga whales migrate to and from summer feeding grounds off the Mackenzie River delta.

Arctic Tundra

Our walk southward now takes us inland of the lagoons to the open tundra of the Arctic coastal plain and foothills. Because the mountains are near to the Arctic Ocean in the refuge, the north-flowing rivers have a steeper gradient than those west of the refuge, where the distance from mountains to coast is much greater and the land is flatter. Thus there is more variable terrain in the Arctic Refuge coastal plain, especially where the swift-flowing rivers have cut through hills, leaving banks and bluffs. These incised areas lie perpendicular to the prevailing east and west winds and collect deep snowdrifts earlier in winter than occurs in areas along rivers west of the refuge. These are the early forming snowdrifts that pregnant polar bears select for their maternal dens in late October. Polar bear cubs are born in mid-winter, and females do not emerge from their dens with their young until March. Studies have shown that a disproportionate number of polar bear dens have been found in the refuge compared to the rest of Arctic Alaska. Some polar bears travel farther inland to excavate their dens in the northern edge of the mountains, bringing them in close proximity with Dall sheep, a situation unique to the Arctic Refuge. The windswept crests of river bluffs are important winter range for muskox, who are year-round residents of the coastal plain.

The steeper slope of the refuge coastal plain and foothills enables water to drain more swiftly, leaving relatively few lakes and ponds and primarily upland tundra vegetation. To the west of the refuge, where the land is flatter, there are extensive lakes, ponds, and wetlands. One of the predominant plants of the refuge uplands is the Arctic cotton grass

(*Eriophorum vaginatum*). This plant occurs in the form of dense, packed lumps of dead leaves and stems from previous years' growth, and is commonly referred to as tussocks. The tussocks extend up out of the soil by as much as twelve inches or more. Wind-blown snow accumulates in the spaces between the tussocks, often leaving only a thin layer of snow covering the tussock tops. When spring comes and melting begins, tussock tops appear before other plants, and due to the insulation provided by the densely packed dead leaves, new plant growth begins in the tussocks earlier than any other species occurring on the tundra. The extensive tussock meadows of the Arctic Refuge coastal plain and foothills constitute the primary calving grounds for the Porcupine caribou herd, currently numbering more than 120,000 animals. It is the green shoots of the cotton grass in early June that enable caribou mothers to produce an abundance of rich milk and assure rapid growth of their newborn calves.

The coastal plain of the refuge bursts with life in spring and early summer, when about seventy species of migratory birds return to nest and raise their young. Another sixty-five species of birds visit the area but have not been observed to nest there. The migrants come from all over the globe. Buff-breasted sandpipers wintering in Argentina arrive to conduct their elaborate, raised-wing courtship rituals. Tundra swans that grace the Chesapeake Bay in winter seek out lakes and ponds in river deltas of the coastal plain for nesting. From the open oceans of New Zealand come three species of jaegers to hunt lemmings on the coastal plain. The yellow wagtail, a robin-sized passerine, returns from Southeast Asia to nest in willow thickets along rivers of the refuge coastal plain.

The ebb and flow of life on the plain reaches its ultimate peak in late June, when great aggregations of the Porcupine caribou herd form in the midst of the teeming bird activity. One evening in early July, I stood on the tundra more than a mile from one of these caribou aggregations. Looking to the northwest with my binoculars, and rotating 180 degrees to the southeast, there was a solid wall of caribou in my field of view. In the background stood the snow-capped peaks of the Arctic mountains (Brooks Range), painted gold in the midnight sun. A rumbling sound could be heard—the grunts of calves and cows and the churning of thousands of hooves on the tundra—reminding me of the stories of bison herds on the great plains during the early 1800s. The caribou herds attract a full component of large mammal and avian predators—grizzly bears, wolves, wolverines, and golden eagles—as well as scavengers such as ravens, gulls, foxes, and jaegers. This diversity of abundant wildlife offers a rare opportunity to observe interactions between several species.

When fall comes to the coastal plain and foothills of the Arctic Refuge, yet another wildlife spectacle begins: the arrival of snow geese from the nesting colony on Banks Island, in northern Canada. The snow geese feed on the root stalks of another cotton grass species, *Eriophorum angustifolium,* which are high in starch. This cotton grass occurs in scattered patches associated with moist areas where water drains over the tundra in small streams. Because of the uneven distribution of this cotton grass, the snow geese need a large area to sustain their needs. While on the refuge coastal plain the geese feed voraciously, rapidly building their fat reserves, which are crucial for successful migration to their wintering grounds, in Oregon and California. In early September, geese reach their peak numbers in the refuge, sometimes exceeding 300,000 birds.

Springs of Life

As our walk to the south approaches the northern front of the mountains, we discover a series of freshwater springs gushing from underground fissures and faults in the limestone substrate. Because of their deep underground sources, the temperature of the springs (about forty degrees F) remains nearly constant year-round and allows for open water areas to persist even in winter. As the water cools downstream of the springs, thick fields of ice form during winter. In summer, these ice fields provide caribou with a cool place to escape harassing insects. In winter, the open water areas host an interesting assemblage of wildlife. The presence of abundant aquatic invertebrates supports populations of overwintering fish such as Arctic grayling and Arctic char. River otters concentrate their winter activities around the open spring water, feeding on the fish. These open water areas also support a small passerine bird, the American dipper, through the winter, feeding on aquatic insect larvae living there. The year-round flow of water at these springs warms the surrounding soil and allows for survival of many plant species, such as the wood fern, that otherwise would occur only much farther to the south. In summer, a rich variety of flowers and rare plants surround the spring areas.

Arctic Mountains (Brooks Range)

Now the walk south becomes steeper, and we have to choose a route through the mountains. A good choice would be a long, straight valley that has a low pass leading over the Arctic Divide, which separates rivers draining into the Arctic Ocean from those draining into the Bering Sea. So let's start up one of these valleys and see what we find first.

At the northern end of the valley and at the margin of the mountains, we encounter side valleys, sheltered from strong winds. Here we find isolated stands of tall willows (*Salix alaxensis*), and in a few

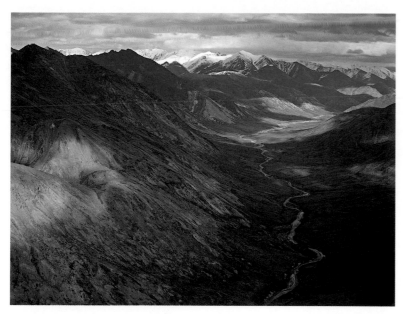

Jago River and the Romanzof Mountains

locations, stands of balsam poplar trees. These oases of forest are well north of the treeline. In summer these protected havens are occupied by a variety of forest birds such as thrushes, flickers, and warblers. In winter they are critical habitat for moose that live here, at the northernmost edge of their distribution.

The mountains constitute the largest ecozone in the refuge, taking in an area approximately a hundred miles wide and two hundred miles long. In the center of the refuge lie the tallest peaks of Alaska's Brooks Range—Mount Chamberlin (9,020 feet), Mount Isto (9,050 feet), and Mount Michelson (8,855 feet). This area also contains most of the glaciers that occur in the Brooks Range.

Not all mountains in the refuge are made up of the same material. Many are composed of layers of limestone, but some are of different types of shale. It is the more limited and scattered shales that are associated with the most productive soils, and thus the most abundant and diverse vegetation types. Limestone, on the other hand, is the most extensive rock type found in the refuge, and supports more austere soils and less vegetation. Due to the relationship between soil nutrients and vegetation, the location and patterns of rock types throughout the refuge have a direct influence on the size and distribution of Dall sheep populations.

Another factor associated with the quality of Dall sheep habitat is the size and shape of the mountain valleys themselves. The valley we are heading up was once filled by a large, powerful glacier that carved out the typical U-shaped valley. The presence of low passes at the top of some valleys allows for wind channeling to occur, as air masses in the interior of Alaska drain across the Arctic Divide and into the basin of the Arctic Ocean. In winter these strong winds scour the snow from the valley floor and neighboring ridges, allowing Dall sheep to find food more readily in winter. These valleys support sheep densities that are sometimes three or four times higher than other valleys that do not have wind channeling. In spring, snow melts earlier in the wind channel valleys due to the thin snow cover and more rapid warming of the ground where exposed soil absorbs solar radiation. This gives plants a longer growing season, resulting in a greater abundance of food for sheep. The presence of mineral salt deposits on the surface of exposed shale areas attracts sheep, especially in early June, when their body reserves are at low levels following the long, difficult winter. In a high-density sheep valley, a few hundred sheep may be found concentrated at a single mineral lick area in early summer.

Near a high mountain ridge we find an ancient stone hunting blind. The blind is situated near a rock outcrop and within twenty feet of a heavily worn sheep trail. Because there is no charcoal or other cultural material left at this site, there is no accurate way to know how old it may be. We try crouching in the blind as an early Eskimo or Indian hunter might have done, waiting for a band of sheep to come down the trail. What thoughts did the hunter have during his vigil here? Was there a family waiting and hoping for a successful hunt in the valley below? One thing for certain is that early hunters knew the best valleys for sheep hunting, and it is encouraging to realize that this hunting blind would still be successful because high numbers of sheep continue to live in this part of the mountains.

The steep terrain of the mountains provides areas of relatively dry soils that are not permanently frozen. It is in such areas, and usually on south-facing slopes, that grizzly bears excavate their winter dens. Some grizzlies also den in the many limestone caves found in the mountains. Caves are also used by Dall sheep, for shelter during snowstorms in winter and as a refuge from heat in the summer. In late winter, wolves excavate their maternal dens at lower elevations in the mountain valleys where there are suitable soils for digging. It is the lack of such conditions on the coastal plain, where the ground is permanently frozen, that prevents wolves from locating dens there. This spatial separation between wolf dens in the mountains and caribou calving grounds on the coastal plain allows the caribou to avoid excessive predation by wolves when their newborn calves are vulnerable. During the calving season, wolves are limited in their travels from the den site as they also have young to feed and care for.

As we approach the summit of the Arctic Divide, the land takes on a barren, moonscape appearance. Suddenly we hear a shrill whistle coming from a steep talus slope leading up to the pass. A careful search with binoculars reveals the perpetrator: a marmot. There is life here

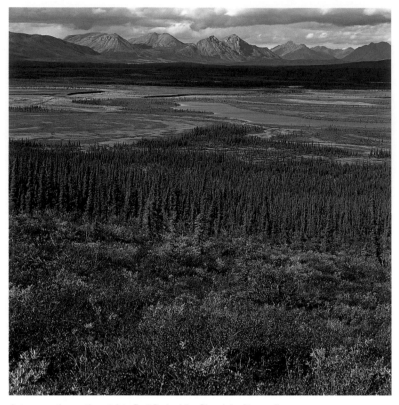
Autumn on the southern taiga, East Fork of the Chandalar River valley

and corrals built of poles and sticks and lashed by strips of bark and caribou rawhide are found at many sites in the taiga zone of the refuge. These structures were used by nomadic Gwich'in hunters to capture caribou for food and other uses. This practice ended around the turn of the nineteenth century, when firearms became more readily available. Current caribou trails through the taiga suggest that some caribou fences would still be effective for trapping caribou if they were repaired.

As we move farther south, the spacing of spruce trees becomes more dense and a thick carpet of mosses and lichens covers the ground. We have reached the Alaskan winter range of the Porcupine caribou herd. Caribou begin arriving on this winter range during late October and remain there until late March or early April. Here the caribou excavate "craters" in the snow to feed on lichens. Because lichens grow very slowly, caribou need very large areas for winter use. Caribou commonly alternate their use of various winter ranges between years. This irregular use allows lichen ranges to recover from intensive grazing.

Caribou are the only species of the deer family in which the females have antlers. Adult male caribou shed their antlers in early winter following the mating season. Pregnant females, however, retain their antlers until a few days following the birth of their calves in early June. During winter, pregnant females bearing antlers are successful in displacing non-antlered caribou from feeding craters that the non-antlered caribou have excavated. This allows the pregnant female to conserve energy and maintain her body condition to grow a healthy calf, and to have adequate energy for the upcoming migration to the calving grounds.

after all! These groundhog-like mammals are sparsely distributed throughout the mountains, never occurring in great abundance. On our descent south of the divide we notice first only slight differences in tundra vegetation, but as we round a corner and look down the valley, in the distance we see the lone sentinels of the spruce forest.

Taiga

The tundra-to-forest transition, or taiga, varies greatly with topography. Tundra vegetation persists at higher elevations well south of the divide; however, scattered spruce trees extend up the valley bottoms well north of some tundra-covered slopes. Gradually, as we descend from the divide, there are more shrubs of willow, alder, and dwarf birch, while spruce trees remain widely scattered. In late summer, after the biting insects have waned, caribou move into this zone of shrubs to feed and rest, and to begin building their fat reserves for the coming winter. At this time the entire landscape takes on the colors of fall, which rival the hardwood forests of New England. There is the flame orange of dwarf birch, bright crimson of the bearberry, gold of willow and birch, and pale yellow of lichens all contrasted by the dark green of solitary spruce trees lightly scattered about the land. The remnants of caribou fences

Boreal Forest

As we continue south, walking through the caribou winter range, we eventually reach the boreal forest. Because the trees are denser here, we must follow caribou trails leading through this portion of the forest. Here there is evidence of fire, and there are many different stages of forest recovery depending on the amount of time that has passed since the last fire. Mushrooms are abundant in some burn areas during the fall, and migrating caribou feed heavily on them to help build fat for the coming winter. The caribou trails lead more directionally to the southeast, toward winter ranges in Canada.

This is the land of the black bear, red squirrel, marten, beaver, lynx, and snowshoe hare. About every ten years the hares increase to very high numbers, then in a few years their numbers crash. Several species of predators, especially the lynx and red fox, increase and crash in response to the hare cycle. The boreal forest zone in the refuge is also home of many forest birds, such as pine grosbeak, white-winged crossbill, gray jay, spruce grouse, goshawk, and great gray owl. This part of the refuge is also the northernmost distribution of wood frogs in Alaska. During winter these amazing amphibians actually freeze quite solid, and then awaken in spring when warming temperatures return. How they do this is an unsolved mystery of the Arctic.

The caribou trails now lead us to yet another feature of the Arctic Refuge: the canyon of the Porcupine River. It is from the seasonal crossing of this river that the caribou herd gets its name. The canyon has two sections: the upper and lower ramparts. The canyons were formed when a large lake measuring about sixty miles across filled with glacial meltwater at the end of the last Ice Age. This lake was in the area that is now Old Crow Flats, in northern Yukon Territory. Eventually the lake broke open to drain into the Yukon Flats basin of Alaska. The catastrophic rush of water quickly carved the canyon from existing limestone and basalt rocks. Today the waters of the Porcupine River are remarkably calm as they flow through the constricted area. The cliffs of the Porcupine canyon are a major nesting area for the American peregrine falcon. During peak years of the snowshoe hare cycles, several pairs of golden eagles also nest successfully in the canyon.

On the canyon rim, the caribou trails are concentrated and cut as much as three feet into the soil due to thousands of years of repeated use by untold numbers of caribou. Some trails are etched in the rock where they wind down precipitous slopes to river crossings in the canyon. These rock-hewn trails of the canyon can be followed all the way north over the mountains and tundra plains to our starting point on the shores of the polar sea—a testament to the interconnected system of lands, waters, and life that is embodied in the Arctic Refuge.

Endowment for the Future?

Now that we have traversed the refuge and experienced some of its ecological character, let us consider its importance in a historic context and its value for future generations. More than five hundred years ago, Europeans began to explore the North American continent in earnest. At that time, the continent's ecosystems were essentially intact, influenced only by hunter-gatherers and early agricultural societies. Today, most of the natural heritage of the continent has been altered by an expanding Western society, with much of our nation's history entwined in a struggle against wilderness. But from that struggle has come our identity as a people. As the movement westward neared a close, we began to realize that, in the course of the conquest, something had been lost. Gone were the great herds of bison on the plains and the natural populations of predators that accompanied them; gone were the endless flocks of passenger pigeons; gone were the vast expanses of unmarred land. Americans discovered that perhaps we had been too effective in our endeavors to take and put the land to our use.

This recognition led to the beginning of the conservation movement, a part of which was the establishment of national parks and other protected areas. Originally these areas were established because of their scenic beauty or to preserve some unique geological feature such as the Grand Canyon or the geysers of Yellowstone. Later we learned that natural ecological systems and the resource of wilderness have great intrinsic value. Unfortunately, this realization has come too late to allow for protection of most examples of our natural heritage. Furthermore, most of what we have set aside are only remnants of wilderness at a scale woefully too small to assure the long-term survival of key large mammal species and their ecosystems. Today, over most of the continent, an army of scientists, managers, and citizens are in an ecological triage situation, struggling to keep species from extinction and trying to restore fragmented ecosystems. We have a lot to learn and there is little time left to act.

In the far northeast corner of Alaska there is still hope. With establishment of the Arctic National Wildlife Refuge, we were able to protect an entire spectrum of Arctic and sub-Arctic systems in their original condition. How rare and valuable is this area? We can scarcely imagine. Wallace Stegner eloquently described the importance of wilderness as "the geography of hope." Here hope exists for improving our knowledge of how natural ecosystems function. Here there is hope that, with such knowledge, we may begin to transform how we relate to nature outside of protected areas. Here there is hope that this place, the Arctic Refuge, can inspire us to seek more sustainable ways of existing on our planet. In the refuge we have both a touchstone to our past and a guiding light to our future. It took great vision and wisdom to advocate for establishment of the Arctic National Wildlife Refuge and the preservation of its wilderness. Do we have the same resolve to keep it wild, forever?

Fran Mauer

Overleaf • Porcupine caribou and calves on the coastal plain

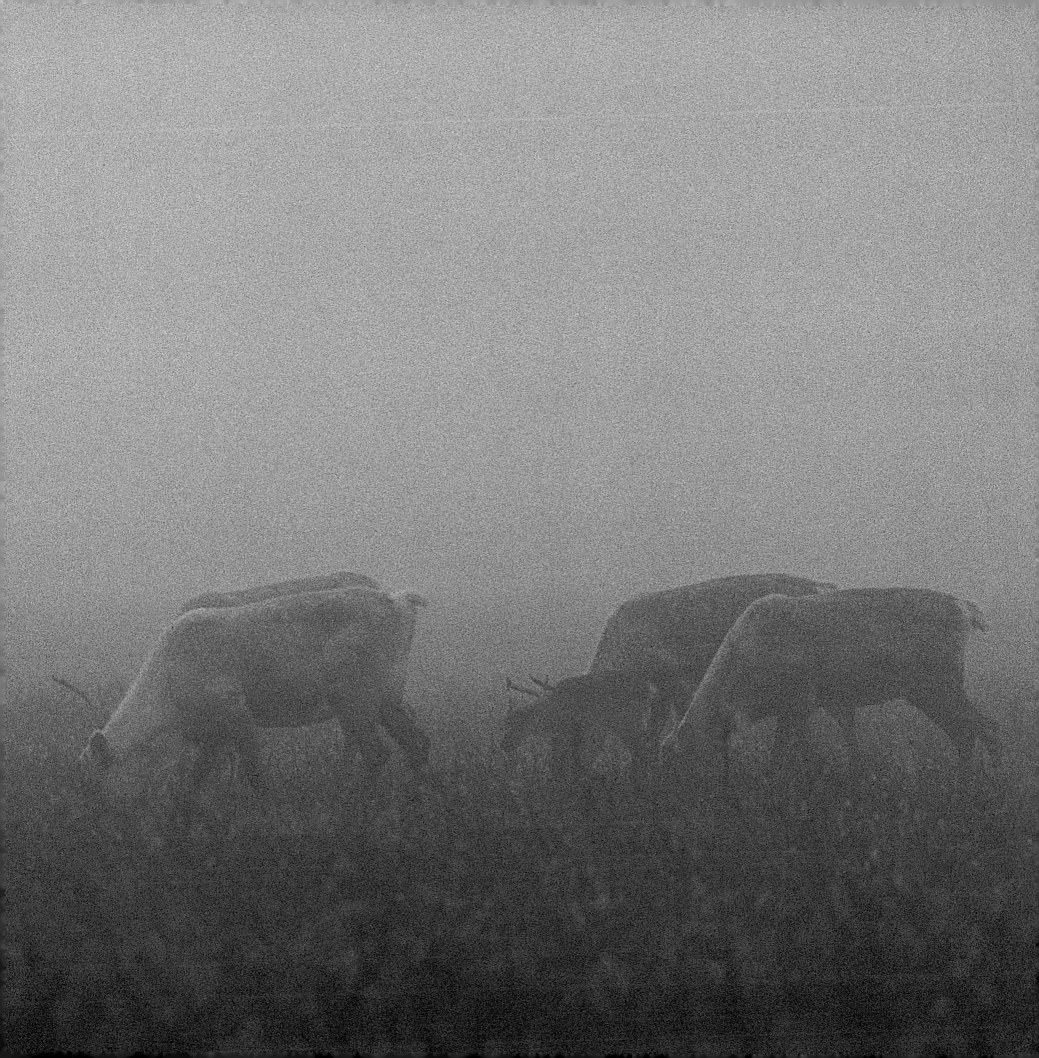

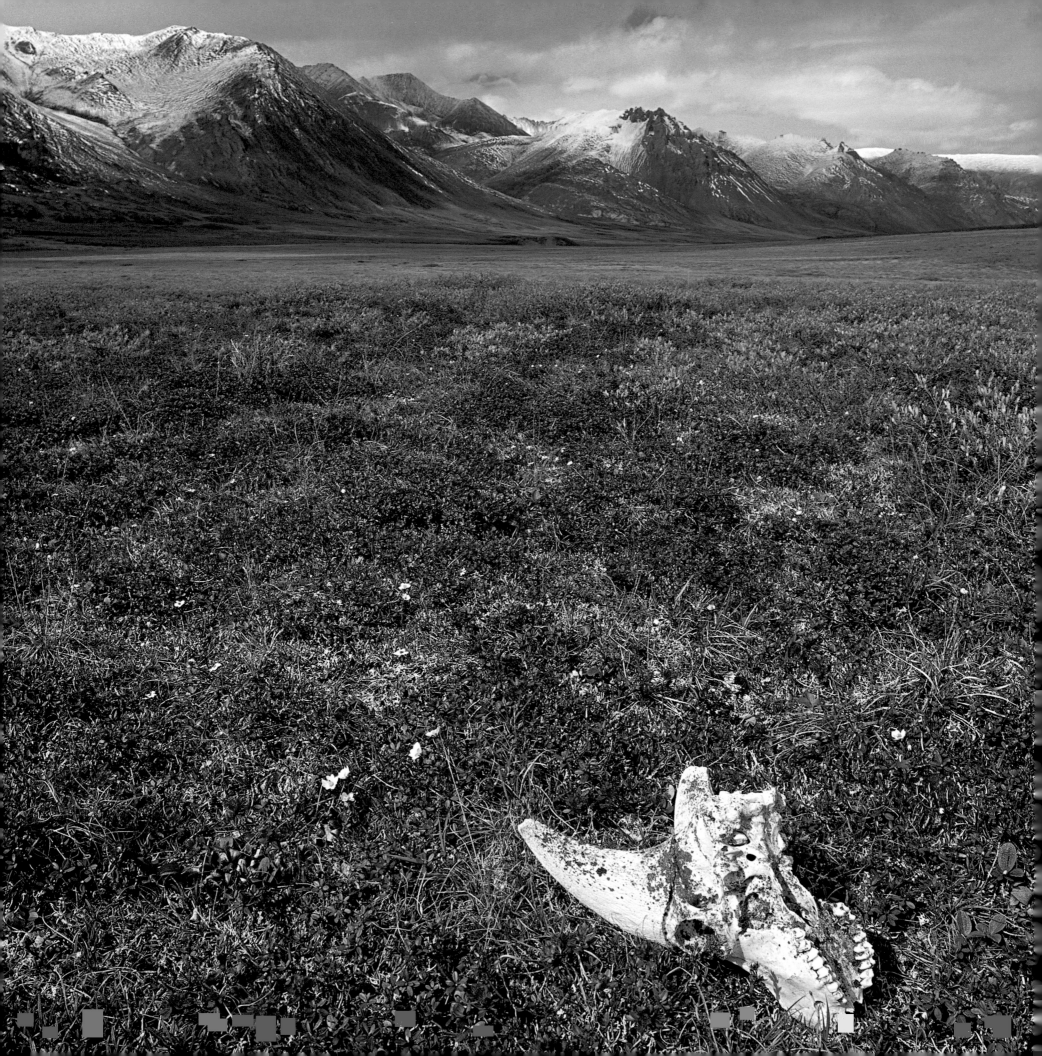

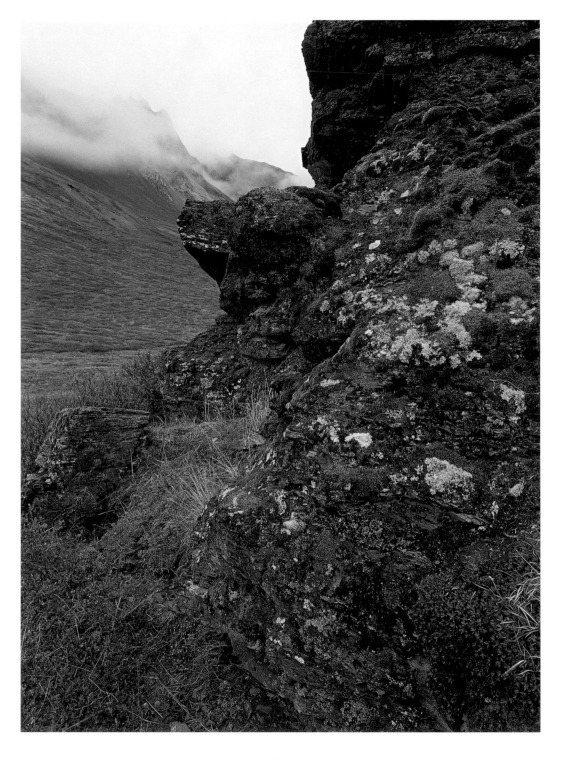

Rock lichens

Opposite • Dall sheep skull on Lapland rosebay-covered tundra, Hulahula River valley

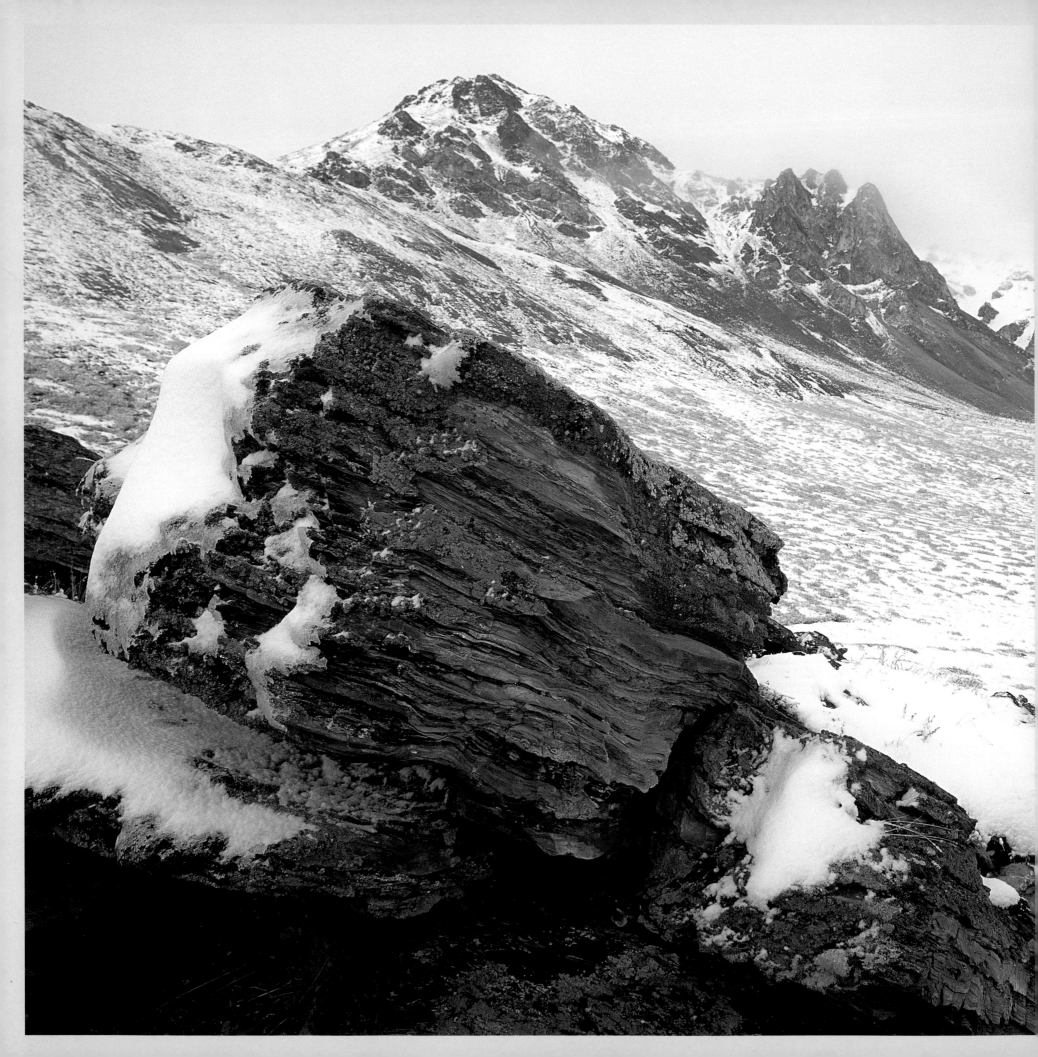

Dall Sheep: Dwellers of the Alpine Brooks Range

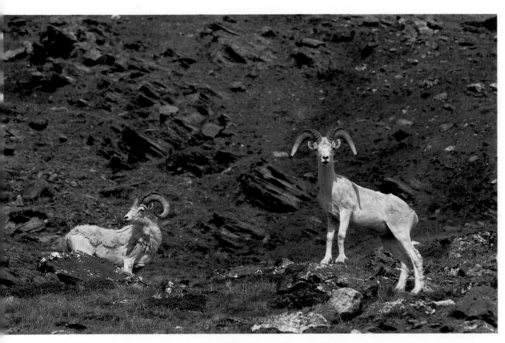

Opposite • Summer snowstorm in the Hulahula River valley

June 17, 2002: Walt drops Robert and me at a landing strip at the upper end of the Hulahula River valley. The hills of the Romanzof Mountains on both sides of the river are scattered with small bands of Dall sheep. Robert and I hike several miles then pitch our tent at the base of one of the hills. There are several sheep grazing on the upper reaches of the hillside, and I have already spotted many lambs with my binoculars. Robert and I spend most of the day observing the sheep from inside our tent, watching as they effortlessly walk the steep hills. Both of us are tired and we turn in for the day.

Suddenly I hear, "Baa, baa. . . . " I wake Robert and say, "Did you hear that?" We peek out our tent door and, sure enough, it is the ewes. Robert is surprised. He has never heard a Dall sheep make that noise, which sounds just like a domesticated sheep. Later I find out that ewes call their lambs with such a noise, and each one knows their offspring. I fall back asleep listening to the soothing, wild call of the ewes, "Baa, baa. . . . "

June 20: I awaken in the morning to find it snowing. The tundra is covered with snow, and there are no signs of Dall sheep anywhere. It looks like a winter landscape except that, when I look closely at the ground, I see a variety of wildflowers trying to make their presence known through the snow. All day long Robert and I walk as I photograph wildflowers and rock lichens in the snowstorm. It is a fleeting and rare day in the Hulahula River valley.

The next morning the only sign of the snowstorm from the previous day is a faint dusting of snow on top of the hills. After breakfast I decide to hike to the top of a hill to observe the sheep at close range. A beautiful, big ram comes as close as twenty feet. Then comes another, then another. . . . Once the rams are comfortable with my presence, the lambs and ewes settle down and continue grazing or nursing or just resting. I am tremendously surprised and elated that they feel at ease around me.

The next day Robert and I follow a creek uphill, photographing wildflowers along the way. Down below a fog system suddenly moves in from the south, obstructing our view of the river. Soon after another fog bank moves in from the north, and we watch in awe as the two fronts collide, sending massive rolls of fog up the creek. We sit together sharing stories for some time, and then start hiking slowly back toward our tent.

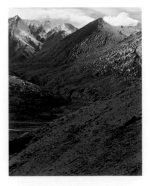

—S.B.

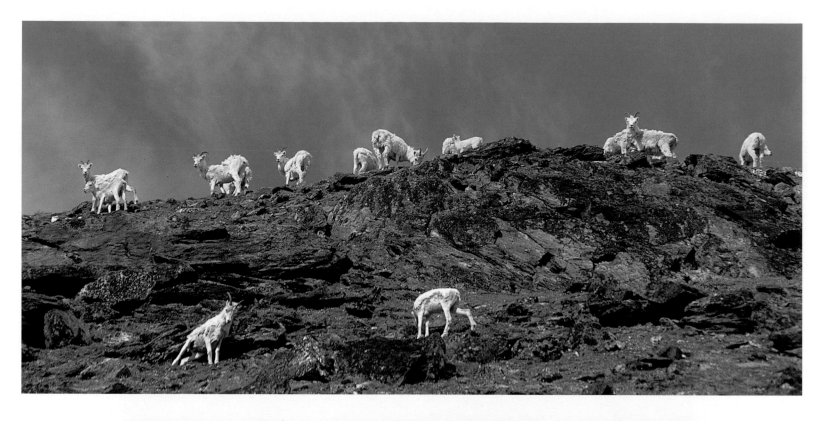

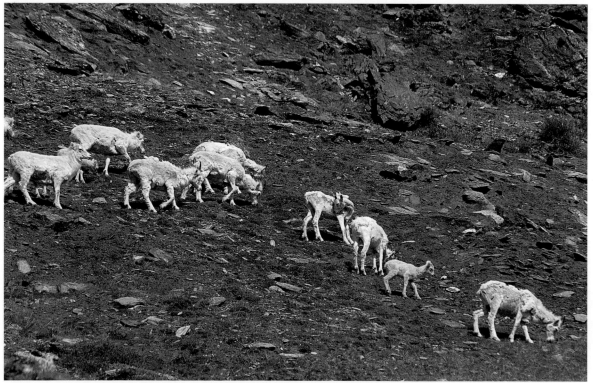

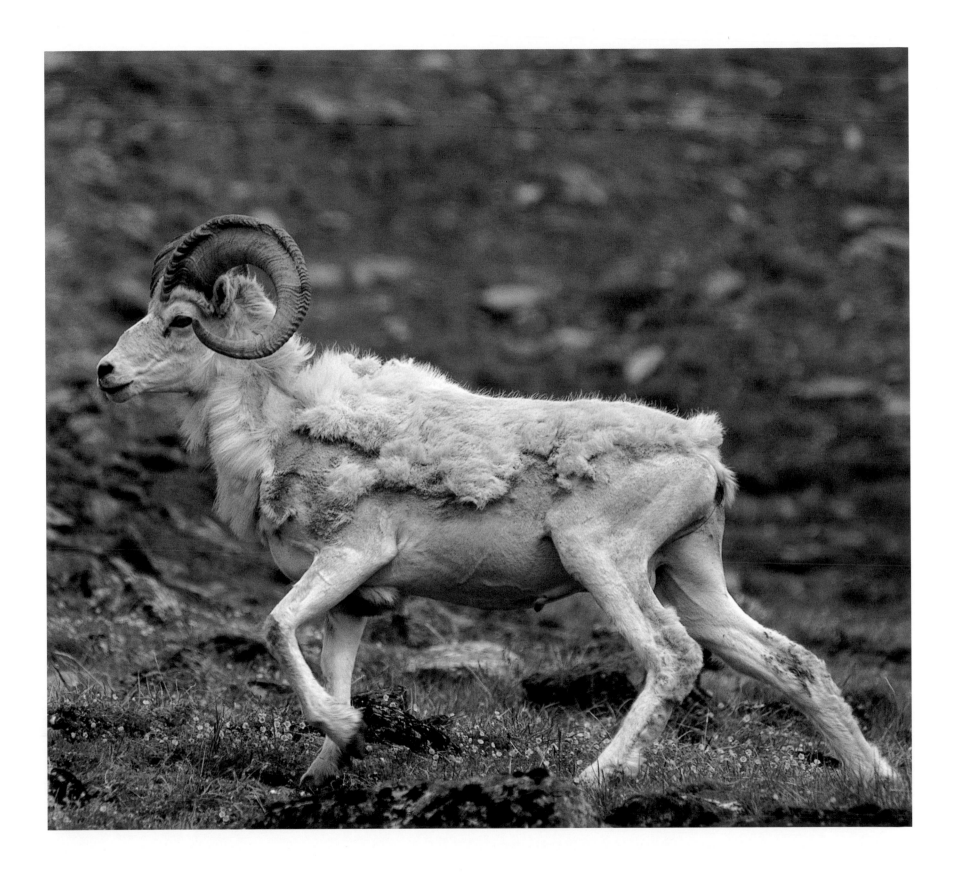

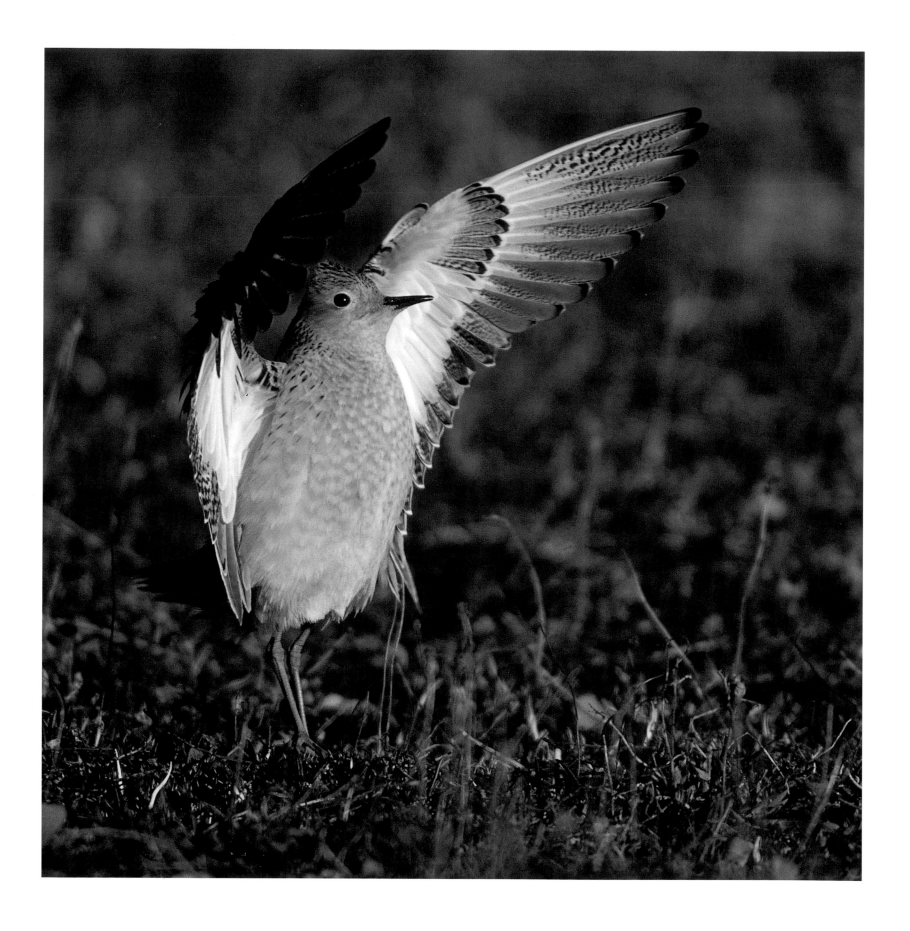

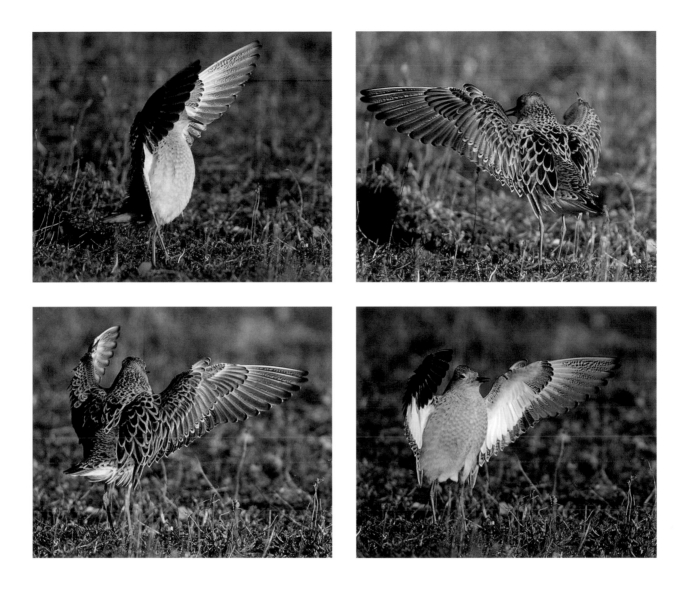

A buff-breasted sandpiper engages in a courtship display on the coastal plain; Jago River. This species, a long-distance traveler that migrates each year from Argentina to the Arctic Refuge coastal plain to nest and rear their young, has a tiny world population—only about 15,000 birds. Their nesting habitat in the Arctic is on the drier coastal terrain where oil facilities tend to be constructed. This bird has been placed on the Audubon Alaska WatchList, which notes birds with declining or vulnerable populations and serves as an early warning to alert land owners, industry, resource managers, and the public to take steps to prevent populations from becoming threatened or endangered with extinction. The buff-breasted sandpiper has been identified as one of the top five species at greatest risk if there is oil development on the Arctic Refuge coastal plain.

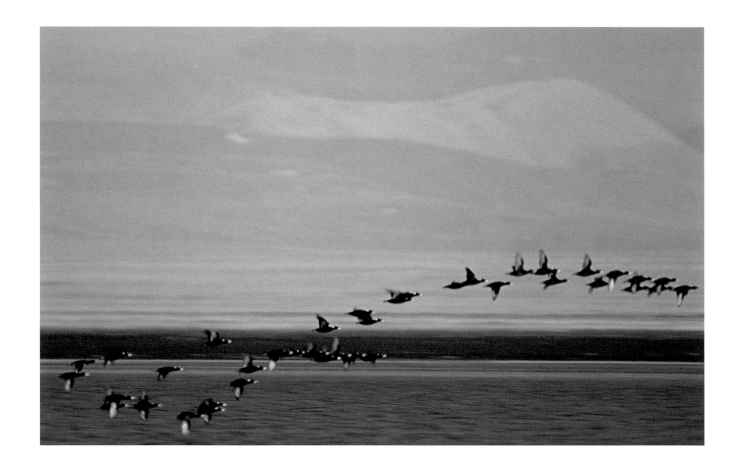

Surf scoters fly over Beaufort Lagoon, coastal plain and the Romanzof Mountains in the background

Opposite • Tundra swan pair on the Aichilik River

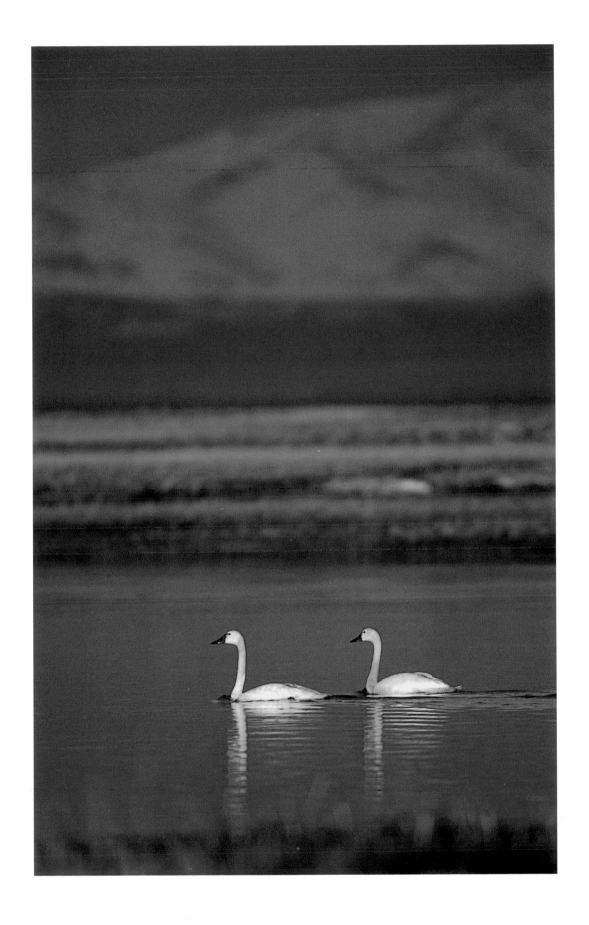

david allen sibley

VISITING THE BIRDS AT THEIR SUMMER HOME

This we know: the earth does not belong to man, man belongs to the earth. All things are connected like the blood that unites us all. Man did not weave the web of life, he is but a strand in it. Whatever he does to the web, he does to himself.

CHIEF SEALTH
of the Suquamish Indians, 1854

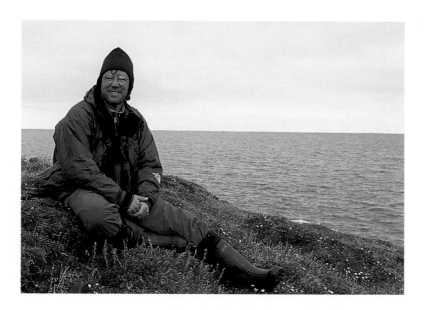

DAVID ALLEN SIBLEY, *son of the well-known ornithologist Fred Sibley, began seriously watching and drawing birds in 1969, at age seven. He has written and illustrated articles on bird identification for many regional and national publications, as well as several books. Since 1980 Sibley has traveled throughout the North American continent in search of birds, both on his own and as a leader of birdwatching tours, and has lived in California, Arizona, Texas, Florida, Georgia, New York, Connecticut, and New Jersey. This intensive travel and bird study culminated in the publication of his comprehensive guide to bird identification—National Audubon Society,* The Sibley Guide to Birds—*in the fall of 2000, and the companion volume—National Audubon Society,* The Sibley Guide to Bird Life and Behavior—*in the fall of 2001. Sibley now lives in Concord, Massachusetts, where he continues to study and draw birds. You can see his artwork at* www.sibleyart.com.

In the summer of 2002 I found myself, willingly but very abruptly, jolted out of a warm Cape Cod summer and transported to the Arctic coast of Alaska. I have come to meet Subhankar Banerjee and Robert Thompson, and to experience birding in the Arctic National Wildlife Refuge. So on July 3 here we are, Subhankar and I, in a small plane loaded with camping gear, banking sharply 150 feet above the wet tundra. We are looking at ponds still mostly covered with ice, while snow falling from the heavy gray clouds is being whipped across the ground by twenty-five-knot winds into what looks from the air like a sort of frigid dust storm. This is not like July on Cape Cod!

We are circling over the delta of the Canning River, one of the main rivers flowing north out of the Brooks Range and into the Arctic Ocean through the Arctic National Wildlife Refuge. The low, flat tundra, with scattered ponds and mudflats, makes the delta one of the most productive bird nesting areas in the refuge, but it certainly doesn't look that way from the air.

I had arrived a day earlier, flying from Boston to Fairbanks and from Fairbanks to the village of Kaktovik. Even before the plane touched down in Kaktovik I saw my first Arctic birds—a pomarine jaeger and a glaucous gull resting on ice floes along the runway. As I tried to adjust from the eighty-five-degree warmth of Cape Cod to the thirty-five-degree chill of Kaktovik in the next twenty-four hours, I was entertained by the ubiquitous snow buntings and Lapland longspurs, by red-necked phalaropes feeding in the front yards of the houses, and even a semipalmated sandpiper singing from an overhead wire. Red-throated and Pacific loons flew overhead every few minutes, and their croaking and crooning sounds were always in the background. Long-tailed ducks and surf scoters passed by in small flocks. Baird's sandpipers were hanging around the small ponds along the gravel airstrip. Several common eiders and a semipalmated plover were sitting on nests there, while long-tailed jaegers flew over the tundra beyond and a snowy owl perched on a tall snow-fence.

A trip to the town dump (a required stop on the itinerary of any birding trip) produces a slaty-backed gull among the two hundred or

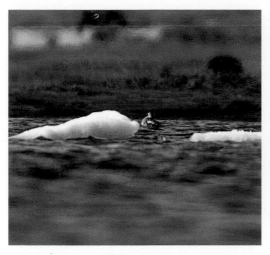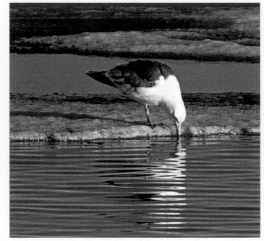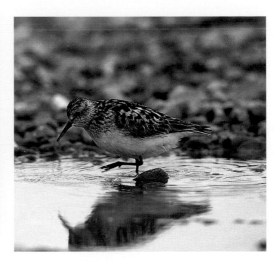

Smew and slaty-backed gull, rare visitors from Siberia; Baird's sandpiper

so glaucous gulls—one of the easternmost records ever in Alaska of this Siberian species. Looking into the bay we spot a yellow-billed loon, and as we watch it is joined by two others and then two more—five yellow-billed loons swimming together. In thirty years of birding I have never seen more than one at a time. The rarest bird by far is a female smew, a small Eurasian duck that flies in from the east on July 3 with some red-breasted mergansers and lands in the bay. This species has been recorded a number of times in the western Aleutian Islands but very few times elsewhere in North America, and never anywhere on the north coast of Alaska.

Late in the evening on July 3 we are in the plane sixty miles west of Kaktovik, looking down at the frozen tundra of the Canning River delta. After a brief conference we decide to look for a more inviting place and fly back to the east, getting a quick sightseeing tour of much of the Arctic National Wildlife Refuge coast. We end up landing about thirty miles east of Kaktovik at an airstrip left over from an old Distant Early Warning (DEW Line) system installation on the edge of Beaufort Lagoon, at a place that I would later learn is called Nuvagapak Point. A few military personnel had lived here in Quonset huts, but the site has been abandoned for many years and all the structures were dismantled and hauled away a year ago. All that remains is a gravel airstrip, but that gives us easy access to the surrounding tundra and ponds. We think it will be interesting to explore a more or less randomly selected area of "typical" coastal plain tundra rather than the prime birding area of the river delta, but it is a place none of us knows about, and we question the decision as we set up camp on a windy night.

The next morning is even windier, but starts auspiciously when the first bird I see as I step out of the tent is a bald eagle—only a very rare visitor to the north coast—and the date is the Fourth of July.

The coastal plain around Nuvagapak Point is only about twenty miles wide, grassy and golden-brown with patches of green at this season, rising gently to the barren gravel slopes, snowfields, and 7,000-foot peaks of the Brooks Range to the south. Looking east or west, you see this broad band of gently rolling tundra stretching away into the distance. The parallel strip of water to the north along the coast is a nearly continuous shallow lagoon (a mile or two wide and mostly ice-free in early July) bordered by low, sandy barrier islands. And beyond the barrier islands is the Arctic Ocean—1,200 miles of ice to the North Pole. It's a deceptively simple landscape—a strip of grass between the barren mountain slopes and the icy ocean—but it is subtly and richly varied. Higher ground is drier, with more lichens and mosses and less grass, while wetter areas are covered by taller, dense grass. The grasses and sedges are sparse or dense, growing in tussocks in some areas, uniformly in other areas. The ground may be spongy, muddy, or relatively dry, and the birds respond to all of these variations in plants and soil.

Part of the uniform appearance of the landscape is due to the fact that the many scattered ponds are sunken below the level of the rest of the tundra. From a normal eye-level view you see only the grass, but as you walk, you are constantly surprised by small ponds, damp gullies, streams, and other hidden variations that come into view. One pond might have a nesting pectoral sandpiper around it, while a pair of long-tailed ducks and a red-necked phalarope take off from the next pond. An area of wet tussocks provides a home for semipalmated, pectoral, and stilt sandpipers, and everywhere are the Lapland longspurs.

On our first full day at Nuvagapak Point we walk east about two miles, ostensibly trying to reach the Aichilik River delta, about four miles away. We don't make it, partly because a smaller river blocks our path, partly because we don't really feel driven to do it, but mostly because

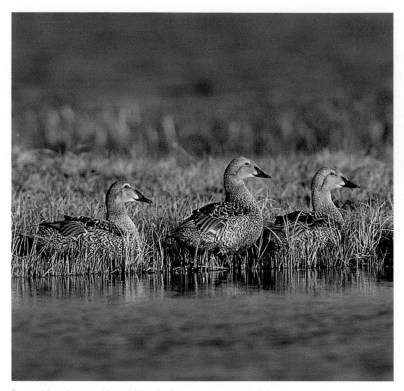
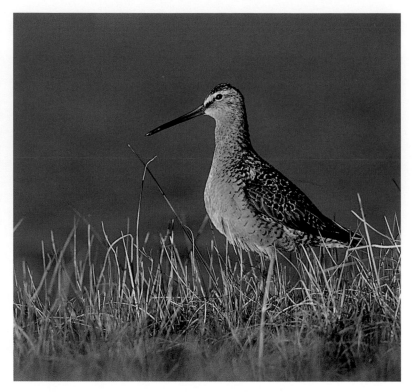

Female king eiders and long-billed dowitcher on the coastal plain

we walk a very erratic course and every few yards we stop to watch and photograph birds. We find the nest of an American golden plover; we try to find the nest of a long-billed dowitcher; we see chicks of a pectoral sandpiper. We watch flocks of long-tailed ducks roosting on the edge of the ice at Beaufort Lagoon, while on the lagoon and resting around the edge are common and red-breasted mergansers, king eider, and brant, as well as red-throated, Pacific, and a couple of yellow-billed loons. Parasitic and long-tailed jaegers appear every so often across the tundra, a family of sandhill cranes walks along, and every pond or wet swale has a nesting sandpiper of one species or another.

On our return to the tent we walk up a ridge and there, spread out between us and our camp, is a system of ponds about a half-mile across, hidden in a depression so that we hadn't seen it earlier, even though it is only a few minutes' walk from our campsite. Here over the next few days we find a great variety of nesting birds, including Canada and white-fronted geese, red and red-necked phalaropes, long-billed dowitcher, dunlin, and others; while Pacific loon, tundra swan, and king eider are always there and possibly nesting.

You develop a new sense of scale and distance in this place. In Kaktovik, as in most of the world, roads and houses obscure the land and stop the eye. You tend to look at close range and use the car to move from point to point along the roads. On the tundra, your world becomes

the few square miles that you can walk to; you get to know the area based on the natural contours of ponds, streams, and hills. You are keenly aware of the surrounding countryside, and you can see for miles.

Not only is perception different, the birds themselves are different on the open tundra as compared to those found in the village. At Kaktovik I saw a greater diversity of species, and the rarest birds of my trip were all seen around the village. But these individual birds are immatures, the "unemployed drifters" of the bird world, attracted to easy foraging at the concentration of food that any human settlement provides. Also attracted to the artificial concentration of food are predators—ravens, gulls, foxes, and others—and these, combined with the constant human presence, greatly reduce the success of birds nesting close to the village and alter the ecosystem far beyond the man-made structures.

The tundra and beaches of the refuge are not pristine, and certainly not beyond the reach of human influence. Signs of people are scattered around—charred logs from a campfire on the beach, soda cans, bits of plywood and Styrofoam—the ordinary flotsam and jetsam of occasional visitors here. There are also contrails of jets high overhead, and the mostly invisible effects of air pollution and global warming. The remains of the DEW Line site at Nuvagapak Point—mounds of gravel mixed with various metal artifacts—are obvious, but the gravel road that extends east

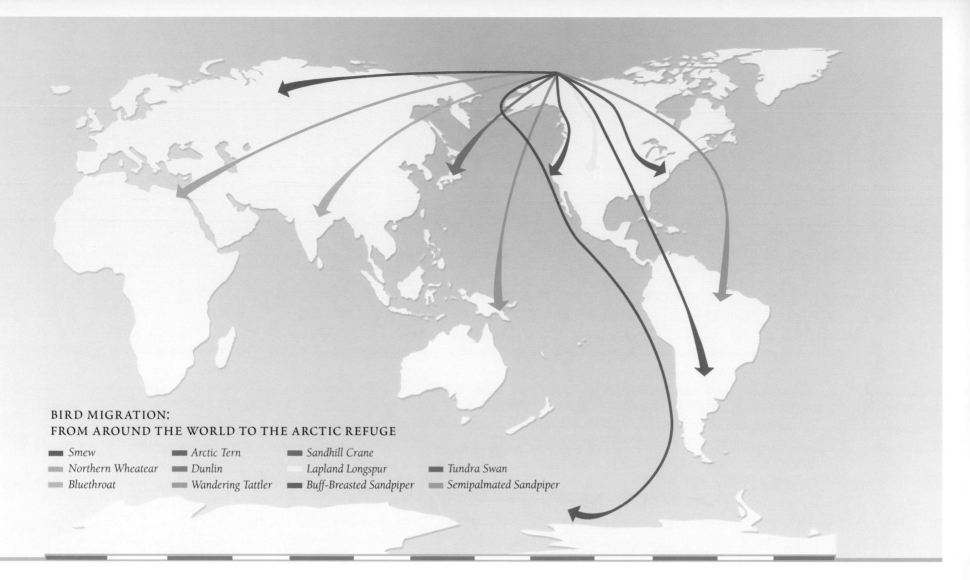

BIRD MIGRATION:
FROM AROUND THE WORLD TO THE ARCTIC REFUGE

- Smew
- Northern Wheatear
- Bluethroat
- Arctic Tern
- Dunlin
- Wandering Tattler
- Sandhill Crane
- Lapland Longspur
- Buff-Breasted Sandpiper
- Tundra Swan
- Semipalmated Sandpiper

for a mile or two is sinking into the tundra, creating ponds and becoming part of the tundra landscape once again.

The refuge is, without a doubt, vast and virtually uninhabited. Just the region referred to as Section 1002, where drilling is proposed, is about 1.5 million acres, about the size of Long Island, with the only human habitation at Kaktovik (population 280). No other permanent human settlement exists for over 150 miles in any direction. Just west of where we are camping, the three-mile-long peninsula that juts into Beaufort Lagoon doesn't even have a name on the map. Neither does the half-mile-long lake where we see families of Canada and white-fronted geese, Pacific loon, and other birds; nor the fifteen-mile-long creek we cross to explore the lakes and ponds to the south.

Looking south toward the Brooks Range from Nuvagapak Point, ignoring the wet spongy ground and some other details, I can imagine that this is what it might have been like to stand just east of the Rocky Mountains in Colorado two hundred years ago: open prairie extending for hundreds of miles around, rivers and lakes and mountain peaks without names, birds and animals moving freely, without roads,

powerlines, houses, or shopping malls to divert them. The flocks of surf scoters that pass our camp as they migrate west might not see another person or a man-made structure in a whole day of flying along the coast. They can settle in on one of these lagoons for the summer and molt without ever being disturbed by a boat.

This is a place where birds can carry on their lives without being distracted by people, but they are not here for a vacation. The birds are intensely focused on the challenges of raising young. Some of that intensity is in response to the weather, which is extreme and changeable, from sunny, calm, and sixty-five degrees one hour to cold and windy, raining, or snowing the next. The adult birds must shelter their eggs or young from all weather that comes along. They must also find food. They face off with (or hide from) jaegers, gulls, snowy owls, foxes, and other predators, and defend territories and mates against other members of their species. There is a sense of urgency to all the activities of birds in the Arctic. The sandpiper that is feigning injury to distract me from its nest or young still pauses compulsively to grab a mosquito or a spider from the grass. Activity continues twenty-four hours a day.

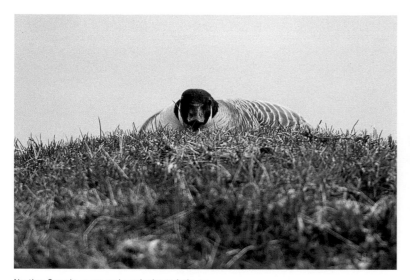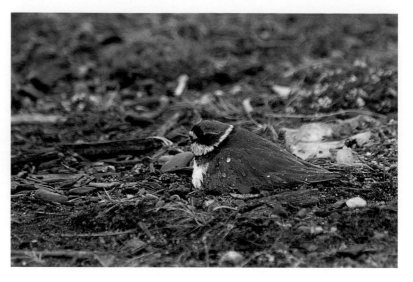

Nesting Canada goose and semipalmated plover

Time is precious. And in the Arctic, time when liquid water and insects can be found is even more precious. Most species return in the spring even before the tundra is exposed, and sandpipers display over an expanse of snow that they know will turn into a suitable nesting territory, taking care of the business of pairing and courtship even before the snow melts. Eggs are laid as soon as possible so that young can grow up and migrate south before the cold weather returns in the late summer. Many of the adult sandpipers head south before their young are fully grown, leaving the juveniles to build up their flight muscles and fat reserves and find their own way to the wintering grounds a few weeks behind the adults.

Virtually every species of bird that occurs in the Arctic National Wildlife Refuge is migratory, and even in the middle of summer birds are constantly moving. A few birds—such as the rock and willow ptarmigan, raven, and snowy owl—will stay in the refuge for the winter and endure the months of twilight and subzero temperatures, but the vast majority of the birds here are migrants, coming to take advantage of the long days and abundant insects to raise young quickly and efficiently. These advantages must outweigh the disadvantages of the long migrations required to get to and from the Arctic, because so many birds do it.

In the first week of July the rhythm of bird movements is like a complex dance: Millions of birds spread out across this vast area, with each of the sixty or so breeding species on their own agenda and in constant motion. Flocks of male surf scoters and long-tailed ducks, finished with breeding chores, can be seen flying west every afternoon and evening to spend the next few weeks on the lagoons of the Arctic National Wildlife Refuge for their complete molt. Small flocks of male pectoral sandpipers, also finished with their breeding responsibilities, are flying east, low over the tundra, beginning the trip toward their wintering grounds in South America. Flocks of Arctic terns cruise east and west along the barrier islands searching for food. Flocks of long-tailed ducks beginning to molt drift around the lagoon and gather in the evening along the shore wherever they are protected from the wind—the east side of the point on one day, the west side the next. All the while Pacific loons are flying from the tundra nesting ponds to the lagoons and back again, and Lapland longspurs are flying back and forth, bringing beak-loads of mosquitoes, flies, and spiders to their young hidden in the grass.

And the brief and chilly summer marches on. In early July the sandpiper chicks are hatching, longspur chicks are fledging, adults without nesting responsibilities are migrating away. The sandpipers and ducks that have not yet started nesting are out of luck this year. They do not have enough time to lay eggs and raise young before the snow flies in the fall. Soon all the juvenile shorebirds will gather on the coastal lagoons in preparation for fall migration. Flocks of ducks will build up in the lagoons and ponds as adults molt and young grow their first flight feathers. Robert says that in August the feathers from thousands of molting ducks pile up in windrows on the shores of the lagoon. By September hundreds of thousands of snow geese will gather on the tundra. The jaegers will migrate west along the coast and then out into the Pacific Ocean. The gyrfalcon and peregrine falcon feed on the young and inexperienced shorebirds and ducks. And by mid-September almost all of the birds will be gone to the south.

The tundra may seem like a world apart, but to the birds, and the birdwatchers, every place is connected. The male pectoral sandpiper migrating east across the tundra on July 5, while its mate is leading its day-old chicks away from me through the grass, might be the same

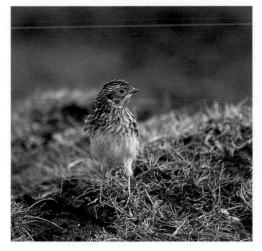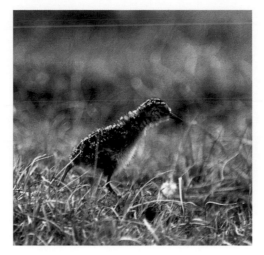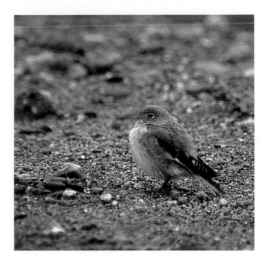

Fledgling chicks: Lapland longspur, pectoral sandpiper, snow bunting

pectoral sandpiper I will see on Cape Cod on July 20. The fluffy chicks struggling to make their way through the tundra grasses will gather in flocks and arrive in the northeastern United States in September. I can imagine seeing the sandhill crane with its young, still traveling as a family, wintering with hundreds of other crane families in the Central Valley of California.

The Arctic terns, champion distance migrants, have just returned in early June from the Antarctic, where they spent a cold southern summer among the ice floes. Now they have just finished the twelve thousand-mile trip to their breeding grounds to spend the northern summer among the ice floes here in Alaska. In a few weeks they will leave to fly south, to find the southern ice again. Fueled by krill and tiny fish, these four-ounce birds travel almost pole to pole twice a year, and spend most of the year in transit.

The semipalmated sandpiper that we found nesting here might be on its way in just a few weeks to the coast of New England or the Bay of Fundy, where it will fatten up on abundant marine invertebrates and take off on a spectacular over-water flight, non-stop from there to South America. While we are accustomed to looking at two-dimensional maps of the earth, birds understand that the earth is a globe, and just like modern jet pilots, these birds follow the shortest route around the globe from the Arctic Refuge to Surinam—across New England and over the Atlantic.

The Baird's sandpiper, only slightly larger than the semipalmated at 1.3 ounces, migrates south from the Arctic coast through the Great Plains to southern South America. Most make a long flight over Central America and then move south along the crest of the Andes. The birds we saw nesting along the runway at Kaktovik might be feeding just a month later along the shores of a lake at 12,000 feet elevation in Peru.

The Lapland longspurs that populate the tundra, each weighing only about half an ounce, will gather in flocks in September and migrate to the northern Great Plains, from Alberta to as far south as Kansas and Oklahoma, where they endure winter conditions that can be harsher than anything the Arctic coast in summer has to offer.

The male surf scoters that came west out of Canada to spend the summer molting in the coastal lagoons of Alaska will, after they finish molting, migrate south—some of them through the passes of the Brooks Range and across Alaska, some around western Alaska, and others back through the Mackenzie delta and south through Canada. In any case they will all meet in winter along the rocky Pacific Coast, from British Columbia to southern California.

Many times when we encounter a new species during the week, Robert and Subhankar ask, "Where does that bird come from?" Each time the question catches me off guard. I think, "What does this question mean? We're looking at a female with young—right here is where these birds come from!"

From my southern perspective, these are all Arctic breeding birds. I am excited to be here because it is an opportunity to see these species —birds I know from migration and winter—and to see where they come from. But from an Arctic perspective, these birds are brief visitors. Like the summer people visiting cottages on Cape Cod, some of them only visit for a few weeks and, obviously, they must come from somewhere else. The fact is that, while they are born in the Arctic Refuge, most of these species don't have a "primary residence." They have a summer home, a winter home, and perhaps even spring and fall homes. Arctic terns and semipalmated sandpipers might spend eight weeks in the refuge, then six to twelve weeks in transit and at a few carefully selected stopovers, and then eight to ten weeks

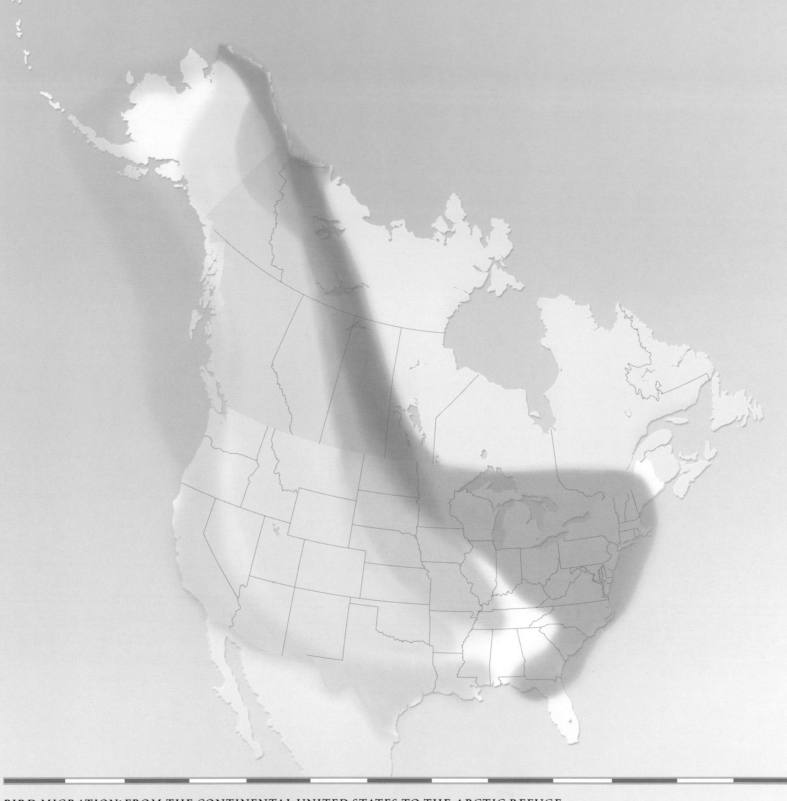

BIRD MIGRATION: FROM THE CONTINENTAL UNITED STATES TO THE ARCTIC REFUGE

Pacific
- *Pacific (Black) Brant*
- *Snow Goose*
- *Sandhill Crane*

Central
- *Rough-legged Hawk*
- *Smith's Longspur*
- *Northern Shrike*
- *Golden Eagle*

Mississippi
- *Red-throated Loon*
- *Northern Flicker*
- *Yellow-rumped Warbler*
- *American Pipit*

Atlantic
- *Tundra Swan*
- *Lapland Longspur*
- *Peregrine Falcon*
- *Long-tailed Duck*

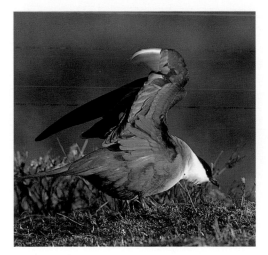

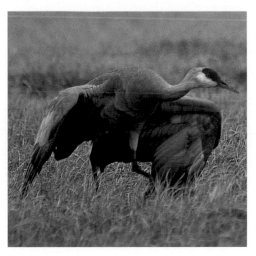

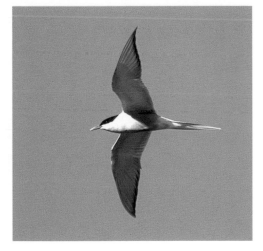

Pomarine jaeger

Sandhill crane in a broken-wing display, a tactic used to lure predators from its chicks

Arctic tern makes the longest migration of any animal on the planet.

on their wintering grounds before starting the return trip to the refuge. The Arctic Refuge is the pivotal northern point on a continuous loop.

All of the waypoints in the birds' year are important, and the birds in turn are an important part of the natural community at each place. The refuge is especially significant as the nesting grounds of many species. It is equally significant as the molting grounds of the long-tailed duck and as a migratory staging area for species such as the snow goose. Many of these species are also key elements in ecosystems far to the south, so that a disruption at the refuge could have far-reaching effects. The ecosystems of the world are linked by birds. A disturbance in one place can begin a cascade of effects across the globe.

Today, the greatest threat of disruption in the refuge—specifically the coastal plain—is the proposed exploration for oil. There are countless reasons for not drilling in the refuge. The biological argument is that, even without a major oil spill, drilling would inevitably degrade the habitat, oil and other chemicals would pollute the water, helicopter traffic and human presence would disturb the birds, while the buildings and human refuse would attract predators such as gulls, ravens, and foxes, which would in turn make it difficult or impossible for some bird species to nest successfully. This could lead to population declines, which could lead to unforeseeable consequences around the world.

My own reaction to the proposed drilling is that it would be a tragedy simply because it would alter a landscape that has been little altered by humans. The value of wilderness seems so self-evident that it is difficult to articulate a response to those who would destroy it. We preserve works of art in museums. We preserve buildings and other objects of great beauty or historical significance. Why do we question the value of preserving an intact ecosystem? To me the proposed drilling in the Arctic Refuge is comparable to cutting holes in the ceiling of the Sistine Chapel.

What benefit could possibly justify such an action? Certainly not the extraction of a small amount of oil—only enough to satisfy U.S. consumers for 180 days—when many alternatives exist. Even restricted development on the refuge would eliminate forever the feeling of being alone in nature in this place. No longer would the birds and other wildlife be able to carry on their lives without seeing any sign of human life. No longer would they move unfettered across the coastal plain. No longer would the air be filled with the perfect refrains of bumblebees, wind, and the trilling songs of the sandpipers, without a mechanical sound of any kind.

I believe that if we truly and honestly weigh the economic benefits of development against the aesthetic and environmental costs, there can be no debate about the future of the Arctic Refuge, and I believe that future generations around the earth will agree. We have a unique opportunity to preserve something that is in danger of vanishing completely from the earth—a whole and natural place, a true wilderness, where the birds are at home and we are visitors.

David Sibley

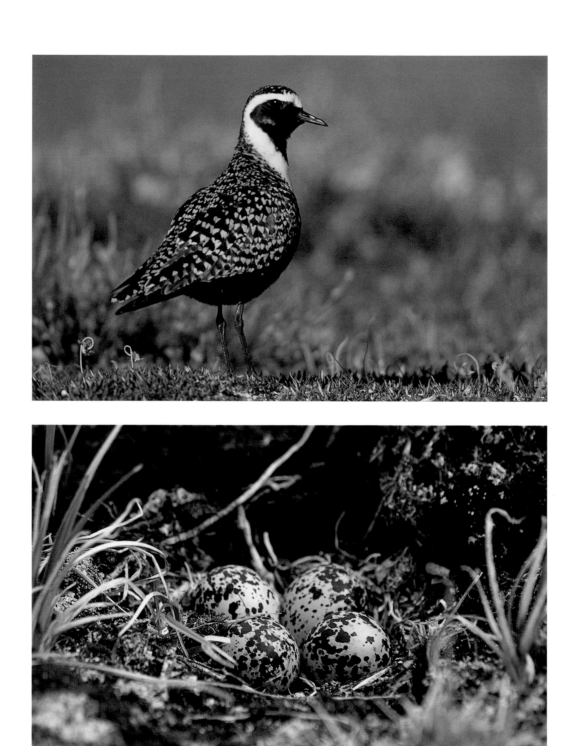

American golden plover nests on the coastal plain near Nuvagapak Lagoon.

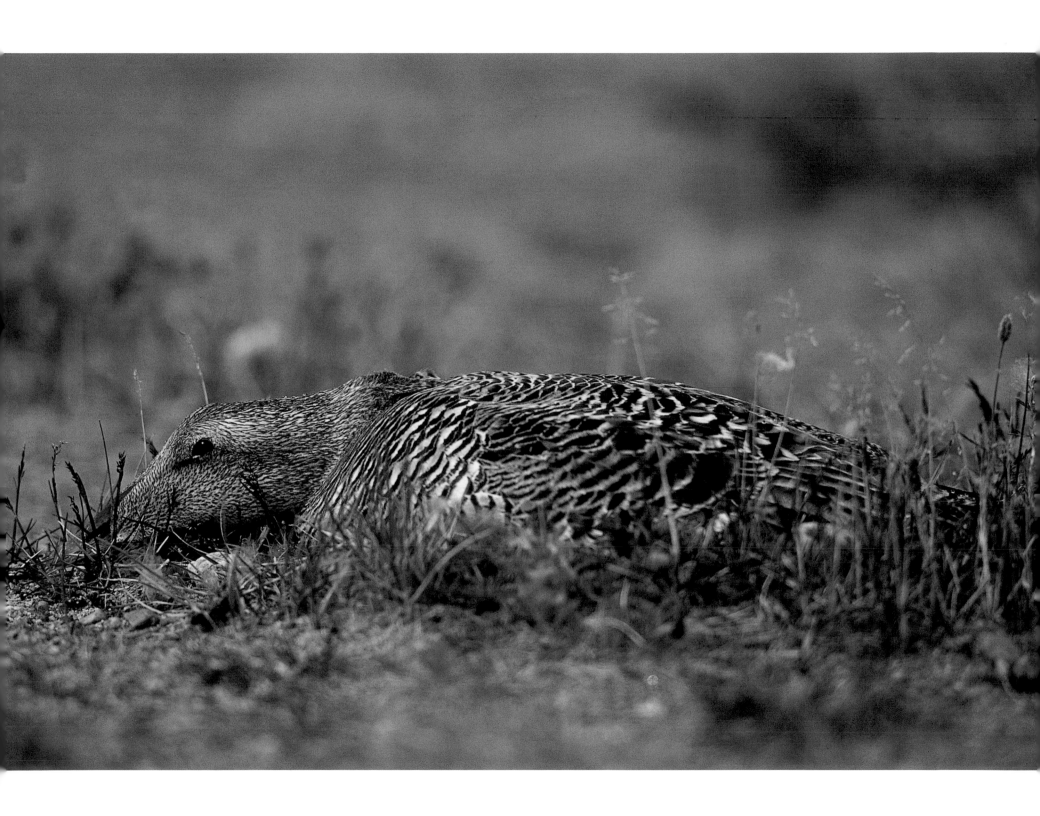

Common eider attends her nest.

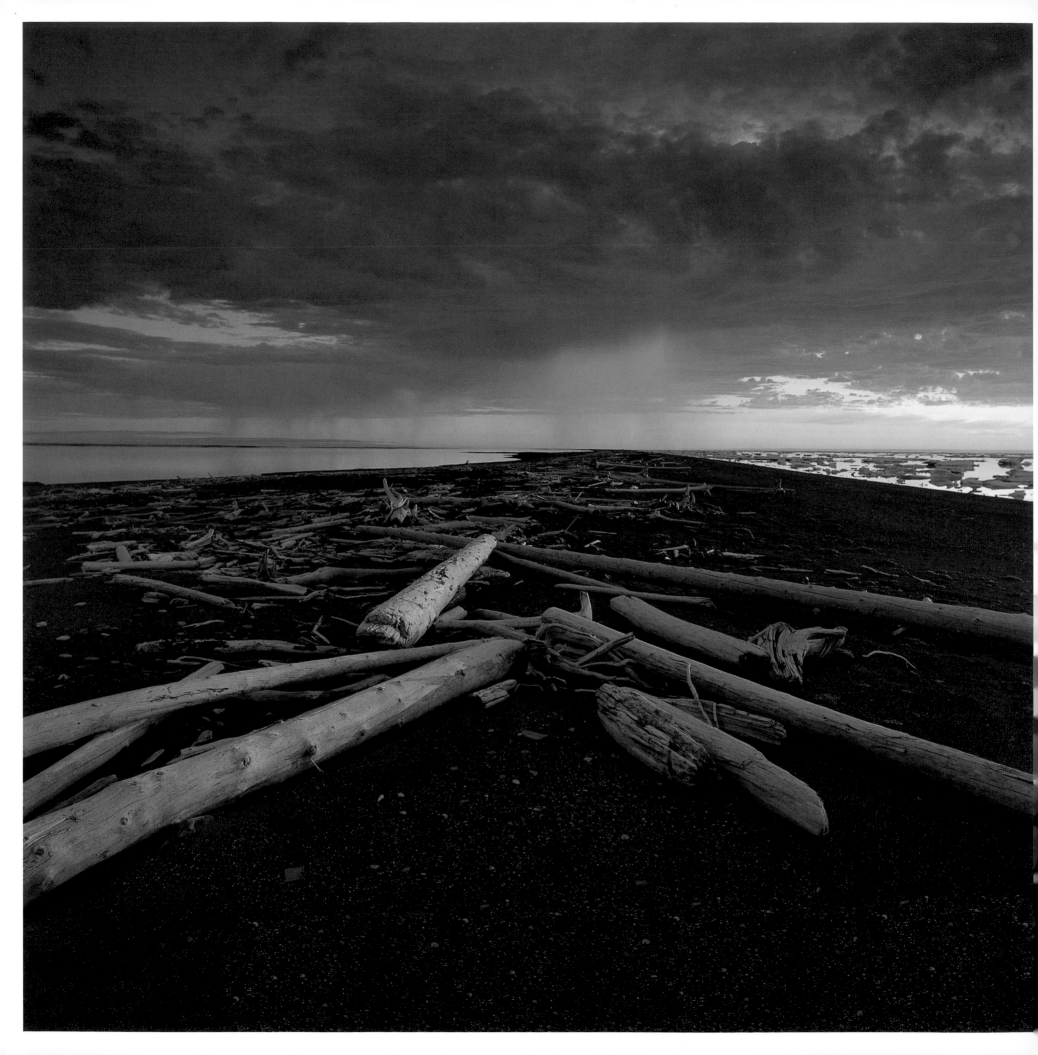

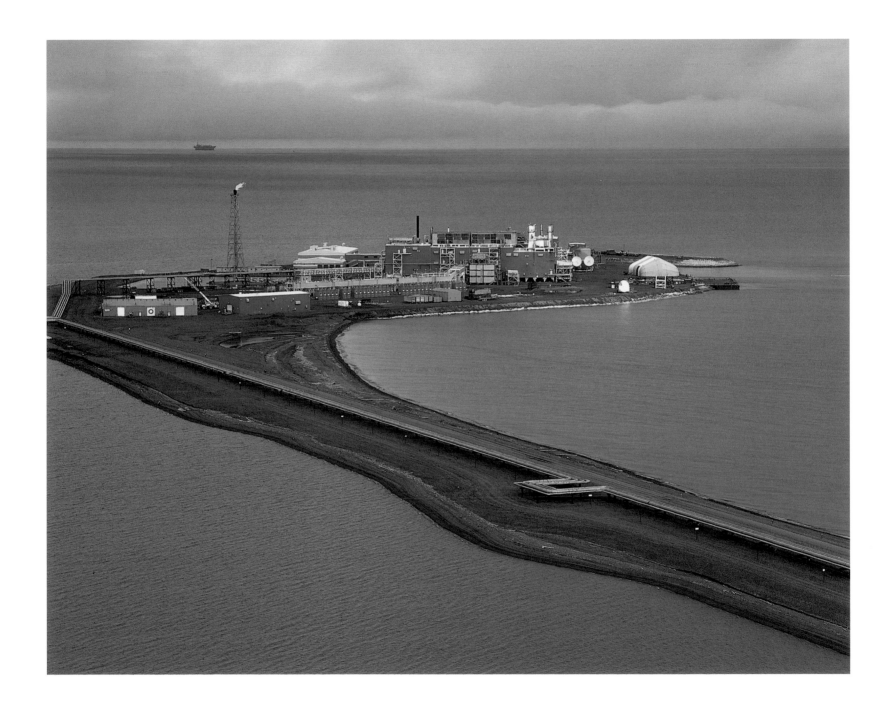

Endicott: An offshore drill site near Prudhoe Bay

Opposite • Icy Reef: A narrow stretch of barrier island, with Arctic coastal waters to the north and a coastal lagoon to the south, creates an important ecological habitat for a variety of species.
These barrier islands are important nesting habitat for many migratory bird species.

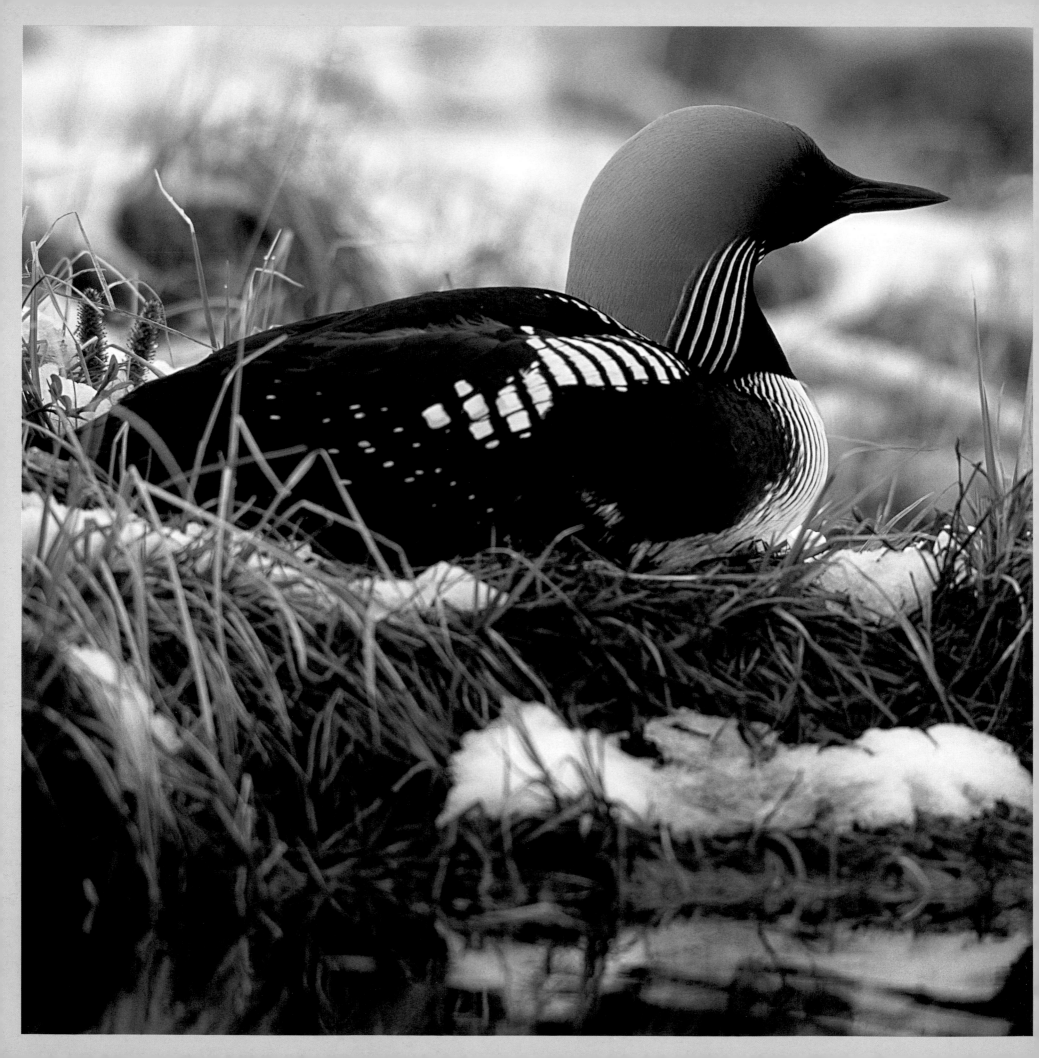

Pacific Loon: Nesting on the Coastal Plain

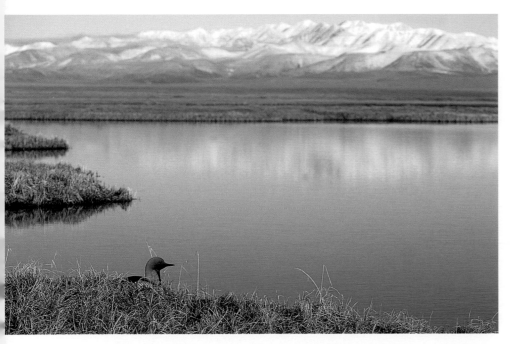

Below right • Male Lapland longspur on the coastal plain

June 28, 2002: While camping out on the Arctic tundra during the summer months, I shared the experience that Debbie Miller portrays in her book *Midnight Wilderness* when she writes, "The Arctic music is as constant as the twenty-four-hour daylight." However, on this morning the snow-covered tundra is utterly silent.

I am camped at the mouth of the Turner River. Every morning a male Lapland longspur appears on a small mound ten feet in front of my tent. He sings his beautiful and magical songs to distract me from the nest nearby that his mate is attending, a lovely good morning welcome. But this morning he is not there to greet me, and I surmise that the birds are preserving their energy on this cold, snowy day. I walk to the little nearby pond where a Pacific loon is nesting. I was introduced to the nest the previous day by my friend and fellow photographer, Izuro Toki, who is camping nearby. Today the loon sits on the nest quietly, her head sometimes falling back while she sleeps. I sit for a long time, until finally the air begins to warm and the snow starts melting.

During breakfast Izuro tells me that both loon parents attend the nest, switching at regular intervals to feed. His dream is to photograph the "swap at the nest," which he has tried unsuccessfully to capture for five seasons.

After the snow has melted, a male loon flies in to the pond, making a magnificent landing like the grandest of airplanes. He starts calling his mystical call, as this species has done for millions of years. With this sound the tundra is back to normal.

Izuro and I walk back toward the pond and sit in quiet anticipation. Slowly the male swims closer and closer to the nest; the two mates exchange looks as he approaches. When he arrives at the edge of the shore, the female steps off the nest, exposing two brown eggs. She walks to the water as he climbs the bank and sits on the nest. He pulls up tufts of grass to throw around the nest; then he checks the eggs and settles down. Those brief moments when the eggs are visible are the most vulnerable for this pair.

I leave on June 30, while Izuro stays behind; he hopes to see the chicks hatch. Over the next three weeks I spend time with Peter Matthiessen and David Sibley, observing birds and learning from them the magnificence of birding in the Arctic. In late July, Walt Audi, who is in contact with Izuro, delivers the news that an Arctic fox raided the loon nest and ate the eggs. I am very sad; I guess I made a personal connection with those two birds in this faraway land. I wanted them to successfully hatch and raise their young. While they did not succeed, many other birds successfully raised their young and I was there to see it. But it is not the success stories but the story of the two loons that I will remember most many years from now, when I am an old man.

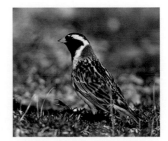

—S.B.

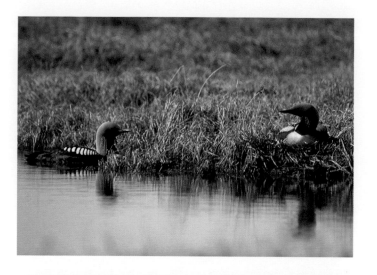

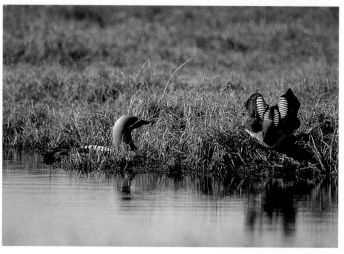

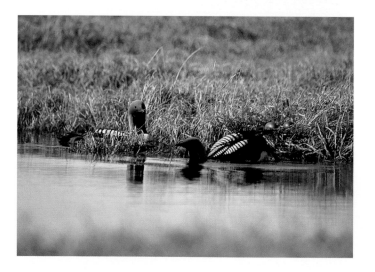

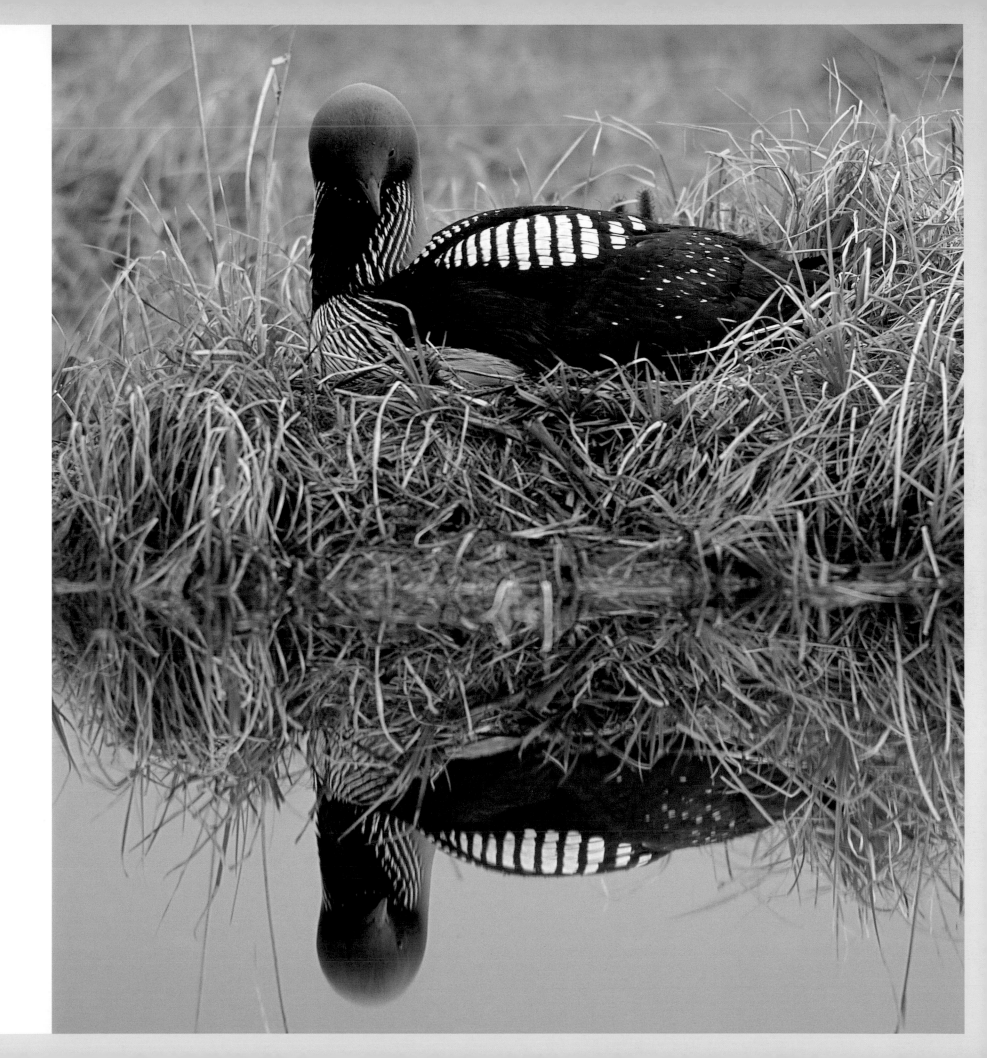

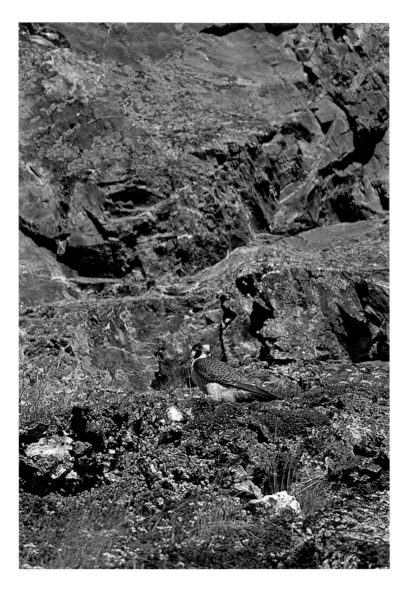
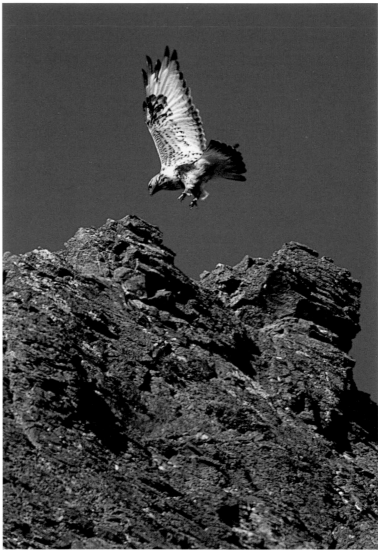

Three raptors nest in the Kongakut River valley: Peregrine falcon, rough-legged hawk, fledgling gyrfalcon chick

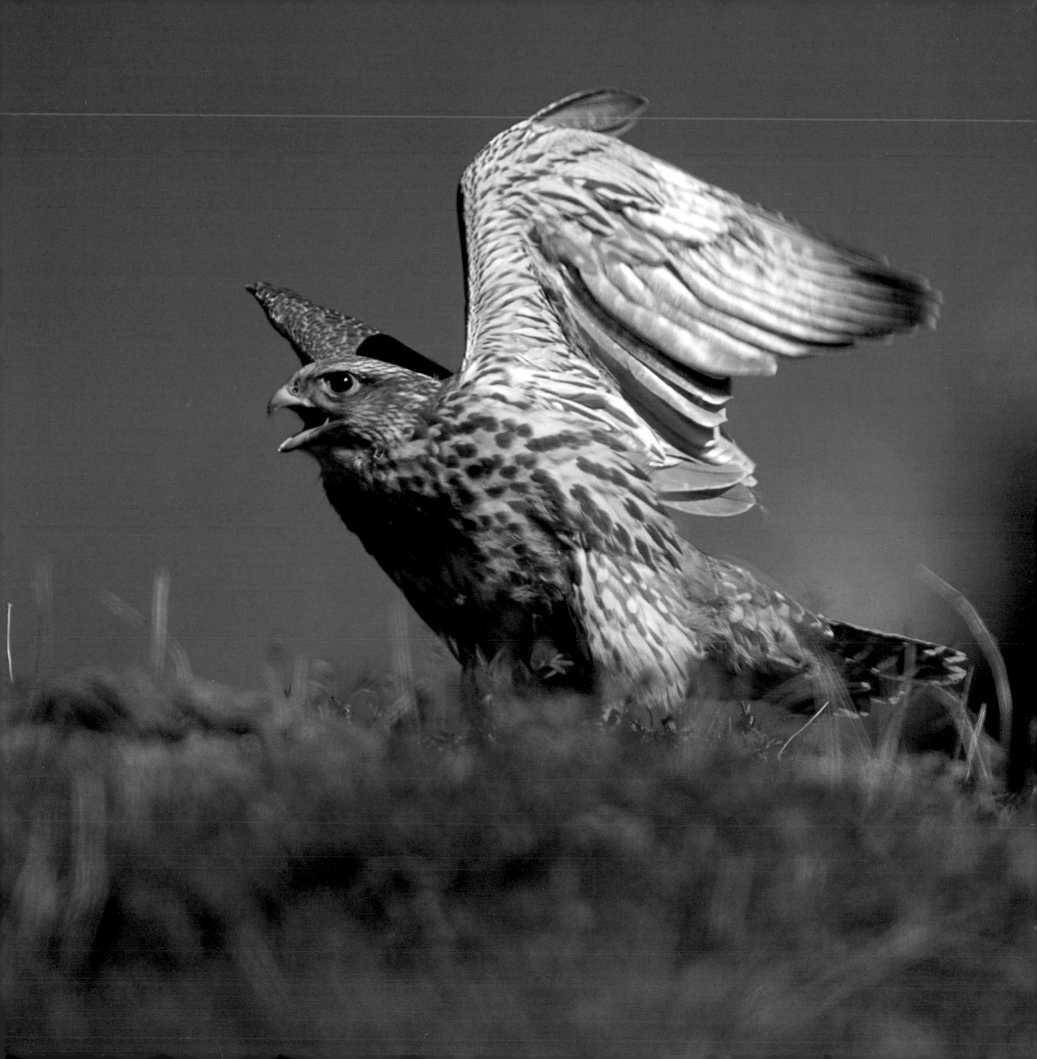

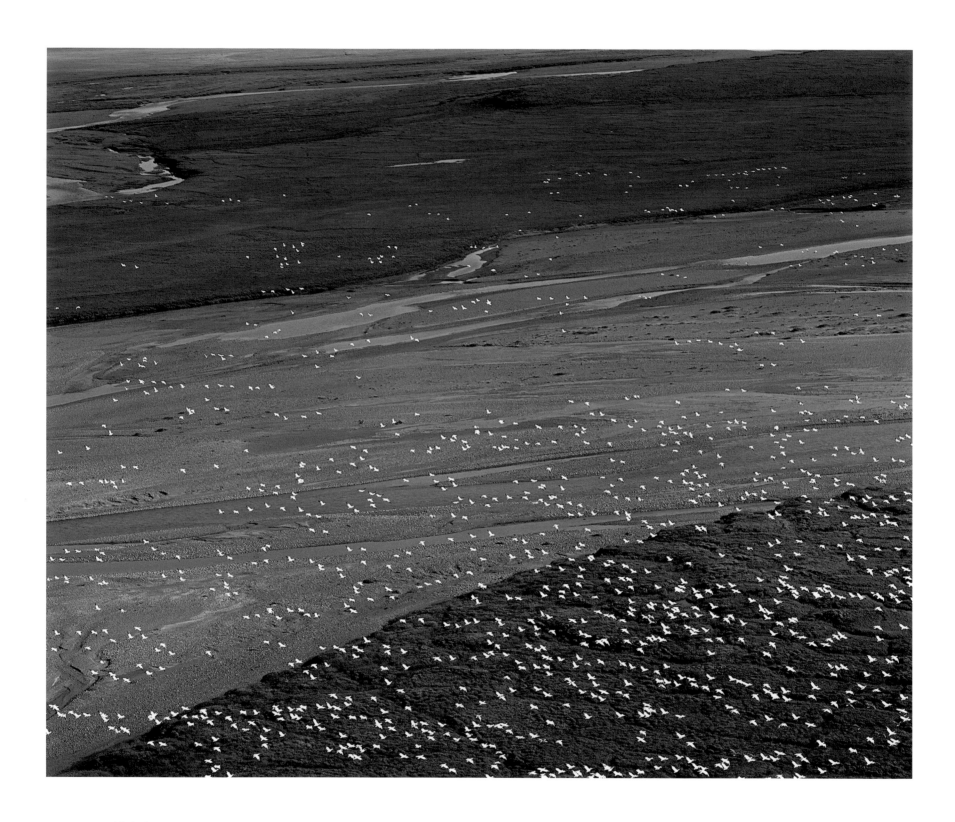

Flock of snow geese over the Jago River and coastal plain: Up to 300,000 snow geese migrate here in autumn to feed on cotton grass, building up fat reserves before heading south.

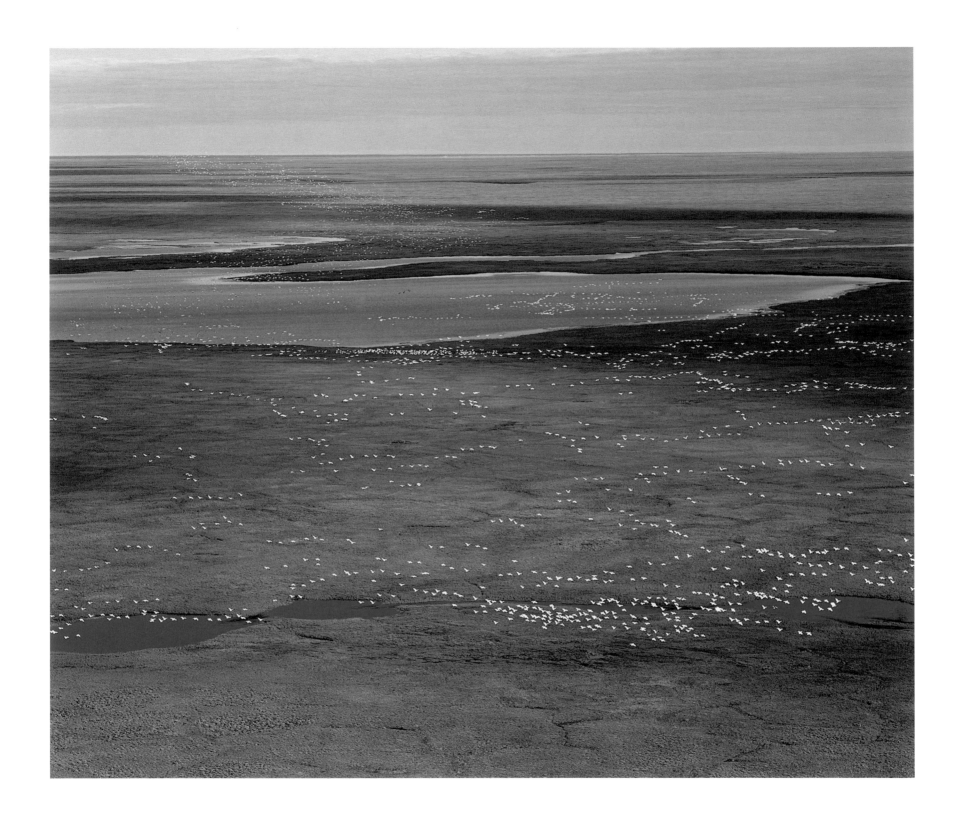

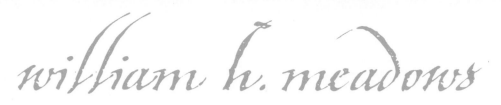

william h. meadows

ARCTIC REFUGE: KEY TO SAVING WILD AMERICA

For a transitory enchanted moment man must have held his breath in the presence of this continent . . . face to face for the last time in history with something commensurate to his capacity for wonder.

F. SCOTT FITZGERALD, *The Great Gatsby*

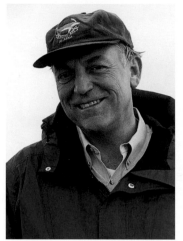

Photo by Sandy Brigg

WILLIAM H. MEADOWS, *president of The Wilderness Society since 1996, has been active in conservation for more than thirty years. He credits Earth Day, founded by his colleague at The Wilderness Society, former Senator Gaylord Nelson, as the catalyst for his involvement. He first became engaged in environmental issues as a volunteer leader in his home state of Tennessee.*

Meadows began his professional career at his alma mater, Vanderbilt University. Later he was Vice President for College Relations at Sweet Briar College in Virginia. His professional conservation career began in 1992, when he became director of the Sierra Club's Centennial Campaign. He has worked on national efforts to protect the Arctic National Wildlife Refuge, the Rocky Mountain Front, the Northern Forest, and the Southern Appalachians, and provides leadership on wilderness campaigns in Utah, Alaska, California, and Washington State.

Besides serving on the Steering Committee of the White Cloud Council and on the Advisory Council for the Biodiversity Project, Meadows has also been an active leader in the Green Group. He is a member of the board of the National League of Conservation Voters, the American Wilderness Coalition, The Murie Center, and the National Wildlife Refuge Association.

For the last quarter of a century, the Arctic National Wildlife Refuge—or more specifically, its northern edge, the coastal plain along the Arctic Ocean—has been at the center of a debate not only about how we use our public lands, but about what they mean to us. When people are first introduced to the issue, they often find this puzzling. The coastal plain is almost impossibly remote, thousands of miles from America's population centers. Few people visit it. Those who do find it is very different from the spectacular landscapes Americans have come to regard as their national treasures, places such as Yosemite and the Grand Canyon. At first glance, it can appear to be a bleak, barren, empty place, of interest more for the views it affords on clear days of the Brooks Range than for itself. But its value does not lie in that first glance; it is not a place that will reveal its beauty up to a casual snapshot.

On the contrary, its value lies in its very wildness, and wildness in turn is valuable precisely because it is difficult to understand, impossible to capture. Before we had any national parks or forests, one of the most influential American thinkers of the nineteenth century, Ralph Waldo Emerson, called wilderness "uncontained and immortal beauty" for the simple reason that wilderness was free. That is what makes the coastal plain so beautiful and so valuable, and what makes it the emblem for millions of Americans of what we hope for from our public lands. We haven't interfered with it, or manipulated it to serve our needs. The wildlife great and small—caribou, polar bears, voles and vetch—live as they have for centuries. The land is uncontained. It is free.

Protecting and preserving wilderness in our country for all time started with the seeds planted by Emerson and his friend and neighbor Henry David Thoreau. It caught on slowly; the first legislation that specifically served that purpose was a New York State law passed in 1885 that declared portions of the Adirondacks "forever wild." Fifty years passed before The Wilderness Society was founded in 1935 for the specific purpose of protecting publicly owned wild lands throughout our country.

One of the founders of The Wilderness Society, Aldo Leopold, was a

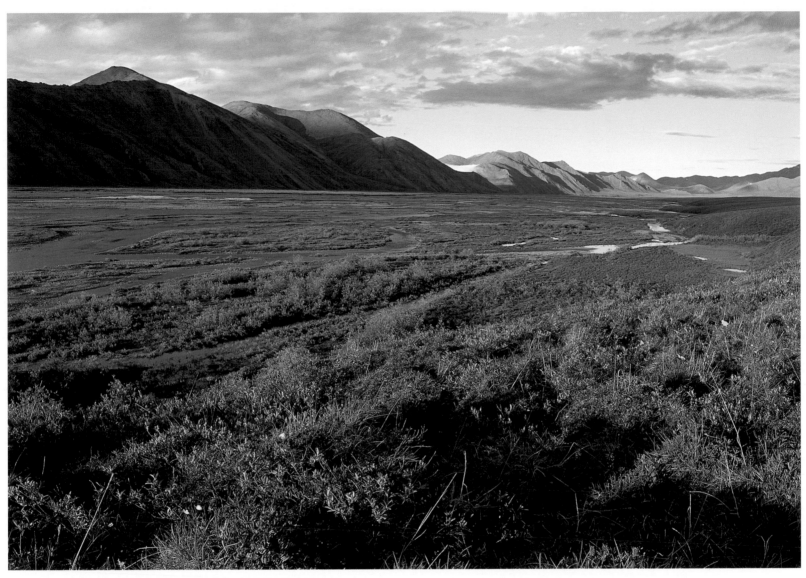

Summer in the Kongakut River valley

Forest Service employee who learned the importance of wilderness from a dying wolf. He had been doing his job, taming the wildlands in the Gila country of southern New Mexico by shooting predators so there would be more deer for hunters. But when he looked into the eyes of a dying wolf he had just shot, he realized that in some places, nature should be left to its own devices, should be left free. Another of our founders, Bob Marshall, also a Forest Service employee, was something of an adventurer, who had his first experience hiking in wilderness in those protected Adirondacks. He realized that not enough of the territory was truly wild, since the protected areas there are a patchwork surrounding small towns and private lands. He was also disappointed that the state government did not fully respect its duty to

keep its lands "forever wild," and was instead building a network of motorized "trails" for maintenance within the protected areas. Thus, they were not as pure and free as he had hoped. So he struck out for Alaska in 1929 to explore the Brooks Range, where he could be hundreds of miles from the nearest road or village.

But it was two of our early leaders, Olaus Murie and his wife Mardy, who found the ideal wilderness in the Arctic's coastal plain. Olaus also worked for the federal government, for a forerunner of the Fish and Wildlife Service. Part of his job as a wildlife biologist was to study the habits of the caribou. He and Mardy first visited what is now the Arctic National Wildlife Refuge in 1926, but they didn't just study wildlife. They fell in love with the place, with its openness, with its serenity,

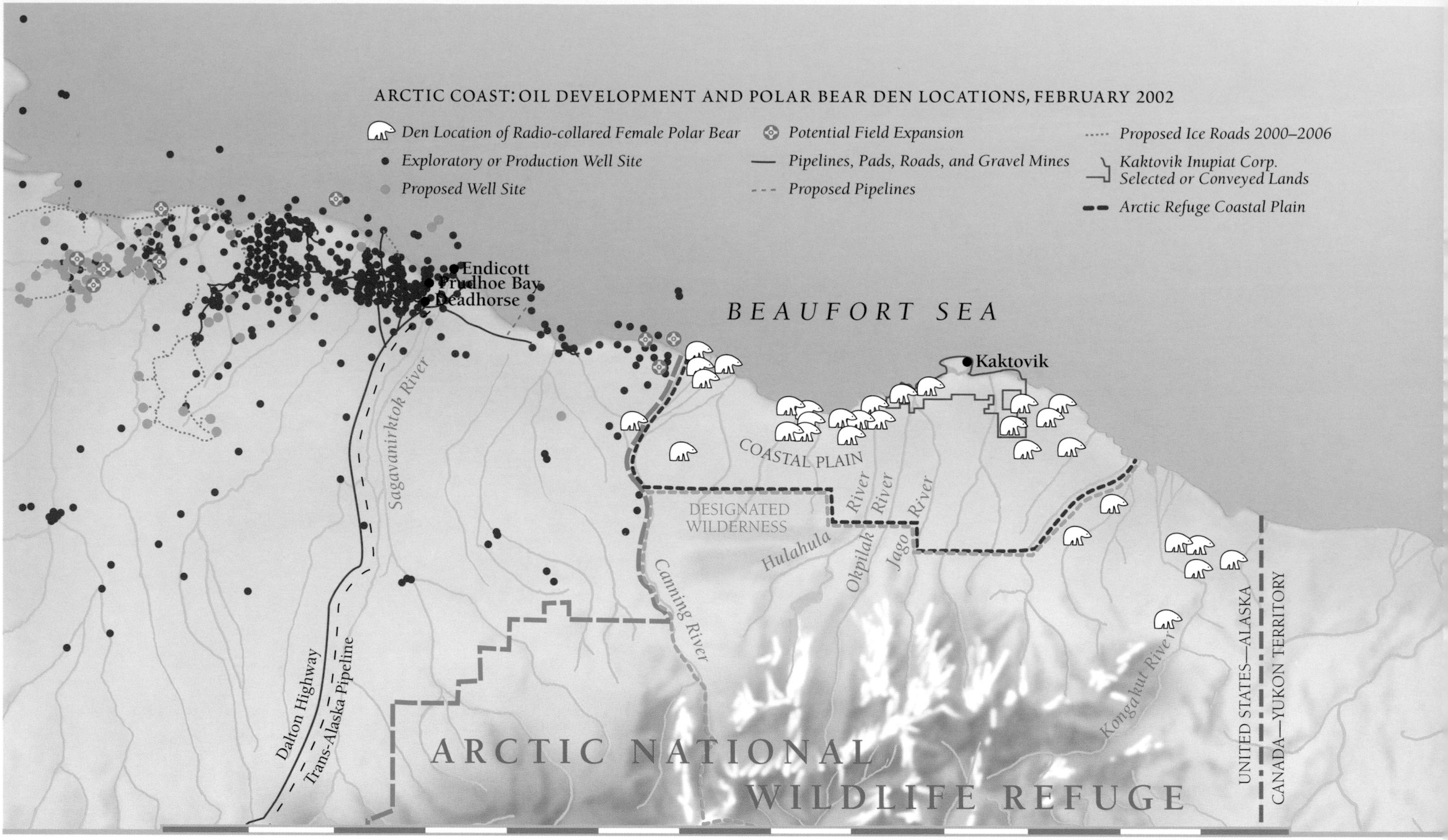

ARCTIC COAST: OIL DEVELOPMENT AND POLAR BEAR DEN LOCATIONS, FEBRUARY 2002

Den Location of Radio-collared Female Polar Bear
Exploratory or Production Well Site
Proposed Well Site
Potential Field Expansion
Pipelines, Pads, Roads, and Gravel Mines
Proposed Pipelines
Proposed Ice Roads 2000–2006
Kaktovik Inupiat Corp. Selected or Conveyed Lands
Arctic Refuge Coastal Plain

BEAUFORT SEA

Kaktovik

COASTAL PLAIN

DESIGNATED WILDERNESS

Endicott
Prudhoe Bay
Deadhorse

Sagavanirktok River

Canning River

Hulahula River

Okpilak River

Jago River

Kongakut River

Dalton Highway
Trans-Alaska Pipeline

ARCTIC NATIONAL
WILDLIFE REFUGE

UNITED STATES—ALASKA
CANADA—YUKON TERRITORY

with its freedom. Although they did not return for thirty years, the place never left them. Mardy later wrote of its meaning to them: "This is the value of this piece of wilderness—its absolutely untouched character. Not spectacular, no unique or 'strange' features, but just the beautiful, wild country of a beautiful, wild free-running river."

When they did return, in 1956, it was with a purpose. Some people within the Interior Department had put forward the idea of establishing a park or wildlife refuge in northeastern Alaska, and the Muries wanted to do all they could to advance the idea. It was on that visit that they witnessed the migration of the caribou one evening. "The quiet, unmoving landscape I had scanned so carefully from the ridge before dinner had come alive," Mardy wrote. "The rightful owners had returned."

For the next four years, working through The Wilderness Society, they pressed for protection of this place they loved. The legislation they supported failed, but their mission succeeded: In the closing days of the Eisenhower Administration in 1960, Interior Secretary Fred Seaton

used his executive authority to designate almost 9 million acres in northeast Alaska—including not only the coastal plain, but parts of the Brooks Range and the land to the south of it—as the Arctic National Wildlife Range, later to become the Arctic National Wildlife Refuge.

Of course, the story does not end there. Designation as a wildlife refuge grants some protection to a place, but allows a wide range of activities, including farming, drilling, and road building, that can damage its wild character and put an end to its freedom. The Wilderness Society had been working since the late 1940s to secure passage of legislation that would allow federally owned lands to be designated as permanent wilderness, which would prohibit the intrusion of roads and machines and keep land "forever wild" and free. That effort finally succeeded in 1964 with the enactment of the Wilderness Act. But although the original Wilderness Act designated over 9 million acres of federal lands in the Lower 48 as wilderness, it did not designate any lands in Alaska. That would have to wait until 1980, with the passage

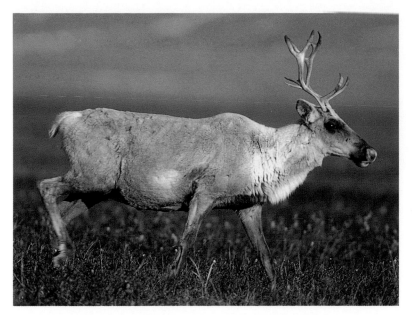
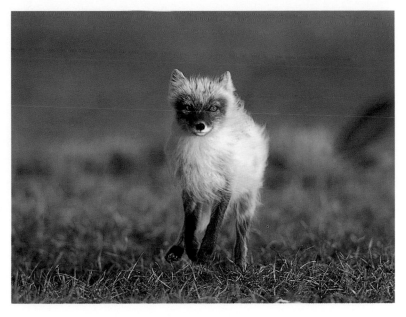

Pregnant Porcupine caribou and Arctic fox in its summer coat, coastal plain

of the Alaska National Interest Lands Conservation Act (ANILCA) in the closing days of the Carter Administration.

ANILCA was fiercely controversial, and the debate over it raged for years. It was during that period that the fate of wilderness in Alaska became the focus of land conservation efforts. The Wilderness Society and other conservation organizations argued that Alaska was still relatively untouched and offered more opportunities than anywhere else for lands to be left free, for nature to run its course. Opponents saw other opportunities in those untouched lands—chiefly opportunities for logging, mining, and drilling. It was a contest for which vision of the "best use" of public lands would prevail.

The enacted version of ANILCA was a victory, but it was a compromise. It doubled the size of the Arctic Range—now called the Arctic Refuge—and protected half of it as permanent wilderness, but the protected areas were in the mountains. The fate of the coastal plain was unsettled. In the time since the Muries had last visited, oil had been discovered on Alaska's North Slope, and surveys indicated that there was some chance that a significant reservoir of oil lay beneath the coastal plain. Some legislators who supported wilderness in the mountains could not get past the promise of possible oil reserves, especially so soon after the embargoes and gas-pump lines of the 1970s. At the same time, they did not want to foreclose future protection. So a provision was added to ANILCA, Section 1002, which left 1.5 million acres of the coastal plain in limbo, to be studied for its oil and gas potential and for its wildlife and wilderness values. A future Congress could declare it wilderness— or open it to exploration and development. That is still the case today.

The debate over the coastal plain's future has continued without interruption since then. As I write this essay, it has reached its most critical moment: The House has approved energy legislation that would open the area to drilling; the Senate has refused to put any similar provision in its version of the bill. The dispute has never had so high a profile: Washington pundits who had barely been aware of the question two years ago can now discuss every aspect of the refuge debate, duel over the latest statistical analyses of it, and claim to speak with unassailable authority for their position. When the Senate voted against opening the refuge, newspapers all over America reported it less as a victory for the environment than as the first major defeat for President Bush.

But few of the pundits or reporters who have covered the story seem to understand why the refuge is so important to those of us who have supported protecting it for the past twenty, thirty, or forty years, or why it has become so central to the broader debate over how we treat our public lands. For now, at least, the fact that they know that the environmental community does see the future of the refuge as the keystone of current land protection issues may be enough: Elevating their awareness represents progress, even if awareness sometimes falls short of full understanding.

Many observers and participants in the debate find the controversy somewhat baffling. After all, as I mentioned, the coastal plain is not a conventionally beautiful place. Its scenery is simple and stark, with none of the cliffs or forests that distinguish Yosemite, no colorful rock canyons like those found in Arizona and Utah, no alpine lakes and aspen forests like those in the Rockies. An oil executive once described

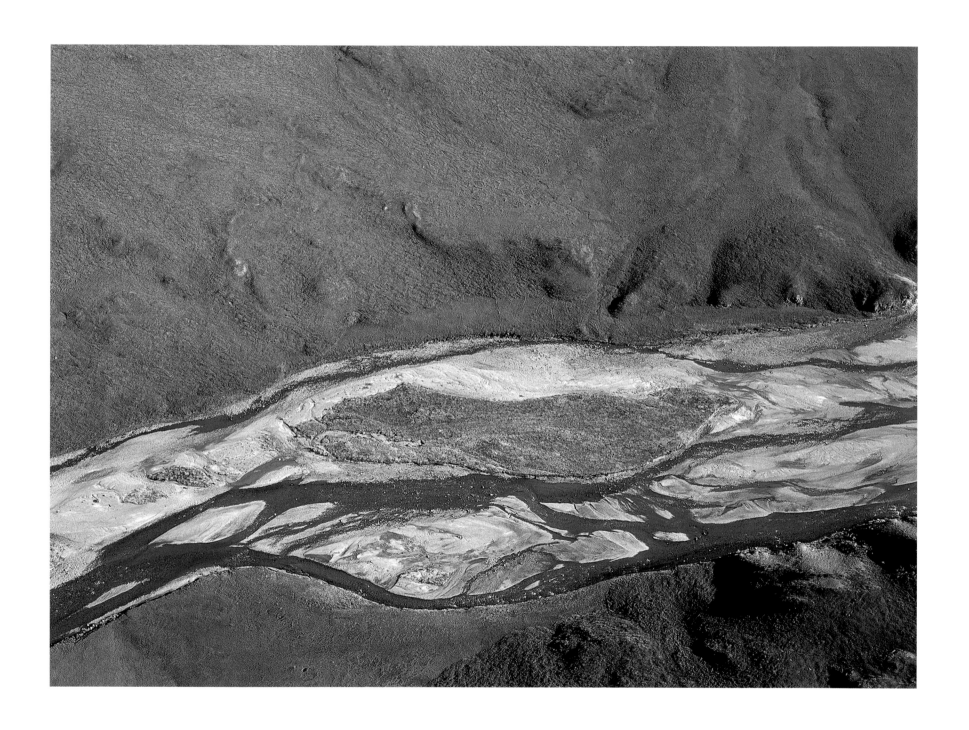

Autumn along the Hulahula River

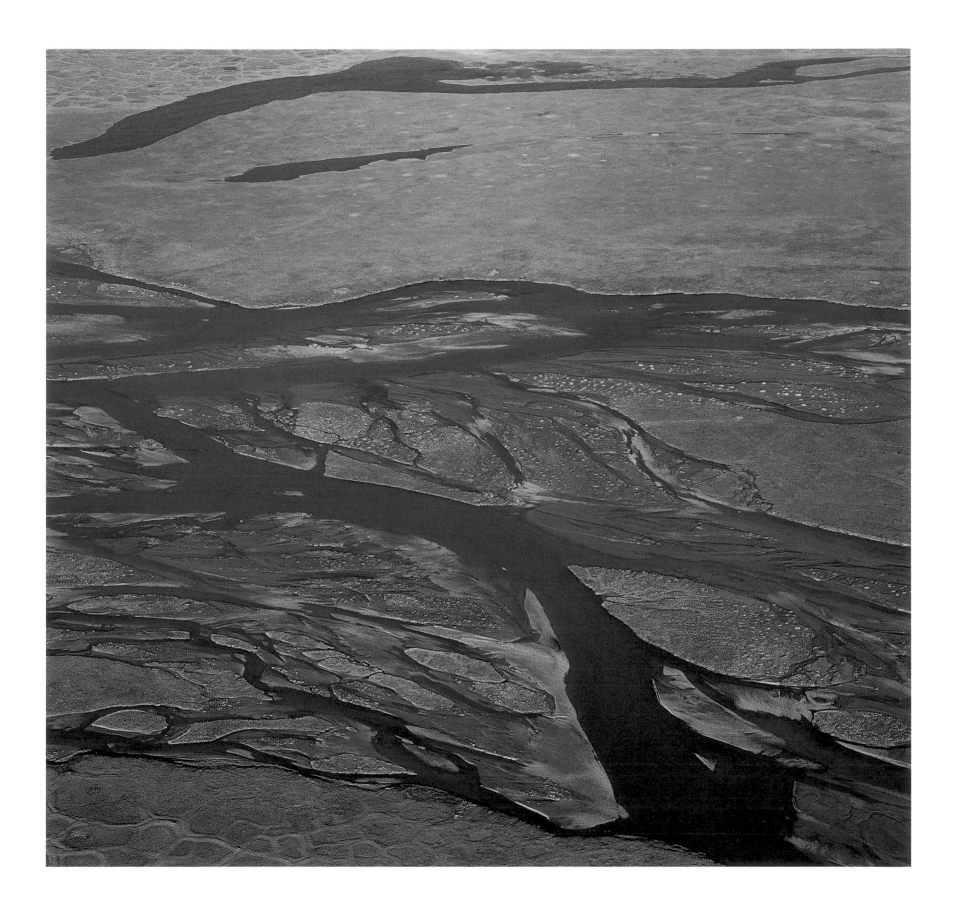

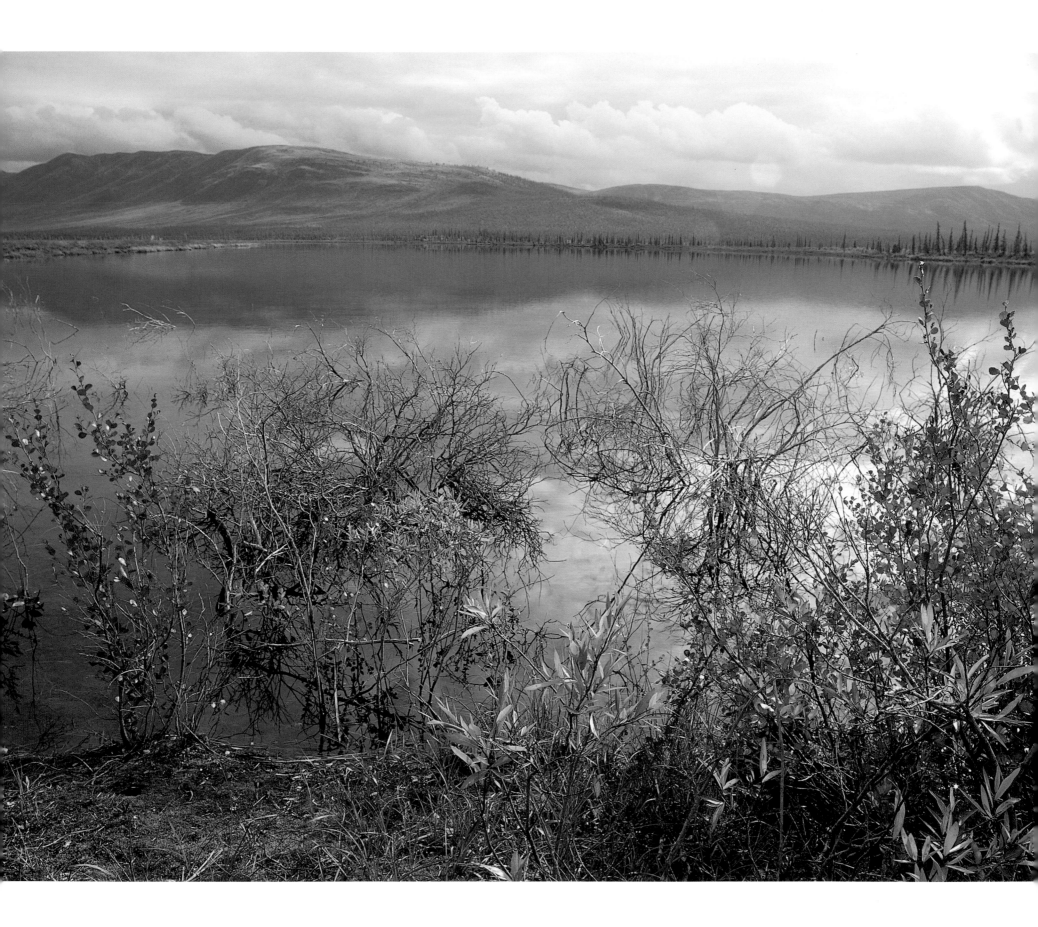

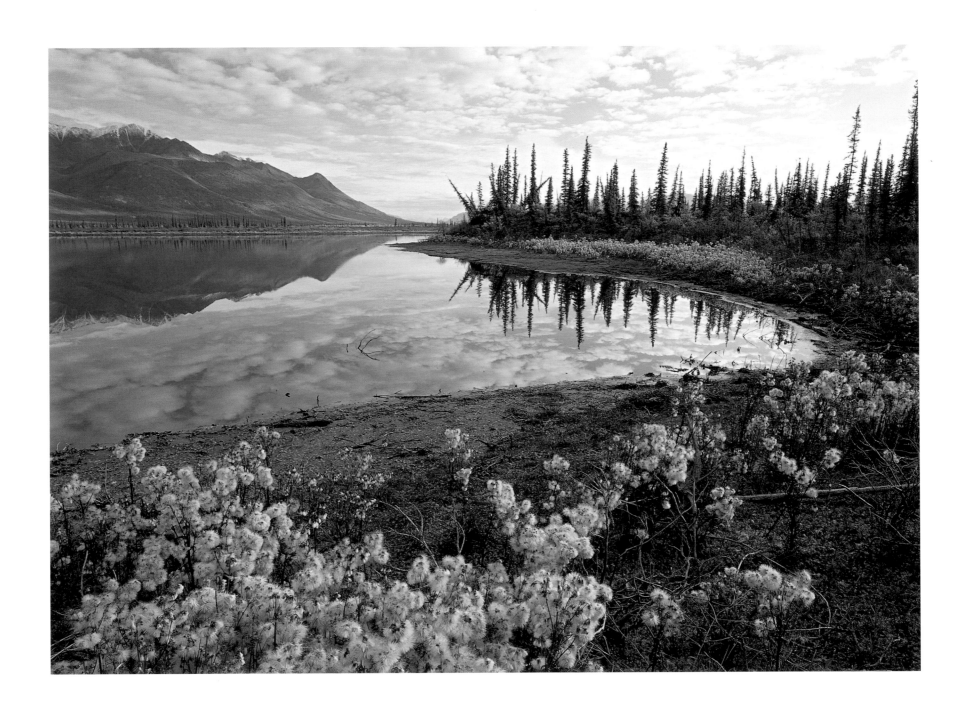

Spruce trees and Nichenthraw Mountain reflect on an unnamed lake, cotton grass in the foreground.

Opposite • Unnamed lake, East Fork of the Chandalar River valley

debbie s. miller

CLINGING TO AN ARCTIC HOMELAND

We often remember ancient or traditional cultures for the monuments they have left behind—the megaliths of Stonehenge, the temples of Bangkok, the pyramids of Teotihuacán, the great ruins of Machu Picchu. Alaska Native people have created no such monuments, but they have left something that may be unique—greater and more significant as a human achievement. This legacy is the vast land itself, enduring and essentially unchanged despite having supported human life for countless centuries. . . .

RICHARD K. NELSON, *Make Prayers to the Raven*

DEBBIE S. MILLER *grew up near the San Francisco Bay. In 1975, she and her husband, Dennis, moved to teach in Arctic Village, Alaska, a Gwich'in Athabascan Indian village located on the southern boundary of the Arctic National Wildlife Refuge. Over the past twenty-eight years, Miller and her family have explored the refuge on many trips through all of its seasons.*

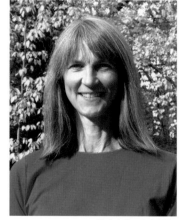
Photo by Dennis C. Miller

Miller has authored two nature books for adults, many children's books about Alaska's environment, and a number of essays and magazine articles. Her children's books have been recognized as Outstanding Science Trade Books for Children by the National Science Teachers Association. In 1998, she received the International Reading Association Teacher's Choice Award. Her adult book Midnight Wilderness: Journeys in Alaska's Arctic National Wildlife Refuge *(Alaska Northwest Books, 2000) describes the natural and political history of the refuge through a series of wilderness adventure essays. She received the 1999 Refuge Hero Award from the U.S. Fish and Wildlife Service for her writing, education, and conservation work.*

Miller lives near the wilderness in Fairbanks, Alaska, with Dennis and their two daughters, Robin and Casey. To learn more about her books and current work, visit www.debbiemilleralaska.com.

Light winds. Unrestricted visibility. The unending view across the vast Arctic National Wildlife Refuge, the homeland of the Inupiat and the Gwich'in, is magnificent.

We are flying north over the majestic Brooks Range beneath a June sky flecked with puffy cumulus clouds. Below us, the rugged spine of the Continental Divide separates two far-reaching watersheds. Countless rivers, streams, and creeks flow either south into the Yukon River and distant Bering Sea, or north toward the ice-mantled Beaufort Sea and Arctic Ocean. More than a geographic delineation, the Continental Divide also separates traditional territories of two distinct cultures: the Gwich'in Athabascan Indians, forest dwellers to the south, and the Inupiat Eskimos, tundra dwellers and sea-faring people to the north.

If a snowflake lands on the south side of the divide, it will eventually journey down rivers such as the Chandalar, passing the Gwich'in villages of Arctic Village and Venetie, whose people have hunted and fished along these south-flowing rivers for at least ten thousand years. If the snowflake blows farther north, it will journey down rivers such as the Hulahula, a traditional hunting and fishing corridor for the Inupiat people, whose village of Kaktovik lies just east of the river's mouth.

Following the Hulahula from its headwaters, we pass over Kanich, meaning "Sources of the River," a traditional Inupiat base camp for sheep hunting. I spot a few sheep grazing on fresh green shoots near the higher ridges. This inland site, about seventy-five miles from Kaktovik, represents one of the more distant hunting areas for villagers whose ancestors once lived in seasonal camps scattered along a thousand miles of Arctic coast. Like the Gwich'in, the once-nomadic Inupiat traveled extensively through their territory to hunt and fish. Both groups occasionally made long journeys over the crest of the mountains to trade with one another.

But relations were not always friendly in historic times. Prior to 1850, battles and territorial skirmishes were not uncommon. Some Inupiat and

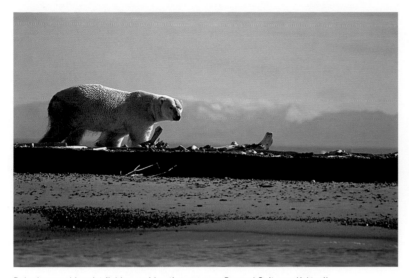
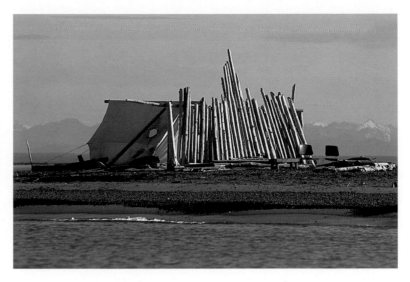

Polar bear and Inupiat fishing and hunting camp on Bernard Spit near Kaktovik

Gwich'in bands fought over resources, such as the taking of caribou.

I begin to think about those old accounts of skirmishes as our plane funnels out of the valley, beyond the glacier-woven peaks and the northern foothills. Walt Audi, a veteran bush pilot, ducks beneath a fog layer that is looming above the expansive coastal plain, tussock-studded ground that some Inupiat and Gwich'in have disputed over for more than two decades. Lobbying on Capitol Hill, political demonstrations, and walks across America have replaced the more primitive warfare of the past.

At issue is what lies on top, and what may lie beneath the Arctic Refuge coastal plain. For the Gwich'in the coastal plain is sacred ground, the place where the Porcupine caribou herd gives birth to tens of thousands of calves each year. This herd is the Gwich'in's lifeblood, their most important cultural resource. They believe the vital birthplace of the herd should be left undisturbed. For the Inupiat, the coastal plain is an important hunting and fishing area, yet the corporate world has convinced many that, if developed, a promising storehouse of oil and gas beneath the tundra would bring them jobs, a fuel source, and millions of dollars. These differing views have polarized America's northernmost cultures.

But are these two peoples, who have survived in the Arctic for thousands of years, so different in their ways of life and world views? I would visit Kaktovik and Arctic Village to gain a deeper understanding.

Soon we reach the northern fringe of tundra that is hemmed in by shorefast ice of the Beaufort Sea. We circle over Barter Island, where Kaktovik's 280 residents are located. As the name implies, Barter Island was an important trading center for centuries, and possibly several thousand years. The Inupiat, Gwich'in, and Canadian Inuit historically traveled here for trading and social gatherings. For a relatively brief time, Barter Island was also an important stop for commercial whalers during the 1890s and early 1900s.

On Barter Island a stiff northeast wind greets us, but it's not strong enough to obliterate the cheery song of a snow bunting that is perched atop the hangar. Temperatures hover around thirty-two degrees F. While I grab my parka out of the bag, Daniel Akootchook appears on his four-wheeler, the runaround vehicle for bush Alaska. Jovial and bundled for sea-ice travel, he invites me to explore Bernard Spit, a thread of land that extends from Barter Island about five miles along the coast. The Arctic Refuge is flanked by many of these spits and narrow barrier islands that provide shelter for a system of shallow lagoons.

Before we leave, Daniel points to a spot on the runway where he once lived in a sodhouse with his older sister, Mildred, and her husband, Herman Rexford. As the youngest of nine surviving children, Daniel has vivid memories of growing up in their sodhouse. He describes the interior.

"In the springtime flowers started growing upside-down from the sod roof, and we had a skylight made out of bearded seal intestines."

The window was placed at the top of the dome-shaped driftwood structure so that animals, like *nanuq* (polar bear), wouldn't break in. Opaque strips of bearded seal intestines were sewn together to form the window. Daniel remembers the skylight often frosted up from moisture and had to be scraped. To keep the home warm, one of his regular chores was gathering a plentiful supply of driftwood from the beaches.

"In the summertime we piled the wood high so that we always had spare wood," Daniel recalled, noting the importance of their only source of heat.

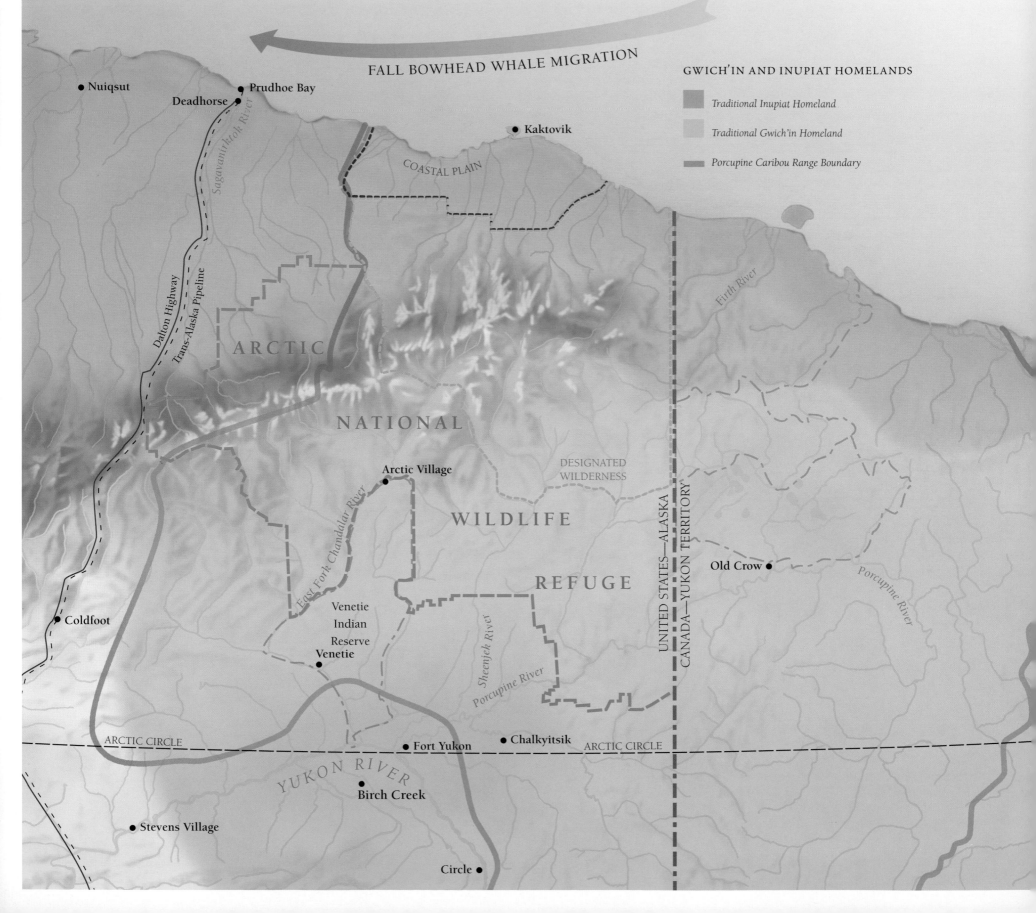

BEAUFORT SEA

FALL BOWHEAD WHALE MIGRATION

GWICH'IN AND INUPIAT HOMELANDS

Traditional Inupiat Homeland

Traditional Gwich'in Homeland

Porcupine Caribou Range Boundary

● Nuiqsut

● Prudhoe Bay

Deadhorse

● Kaktovik

Sagavanirktok River

COASTAL PLAIN

Firth River

Dalton Highway

Trans-Alaska Pipeline

ARCTIC

NATIONAL

DESIGNATED
WILDERNESS

Arctic Village ●

WILDLIFE

UNITED STATES—ALASKA

CANADA—YUKON TERRITORY

Old Crow ●

East Fork Chandalar River

REFUGE

Porcupine River

● Coldfoot

Venetie
Indian
Reserve

Venetie ●

Sheenjek River

Porcupine River

ARCTIC CIRCLE

● Fort Yukon

● Chalkyitsik

ARCTIC CIRCLE

YUKON RIVER

● Birch Creek

● Stevens Village

Circle ●

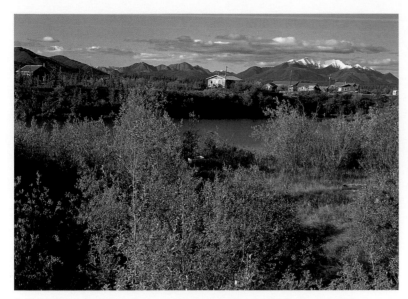

Arctic Village, the Gwich'in Athabascan village on the East Fork of the Chandalar River

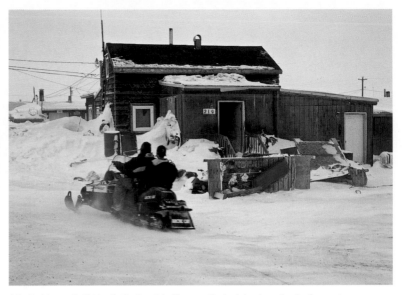

A typical house in Kaktovik, the Inupiat village on Barter Island, on the Arctic coast

Daniel, now seventy, grew up in one of the most isolated, primitive, and harsh settings in North America, having little contact with the outside world. The small number of families who lived on Barter Island in the 1920s and 1930s led a true subsistence existence, depending on hunting, fishing, trapping, reindeer herding, and trading with coastal and inland peoples, including the Gwich'in of Arctic Village.

As a young boy, Daniel remembers snaring ptarmigan and ground squirrels, and killing lemmings with a bow and arrow. He would dry the lemming skins and give them to the younger girls in his extended family, following the footsteps of his uncle who hunted caribou and sheep and gave the skins to his aunt for tanning.

"When the women scraped the skins they used a scraper made from wood and a shotgun shell. We had no other metal," Daniel recalled.

In the wake of World War II, change came very suddenly to Kaktovik. In 1947, the Air Force began construction of a five-thousand-foot airstrip and hangar facility, and the Rexfords, Akootchooks, and others were forced to relocate their village about a mile south of the runway. Bulldozers hauled a dozen sod and driftwood homes to the new village site. As a fourteen-year-old boy, Daniel remembers seeing his first *tannik* (white man) during the relocation.

The postwar military build-up brought major changes to Kaktovik, including the introduction of a wage economy. Barter Island became one of the many radar sites of the Distant Early Warning (DEW Line) system, which extended across the Arctic coast of Alaska and Canada. The development offered jobs to local residents, but also caused two additional village relocations—three moves, three village sites, in less than twenty years. The aftermath of a distant world war brought more

disruption to the far-flung community of Kaktovik than it did to most American towns. Yet the residents of Kaktovik still continued to live off the land with a profound tenacity that comes from thousands of years of experience.

We motor off behind the hangar, crossing a slushy section of the lagoon to reach the spit. I have visions of sinking through the thinning ice, but also have faith in someone who is driving across his backyard. We reach the spit and rock-and-roll our way along the bumpy shoreline. The backbone of the barrier island is several feet higher than the shore, still covered with wind-crusted snow. Daniel slows down and points up ahead.

"*Nanuq* tracks," he says, stopping the four-wheeler.

We follow polar bear tracks the size of dinner plates to the top of the spit's ridgeline. I'm awestruck by the size of the tracks, let alone imagining the bear that matches them. From the spit I gaze north across the ice-covered lagoon and Beaufort Sea, realizing that if we continue toward the North Pole, the next point of land would be Svalbard, Norway. We're truly standing on the last sliver of ground that connects us to the continent.

There is no sign of *nanuq*, but we catch a glimpse of a ringed seal diving into its breathing hole. Beyond this table of ice, a dense fog layer hovers over an open lead of water that has formed between the shorefast ice and the drifting pack ice. Known as water sky, or *qisuk*, the steel-blue underside of the fog layer reflects the dark stretch of water that we cannot see. A jumble of ice and pressure ridges lies between us and the lead.

Daniel manifests his love for the outdoors in his happy outlook and a deep pride in his homeland. He has spent his entire life in Kaktovik, including a twenty-four-year stint as maintenance worker for the local school. Now retired, Daniel noted the dramatic change in his salary over the years, the direct result of enormous tax revenues generated by North Slope oil field developments.

When he began his job in 1964, prior to the Prudhoe Bay oil discovery, he earned two dollars an hour. When he retired in 1988, the oil-endowed North Slope Borough School District paid him $27 an hour. Today, if Daniel were still working, he would earn $41 an hour, or $80,000 per year. By comparison, the most a maintenance worker can earn in the neighboring Yukon Flats School District, which includes several Gwich'in villages, is about $19 an hour. Unlike other political subdivisions in Alaska, the North Slope Borough receives hundreds of millions of dollars in oil field-generated property taxes.

Back on the spit, Daniel crouches down and shows me a round tuft of vegetation that is just beginning to green up. He recalls the time when, in 1945, his family harvested the roots of this beach plant (*Hedysarum,* a member of the pea family) for survival food. It was a particularly poor hunting year. His family ate the roots dipped in bearded seal oil to help sustain them. In the span of a few startling decades, Daniel and his neighbors have gone from living in sodhouses in a truly subsistence-dependent world to a world that is fostered by a wage-based, oil-rich economy.

Yet, regardless of the wage-influenced economy, the Inupiat have continued to value their homeland and the resources that have sustained their traditional culture. In the village's cluster of framed houses, signs of the hunting tradition are apparent: caribou hides draped over porch railings, sealskins stretched and tacked on walls, creative designs etched on whale baleen, jars of frozen bearded seal oil tucked beneath a stairwell. The Inupiat will continue to hunt and fish, as sure as they will breathe.

We bounce along the shore until we come to a small patch of open water, where long-tailed ducks are swimming in easy circles. I count forty-three. Daniel searches the empty sky for eiders and black brant, two of several waterfowl species that the Inupiat hunt each spring.

He points to a thirty- to forty-foot-tall driftwood pole in the distance, erected near the end of the spit. The pole, he explains, helps whaling crews chart their location when they are far offshore. For many years Daniel was a whaling captain, and has since passed down his boat and harpoon gun to Eddie Rexford, one of his nephews. I ask Daniel how far off the coast he traveled in search of bowhead whales.

He explained that, one fall, his crew motored thirty miles offshore, the longest distance traveled. While several boat crews searched for whales, his sister called him on the CB radio to warn them that a dangerous west wind was about to unleash. All but one boat heeded the call and rushed home. The lone crew later became temporarily stranded

due to the powerful gale. This was the only year the village didn't harvest a whale. But Daniel doesn't blame the lack of success on the wind.

"That year there was also a company exploring for oil three miles offshore near the mouth of the Jago River," Daniel recalls.

Daniel and other whalers are convinced that the loud seismic booming disturbed the bowhead whales' fall migration. To avoid the industrial noise, Daniel believes the whales moved farther offshore. The Inupiat villages of Alaska's North Slope, communities that depend on the whale for food, are united in their opposition to offshore oil drilling.

In recent years, Kaktovik has been among ten Native villages that have been permitted to strike and land whales. Kaktovik is allowed to land a maximum of three whales per year, out of a maximum quota of fifty-one. On an average year, Inupiat and Yupik communities harvest about thirty-eight bowhead whales from an estimated population of ten thousand.

"I don't think our people will ever live without the whale," Daniel says, in response to past controversies over their whale harvest.

For the community of Kaktovik, fall whaling is the bedrock ritual that holds the village together. Families and whaling crews work closely together to successfully harpoon, land, butcher, and distribute the whale to each household, and to distant inland villages such as Anaktuvuk Pass and Nuiqsut. Sometimes more than half of the meat and *maktak* (blubber and skin) are sent to other communities

Respectful crew relations and prayer are essential for a successful whale hunt. According to Daniel, if one crew thinks they're better than another, and fails to cooperate, that crew won't get a whale. Praying before the crews head out to sea is also important. Their religious practices have gradually evolved to an acceptance of Christianity while still following their traditional spiritual beliefs regarding the human use of wild animals and the natural world.

"God gives us the whale," Daniel says with reverence.

Later on I sit at the Akootchook's kitchen table, and Daniel offers me bread dipped in bearded seal oil, guaranteed to warm up a chilled *tannik.* His wife, Lillian a well-known mask-maker, is away in Anchorage for medical reasons. While Daniel and Lillian have no children, their home is lively, with a steady stream of nephews and nieces. Their walls are covered with pictures of children. Daniel is an *amaau,* or great uncle, and related to just about everybody in town because of his large, extended family.

In the course of an hour, one nephew drops off two freshly killed black brant, another nephew comes to borrow a battery, and five-year old Damon, a great nephew, stops by to catch a ride to the community hall on Daniel's four-wheeler.

Then the phone rings, and it's Daniel's oldest brother, Isaac, who invites us to a birthday party for his daughter, Ida. Isaac is the Presbyterian minister for the community, having carried on the ministry tradition of their father, Andrew Akootchook. Andrew, in addition to being a minister and leader, helped Tom Gordon, a white trader, establish the first trading post at Barter Island in 1923. This marked the beginning of Kaktovik as a permanent settlement.

Soon we are seated at the table with Isaac and his gracious wife, Mary Sirak Akootchook. Mary was born on Flaxman Island, near the western boundary of the Arctic Refuge. Her Inupiat name, Sirak, means "the Place Where the Polar Bears Go to Cover Themselves up with Snow to have Their Cubs." Many Inupiat elders have names that describe the circumstances or setting at the time of their birth. Daniel tells me his Inupiat name is Nooyak, meaning "Drifting Snow on the Tundra."

Mary has prepared a pot of creamy duck soup that is delicious. While villagers consume more *tannik* food from the grocery store than in earlier days, there continues to be a strong preference for and cultural connection to the diversity of wildlife in the Arctic Refuge and Beaufort Sea. Seals, fish, birds, caribou, sheep, and bowhead whales are all important food sources.

One diet study, conducted about ten years ago, revealed that Kaktovik residents harvested 600 to 800 pounds of wild game per person per year, three to four times the national per capita consumption rate of meat, fish, and poultry. It's important to note that a substantial portion of Kaktovik's harvest includes whale meat and *maktak,* which is shared regionally. These numbers reflect that families, such as the Akootchooks, continue to value wild game on their tables.

We talk about the future. The Akootchooks and other families will soon have running water, as seventy homes will be hooked up to a new $60 million sewer and water system. This major construction project is providing many local jobs and is one example of the benefits that have come from North Slope oil development.

Isaac dreams of the day when Kaktovik residents will heat their homes with the natural gas that lies beneath them rather than barging in more costly fuel. He hopes that, one day, natural gas will be transported through buried lines so that the caribou won't be disturbed and others can access the resource. Isaac and Daniel have adopted the position that limited development on the coastal plain will bring great benefits to the community, with little harm.

Isaac believes that careful oil and gas development in the Arctic Refuge will not hurt the caribou, nor the Gwich'in people. He speaks from the heart.

"We don't want to hurt the Gwich'in."

Yet there are other family members and villagers who feel differently, including Isaac's daughter, Jane, and her husband, Robert

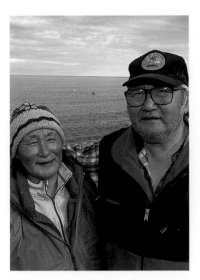
Daniel and Lillian Akootchook of Kaktovik

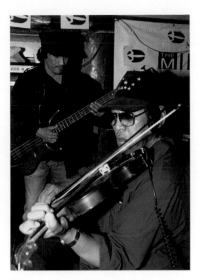
Trimble and Albert Gilbert play fiddle music during a community gathering at Arctic Village.

Thompson. They are outright opposed to any oil drilling in the Arctic Refuge. Robert, one of the most active hunters in the village, feels that the land environment is just as important as the sea, so he is opposed to any offshore or onshore oil development.

"If they develop the coastal plain, huge areas will be off limits to hunting. Security guards will be telling us where we can and cannot hunt. I don't want to live in an oil field for the rest of my life," Robert says somberly.

The Thompson family is so strongly against proposed development that their daughter, Sharon Thompson, is leading a petition drive, and the Thompsons have traveled to Washington, D.C. to lobby Congress. Recent discussions with residents of Nuiqsut, the only Inupiat community surrounded by oil field development, have also set off alarms. Many Nuiqsut residents are voicing their complaints about diminished hunting access, social disruption, pollution, and health problems associated with the North Slope oil fields.

"When development comes, it is detrimental to our culture. Nuiqsut is feeling the impacts, but now they can't undo it."

Leaving Kaktovik, I reflect on a village that has been caught in a political fray over oil for more than two decades. This is a community whose residents still treasure their homeland and subsistence lifestyle, but whose lives and culture have been upholstered by all that comes with the development of North America's largest oil field. Future dollars and benefits are manna for many, but others foresee great losses that might accompany industrialization of their truly wild homeland.

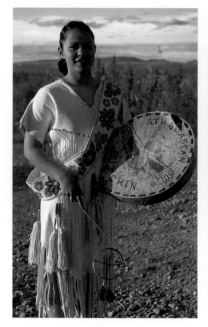
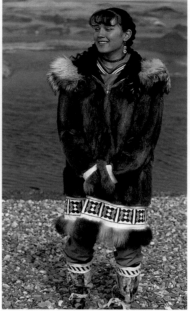

Amy Carroll in a traditional Gwich'in costume during a gathering at Arctic Village

Flora Rexford in a traditional Inupiat parka during the whaling feast at Kaktovik

A few weeks after my visit to Kaktovik, I'm flying along the East Fork of the Chandalar River en route to Arctic Village. It was twenty-seven years ago that I first arrived here as a schoolteacher. For a few years, my husband, Dennis, and I lived near the river's edge, overlooking the Brooks Range. This great land, with its winding rivers, lake-specked valleys, boreal forest, and rising mountains, has not changed. The beauty of this wilderness still takes my breath away.

As we fly above the Chandalar, I picture nomadic ancestors of Arctic Village residents in their seasonal camps near the river. When the French-speaking traders of the Hudson Bay Company explored this area in the 1840s and 1850s, they called the Athabascan Indians *gens du large,* or people at large, because of their highly nomadic subsistence-based culture. That French name was eventually butchered to Chandalar, and the river inherited the nomenclature.

The people of Arctic Village specifically call themselves the Nets'aii Gwich'in, which means "Mountain People," because they live in close proximity to the Brooks Range. This northernmost group of Gwich'in is among at least nine aboriginal Gwich'in bands, each having a specific dialect, who largely inhabit the upper Yukon and Porcupine River drainages. Gwich'in Athabascans are distantly related to the Navajos of the Southwest, speaking a similar language. Today the Gwich'in, at least seven thousand strong, live in fifteen scattered villages, in Alaska and in Canada's Yukon and Northwest Territories.

As with the Inupiat in Kaktovik, much of the Gwich'in's traditional homeland is now protected in the Arctic Refuge. Additionally, the people of Arctic Village and Venetie, a nearby sister village, own title to 1.8 million acres of tribal lands that were initially set aside in 1934 as reservation lands under the Indian Reorganization Act (IRA).

The plane circles over the village that hugs the Chandalar and is surrounded by shimmering lakes. While there are some new homes and buildings, I spot the old footbridge that still arches over Vashraii K'oo, a small tributary that runs through the community. Known for its plentiful fish, Vashraii K'oo means "Steep Bank Creek," and is the traditional Gwich'in name for Arctic Village. Today, about 150 people live in the village and continue to set fishnets near the mouth of Vashraii K'oo.

Trimble Gilbert greets me at the airport on his four-wheeler. His coffee-dark face reveals that he's been camping upriver, bronzed from the twenty-four-hour sunshine. Trimble, sixty-five, has recently finished instructing a group of teachers from surrounding communities about his culture, language, and history. His non-traditional wilderness classroom was located at a campsite on the Chandalar.

Trimble is a strong proponent of teaching youth and educators about the Gwich'in culture through active, land-based learning. Through the week-long course, teachers observed Trimble construct snowshoes, build a traditional fish trap, and carve arrowheads from caribou antlers. Participants also hiked several miles to study one of the many historic caribou fences that were once used to funnel migrating caribou into keyhole-shaped corrals.

"Those teachers were fast learners. I enjoyed instructing them about our traditions and sharing stories about how we survived as a people in the early days," Trimble reflected.

Prior to the introduction of rifles, caribou fences were extensively used to successfully hunt *vadzaih,* or caribou. Men, women, and children cooperated together to build impressive fences that could be several miles long. Once the caribou entered the enclosure, hunters snared the animals and killed them with spears or bows and arrows. The use of caribou fences gradually ended as rifles became more available in the 1900s.

While the hunting technology has changed, and wage jobs and store-bought food are more readily available, the importance of the caribou has not diminished. Like the Inupiat's reliance on the bowhead whale, the caribou is still the most important food and cultural resource for the Gwich'in, often referred to as their "source of life." The caribou provide as much as 80 percent of their diet, and the Gwich'in continue to make clothing from the hides and perform traditional caribou songs and dances. In addition to being people of the mountains, the Gwich'in commonly refer to themselves as "caribou people."

For this reason, the Gwich'in have strongly voiced their opposition to proposed oil development in the calving grounds of the Porcupine caribou herd. They consider the Arctic Refuge coastal plain sacred, calling it *Izhik Gwats'an Gwandaii Goodlit,* which means "the Sacred Place Where Life Begins." In 1988, Gwich'in leaders from Alaska and Canada gathered together in Arctic Village to form the Gwich'in Steering Committee, in an international effort to protect the caribou, their lands, and their way of life. Since the 1988 gathering, dedicated Gwich'in leaders have worked tirelessly to protect the coastal plain from proposed development.

"Without the caribou, I don't think the Gwich'in people of Alaska and Canada would have survived for ten thousand years. No one should touch the birthplace of the herd. It is holy ground for the animals," Trimble says with reverence as strong as steel.

We follow a dirt road up a small hill behind the village store, passing a number of log and frame cabins that make up this village. In the bright summer light, the tundra sparkles with the white blossoms of dryas amidst the soft cushion of mosses and lichens. In the willow bushes, white-crowned sparrows sing their welcoming melody and I hear the voices of children playing outside.

The Gilberts' cabin is perched on the flower-specked hill with a spectacular view of the Chandalar valley, the Brooks Range, and Dachanlee, the low-lying ridge just south of the village where caribou are often first spotted above timberline during their fall migration. Before his passing, Trimble's father, James Gilbert, would set up his spotting scope in front of his cabin to watch for the first migrating caribou along Dachanlee. Trimble's wife, Mary, has continued the spotting tradition, beginning in August. Once sighted, the leaders of the herd are never hunted by villagers, so the rest of the herd will follow.

Mary greets me behind their home. She is a gentle, soft-spoken woman, busy with household chores. She washes a pile of clothes in an old-fashioned Maytag machine equipped with a hand-feeding wringer. This model, which is no longer produced, is highly desirable in rural Alaska for homes that lack running water. Wash water can be recycled more than once, and Mary takes advantage of the free sunshine to hang-dry her clothes.

"I could wash and dry clothes at the washateria, but at six dollars per load, I'd rather do it myself," she says.

The Gilberts are self-reliant people who truly enjoy their subsistence lifestyle. They haul their own water and wood, hunt and fish for their extended family, make traditional clothing and crafts, and even create their own music. Trimble, an accomplished fiddle player, has performed throughout Alaska and produced his own recordings. The Scottish jigs that he plays, originally introduced by Hudson Bay traders in the 1840s, are a favorite for local dancers. Some of the old-style jigs that are still danced in Arctic Village are no longer performed in Scotland.

Walking into their home, I notice a metal pot with thin strips of caribou hide soaking in the water. Trimble tells me that he plans to use the *babiche* as webbing for a pair of snowshoes. In earlier days, *babiche* had many important uses. The rawhide strips were braided together to make strong snares and ropes or wrapped around the handles of spears for better gripping. *Babiche* is still used today for snowshoe webbing, boot ties, and straps.

The Gilbert home is cozy and functional for everyday life. With the exception of a small television nestled in a corner, home life looks the same as it did in 1975. The one-room living room and kitchen includes the essentials: a drum of fresh water, kitchen table with a box of sewing materials, woodstove, refrigerator, sink, slop buckets, a couple of sofas, and a propane stove with whitefish simmering in a pan.

Like the Inupiat people of Kaktovik, the Gwich'in rely on fishing and waterfowl hunting in the spring and early summer for much of their food. While the two groups live about 150 miles apart, in two very different settings, they share common ground when it comes to the hunting and fishing of many species. In the spring, the Gwich'in hunt ducks and ice fish for lake trout, northern pike, and grayling. During summer, villagers set fishnets in the creeks and lakes to catch whitefish, a rich, desirable catch that is shared with neighboring villages.

Trimble caught plenty of whitefish on this particular day, so he boxes up several and sends them to Venetie, where the fishing hasn't been as good. Regional sharing of resources is a common custom for the Gwich'in, Inupiat, and other Alaska Native groups.

After we finish the whitefish, Mary shows me her recent sewing work. Several beautiful articles are set on the table. I pick up a pair of beaded moccasins crafted from a hand-tanned and smoked caribou hide, prepared by Maggie Roberts of Venetie. The soles of the moccasins have a pungent, smoky scent that will always remind me of the Gwich'in culture. Few women still hand-tan the hides of caribou and moose, as the process is very laborious, requiring many hours of scraping.

Mary's sewing and beadwork designs are known throughout the village and region. Stitching two tiny beads at a time, Mary precisely sews floral designs that are flawless. Over the years she has instructed younger girls in the village how to bead and sew clothing items. Her seventeen-year old granddaughter, Cindy, has recently expressed an interest in learning how to make moccasins and fur hats.

Would the Gilberts ever consider living in a big city? They tried living in Fairbanks once.

"We couldn't stand living there. We're used to working outside all the time, whether it's hauling water, wood, or checking the fishnet. In Fairbanks there was nothing for us to do, and when we wanted to do something it cost money," Trimble described the one-time urban experience.

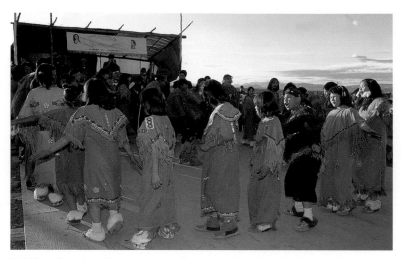
Gwich'in children in traditional beaded caribou dress participate in the Raven Dance at Arctic Village. The Raven Dance symbolizes the sharing of food with other creatures and keeping the earth clean.

Their three sons have followed suit. Albert, Gregory, and Bobby have all chosen to live and raise families in Arctic Village. Their homes form a ring around Trimble and Mary's cabin. Like their father, the boys are self-taught musicians, and they enjoy hunting and fishing. The parents, boys, and their families seem to appreciate one another, helping family members when in need.

"My father taught us that the most important thing was taking care of the children of the village. They heal us. We love having kids around, so we baby-sit a lot," Trimble said.

Trimble also gives of his time as the Episcopal minister of the village. Like Isaac Akootchook in Kaktovik, Trimble carries on the ministry of his late father, James Gilbert. Having attended both Isaac's and Trimble's religious services, I realize they share a deep desire to hold their communities together by supporting one another through prayer and daily life. It is that cooperative working spirit between families that has enabled both the Gwich'in and the Inupiat cultures to survive through the centuries.

According to Trimble, and other accounts, there were many historic fights and skirmishes between Gwich'in groups and the Inupiat. But that changed, Trimble believes, after missionaries visited the region during the later half of the nineteenth century.

"People became more tolerant of one another," Trimble said, referring to the gradual end of tribal skirmishes.

Trimble explained that after the Gwich'in embraced Christianity in the 1860s, they still continued to practice some aspects of their old religion, such as traditional healing. It was not uncommon for a shaman to play a dual role as a lay reader for the Episcopal Church and a medicine man for the old religion. As recently as the 1980s, the late Alice Peter, a traditional healer, used her knowledge about medicinal plants and minerals to treat residents in Arctic Village. Some of her treatments, such as the use of spruce tree pitch for wounds and infections, are still in use today.

Until the 1940s, the Gwich'in occasionally traveled to Barter Island to trade with the Inupiat. Trimble's mother, Maggie Gilbert, once noted that spruce tree pitch and wolverine skins were two popular trading items. Wolverines, known for their water-resistant fur, were scarce on the north side of the mountains. Spruce pitch was also in demand for several medicinal purposes. Trimble recalled hearing Barter Island trading stories from his parents.

"When they got to the seashore, they shot their guns and the Inupiat people would come across in skin boats to take them to Barter Island."

On Barter Island the Gwich'in would trade for items such as gun shells, tea, and rifles. The Inupiat had access to such goods through the commercial whalers and traders. The first rifles acquired by the Nets'aii Gwich'in reportedly came from the Inupiat via the whalers. The Inupiat also traveled into Gwich'in territory for social and trading gatherings. With the drop in fur prices during the late 1930s, trading activity gradually decreased and many trading posts closed.

Over the course of a century, the Gwich'in have transitioned from living a semi-nomadic existence, traveling on foot, by dog team, or caribou-skin boat, to living in a permanent settlement and traveling by snow machine, motorboat, four-wheeler, or airplane. While the Gwich'in have welcomed much of the modern technology, they are also ambivalent. Trimble reflected on replacing his dog team with a snow machine in 1970.

"Dogs are more trustworthy than snow machines. You don't have to worry about parts," he said, somewhat bereaved about the end of the dog team era.

Later on, I attend a Father's Day community gathering and have the chance to see all my former students and their children. We play midnight sun baseball in front of the village store and swat mosquitoes in the cooling air. Bobby Gilbert, Trimble and Mary's youngest son, sets up speakers on the porch of the village store. A festive recording of Trimble's fiddle music livens up the game, while ravens dance overhead with feathers glowing in the Arctic light.

This summer most of the families and working-age men are staying in town because of a massive airport renovation project. Jobs are plentiful, unlike some summers when many residents leave the village to seek seasonal work, such as firefighting. In Arctic Village, there are a limited number of year-round jobs: postmaster, store manager, school and village maintenance workers, health aide, classroom aides, and school cook, a position that Mary Gilbert filled for many years.

Unlike Kaktovik, where residents have greater job opportunities through the North Slope Borough and their Native regional corporation, Arctic Village is not part of any tax-subsidized borough, nor does it draw corporate benefits. Under the 1971 Alaska Native Claims Settlement Act (ANCSA), Arctic Village and Venetie were two of four Native communities in Alaska that chose not to join one of twelve Native regional corporations established under ANCSA, forfeiting any future shareholder benefits. Instead, the Gwich'in elected to seek title to their 1.8 million acres of tribal lands, maintaining ownership of their surface and subsurface rights—a choice they have not regretted.

In short, the Gwich'in value their land more than the money. In contrast, Arctic Slope Regional Corporation (ASRC), which represents Kaktovik and seven other Inupiat villages, is a billion-dollar corporation owning at least a dozen major subsidiaries, from ASRC Aerospace in Maryland to Puget Plastics Corporation in Oregon. Inupiat shareholders each receive annual dividends that average about $1,000 per year, and they are afforded many high-paying jobs through construction-related companies that are owned by ASRC.

While the cash economy differs substantially between the North Slope Inupiat and the Gwich'in, I'm struck by the underlying similarities between the two cultures. Both the Inupiat and the Gwich'in are still deeply connected to the land and the waters around them. They share a profound love for their homeland. They both hunt and fish to feed their families and their neighbors. They share similar religious traditions.

The Inupiat and the Gwich'in both know that all the money in the world can never buy a bowhead whale or a wandering caribou herd. Money cannot replace a wilderness or a homeland, once it's lost. The value of these Arctic resources, which has sustained two distinct cultures for centuries, runs much deeper than any oil well, any pocketbook. The cultural value of this great Arctic wilderness transcends the power of corporations and governments, of dividend checks and jobs.

I sit on a pew inside the old log Episcopal Church. The altar is decorated with a caribou hide that is beautifully decorated with an intricate beadwork design sewn by several women. Behind the altar, a window frames a view of greening willows, an azure sky, and Dachanlee in the distance. Trimble joins the small congregation of villagers. He wears a white robe and a beaded caribou stole. Everyone rises.

The congregation begins singing hymns in their Native language. The 1881 edition of the hymnbook contains songs published in the old Takudh language, as written by Archdeacon Robert McDonald of the Anglican Church. McDonald was one of the first white people to visit the Gwich'in, in the 1860s. He created a simple written language for the Gwich'in so that prayers and hymns could be transcribed and read.

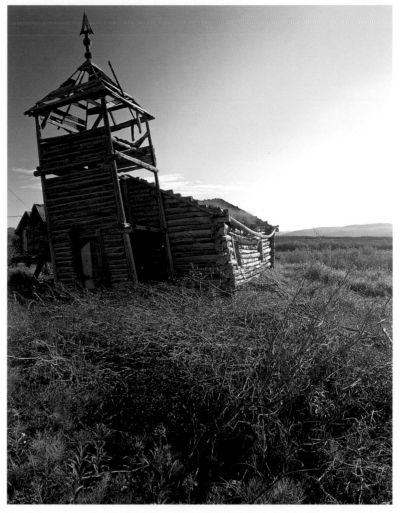

First Episcopal Church at Arctic Village, a National Historic Site built in 1922

Villagers continue to sing the well-known verses. There is a timeless quality to the slow-paced chanting of these songs from another century.

During the sermon, Trimble speaks of the importance of respecting the ways of wild animals, whether it be a raven, ground squirrel, or caribou. He recalls the time when during one church service, a group of caribou could be seen through the window walking behind the church.

"We live with these animals," he says, "and they've always been a part of us."

Leaving the church, I notice that the old door still squeaks as loudly as it did in the 1970s. I walk into the sunshine down the dirt path below the steeple. In one hundred years I hope that the caribou will still walk by the church window and the Gwich'in will sing their oldest songs, clinging to their precious wilderness and way of life.

Debbie S. Miller

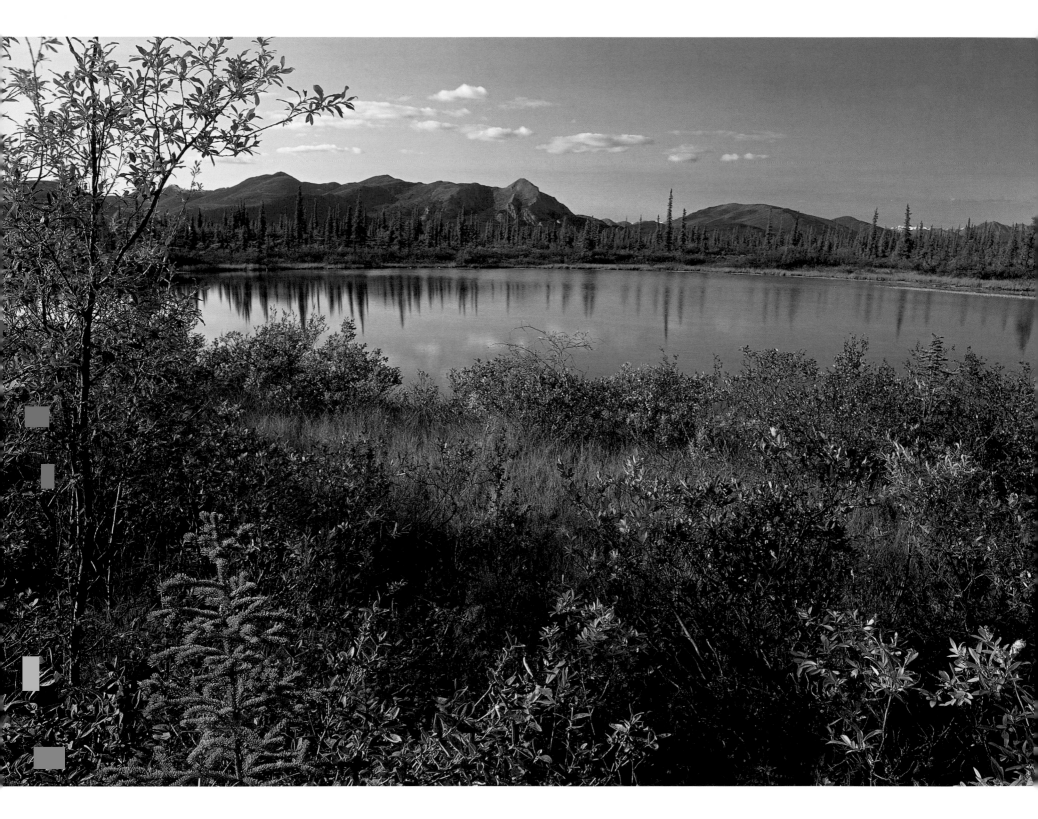

An unnamed lake, Arctic Village

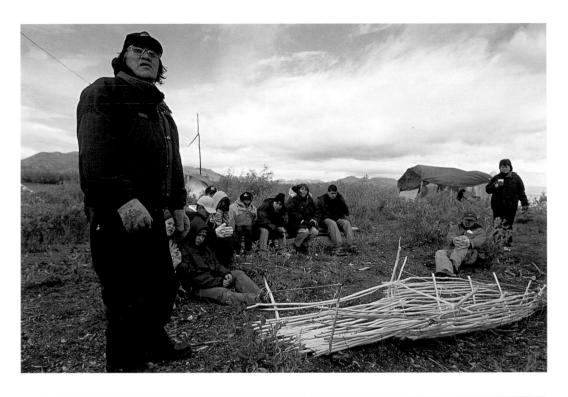

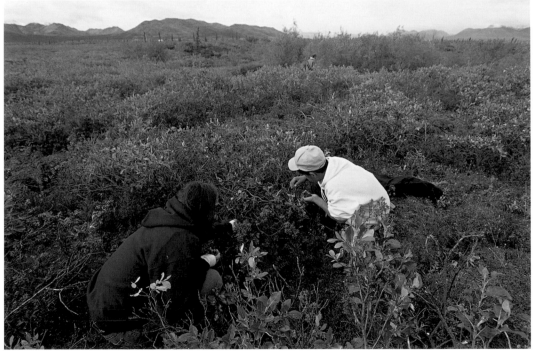

Trimble Gilbert teaches local youth about fish trapping and other traditional cultural activities;
Roxanne Peter and Galen Gilbert pick blueberries near Trimble Gilbert's cabin.

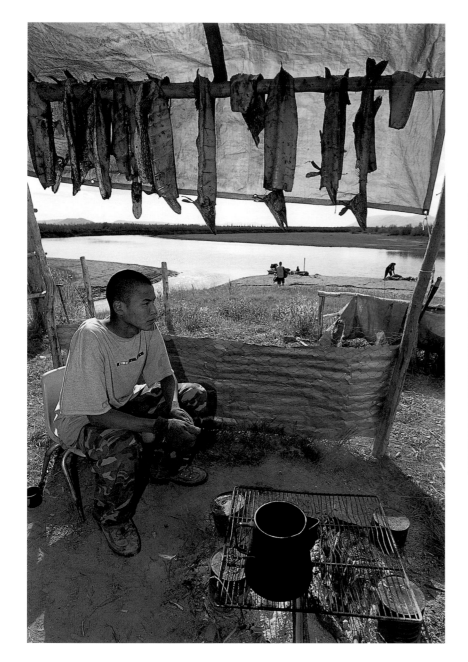

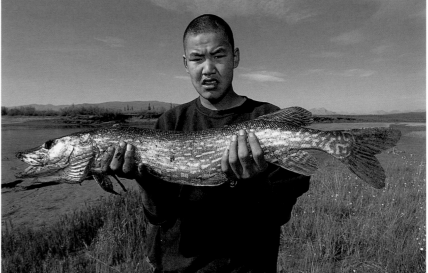

Rockey John dries the northern pike he caught at Charlie Swaney's camp; Gerrald John with freshly caught northern pike

Opposite • Charlie Swaney uses a spotting scope to scan the East Fork of the Chandalar River valley for moose and caribou; his dog, Scooby, waits patiently.

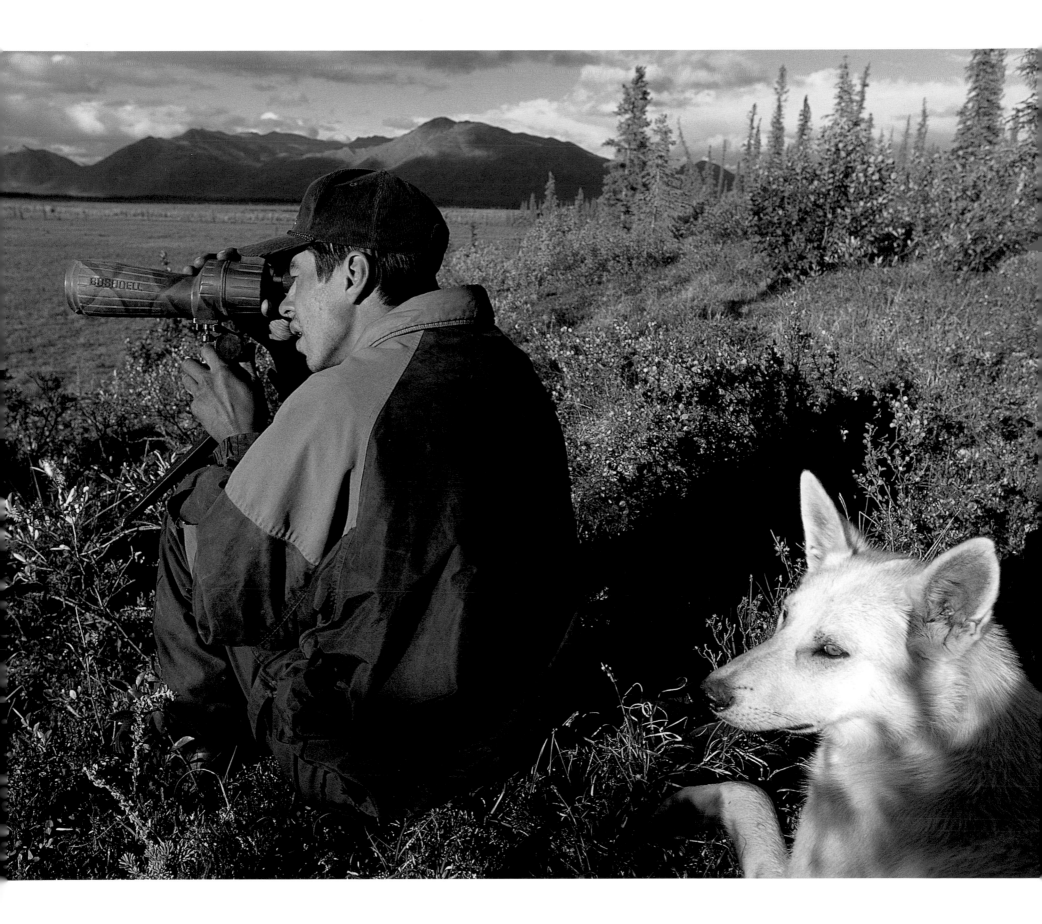

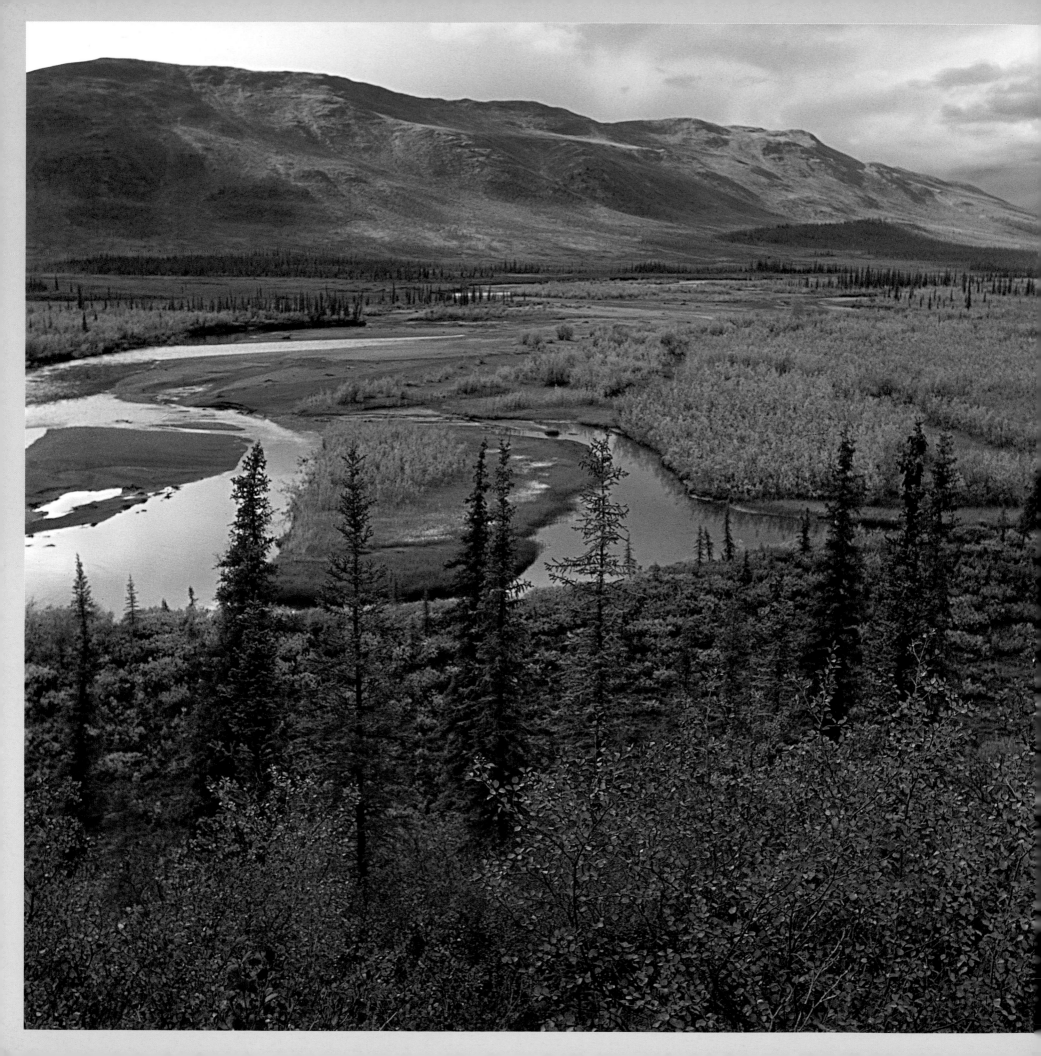

Subsistence: A Gwich'in Way of Life

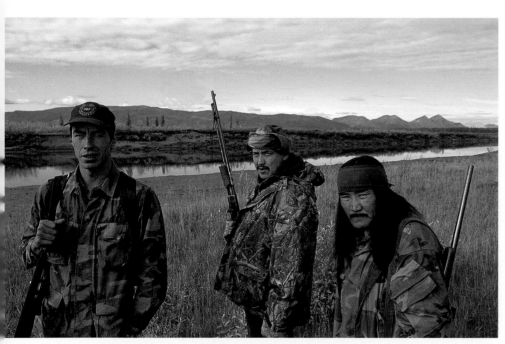

Charlie Swaney, Mike Garnette, and Jimi John

Opposite • Autumn in the Junjik River valley

August 24, 2002: This has been a difficult year for Arctic Village: The caribou have not yet arrived and there is no fresh meat. Charlie Swaney and Jimi John, the two most active hunters in the village, hope to find moose and caribou on this trip.

Charlie, Jimi, Mike Garnette, and I are in a boat on the East Fork of the Chandalar River. It is a clear evening; the leaves on the willows have started to change color, and the hillsides on both sides of the river are draped in the orange and red of berry leaves. We move at a leisurely pace, stopping wherever we spot fresh moose tracks on the sandbars. Charlie, an expert boatman, knows every bend of the river. We stop around nine in the evening. Charlie's hunting camp is modest, with two scouting towers and two wood frames used for cooking and smoking meat and fish.

Early the following morning Charlie and I decide to walk to the Junjik River, a favorite moose-hunting place. Jimi and Mike hike the hillsides and tundra near camp. It is always a pleasant experience to spend time with Charlie. He has an intense love for the wild land and is always happy to share his hunting stories, his knowledge and experience.

Charlie and I walk only a few hundred yards before a small lake comes into view. There is a beautiful display of cotton grass along the lakeshore, and the mountains cast a reflection on the clear, calm water of the lake. This lake has no name and Charlie does not seem compelled to give it one; this is his favorite lake. In midafternoon we reach a hilltop along the Junjik River. From this high point we have an unobstructed view of the valley. Autumn is in full swing here: The tundra and hills look magnificent from this high vantage point.

After much hiking over the next two days, on the morning of August 26 the hunters take down a moose. Charlie, Jimi, and Mike cut golden willow branches to use as a carpet on which to lay the moose. For the next couple of hours, with great care and efficiency, they butcher the moose. "We use almost every part of the animal," Charlie says, and he explains the use of each part while they work on the animal. They lay more willow branches in the boat and slowly load the boat with moose meat.

Back at camp, Jimi cooks fresh moose meat in fat; it is delicious. We collect our gear and head back for Arctic Village. We reach the village around eleven that evening, tired yet happy. The next day Marion Swaney, Lillian Garnette, and other women cut the meat into smaller pieces to share with family members and the community.

August 27: I leave Arctic Village, having spent five weeks in the community. When I am on the plane a strange, sad, empty feeling fills my heart. I know I will miss Arctic Village. I will miss my Gwich'in friends—the elders, the children, and surely the dog Scooby, who followed me everywhere I went. *Mahsi Choo Shalak Nai* ("Thank you, all my relations").

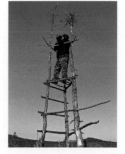

—S.B.

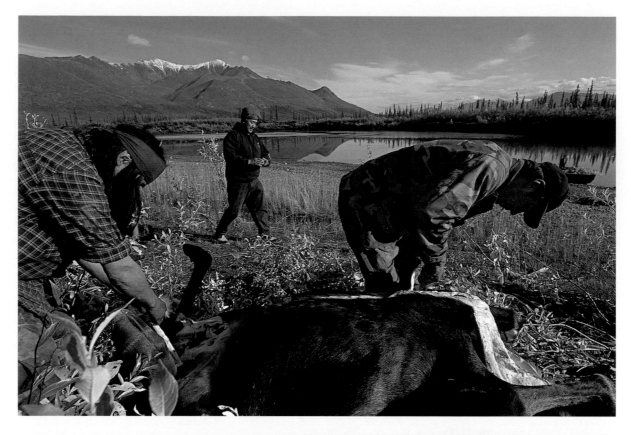

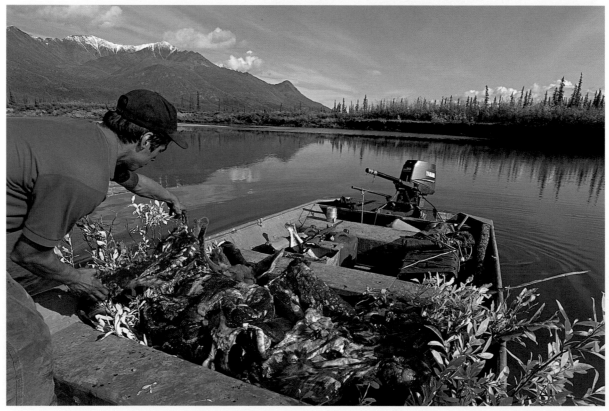

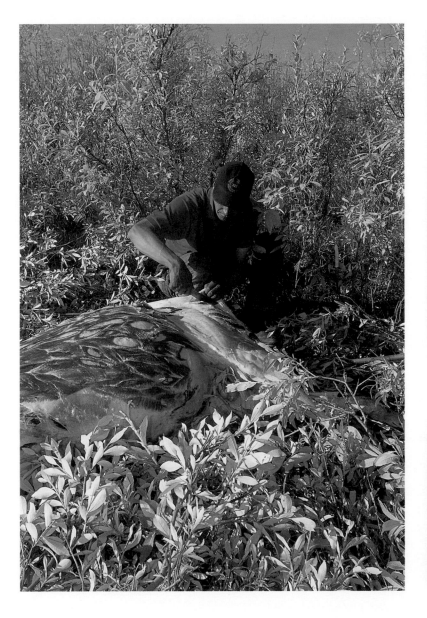

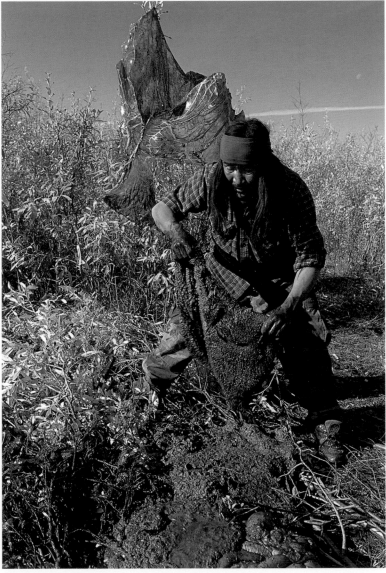

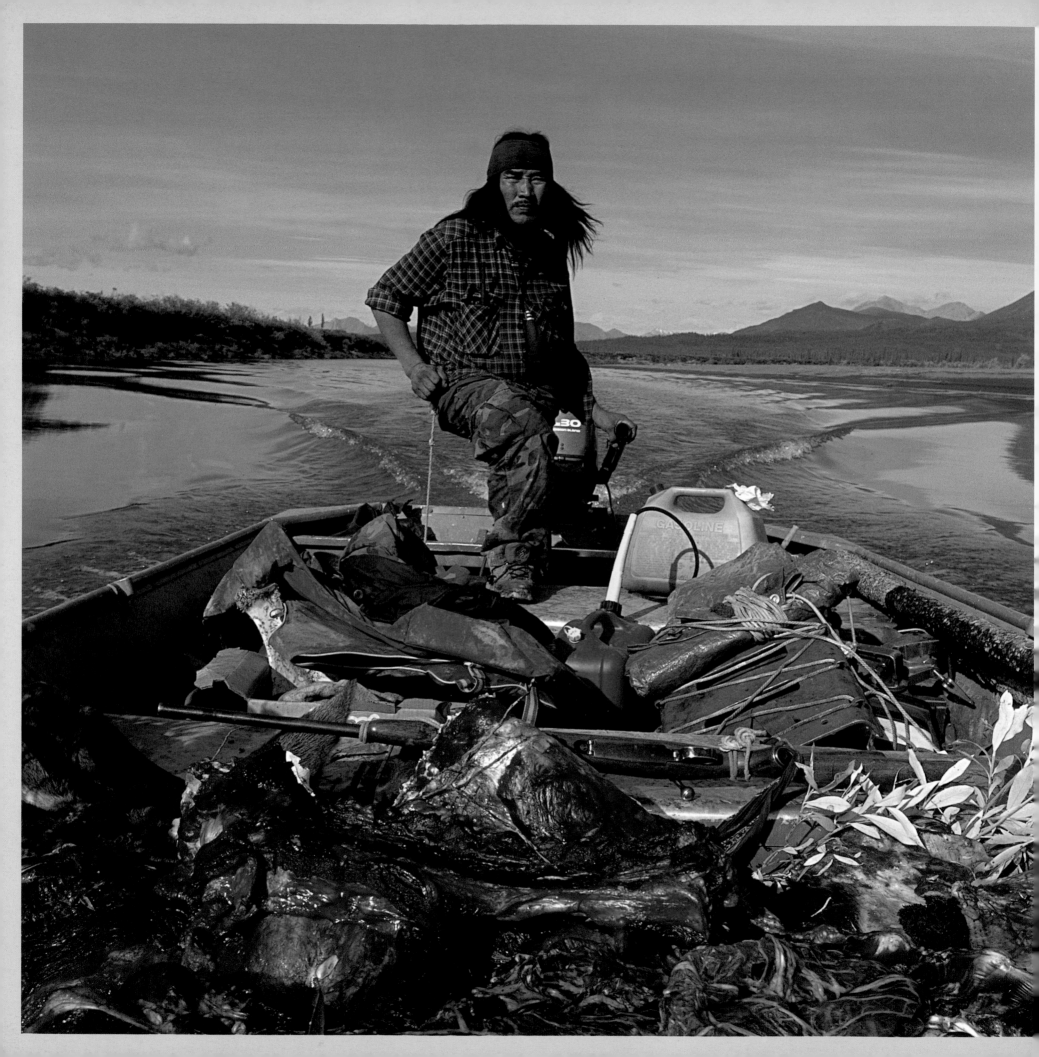

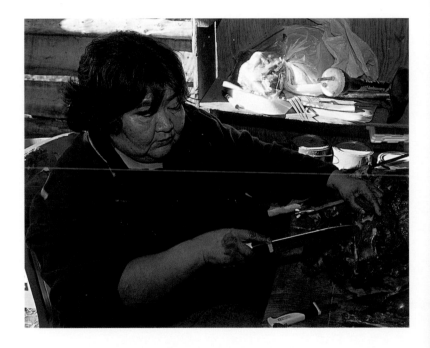

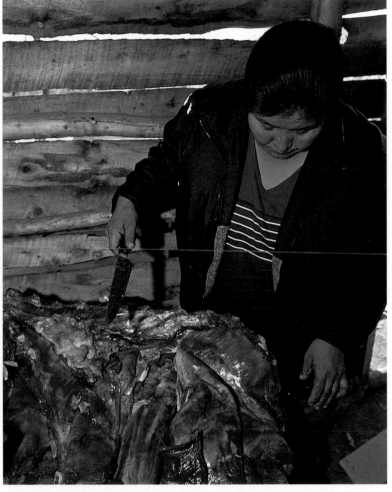

Lillian Garnette and Marion Swaney cut moose meat to be later shared with the community.

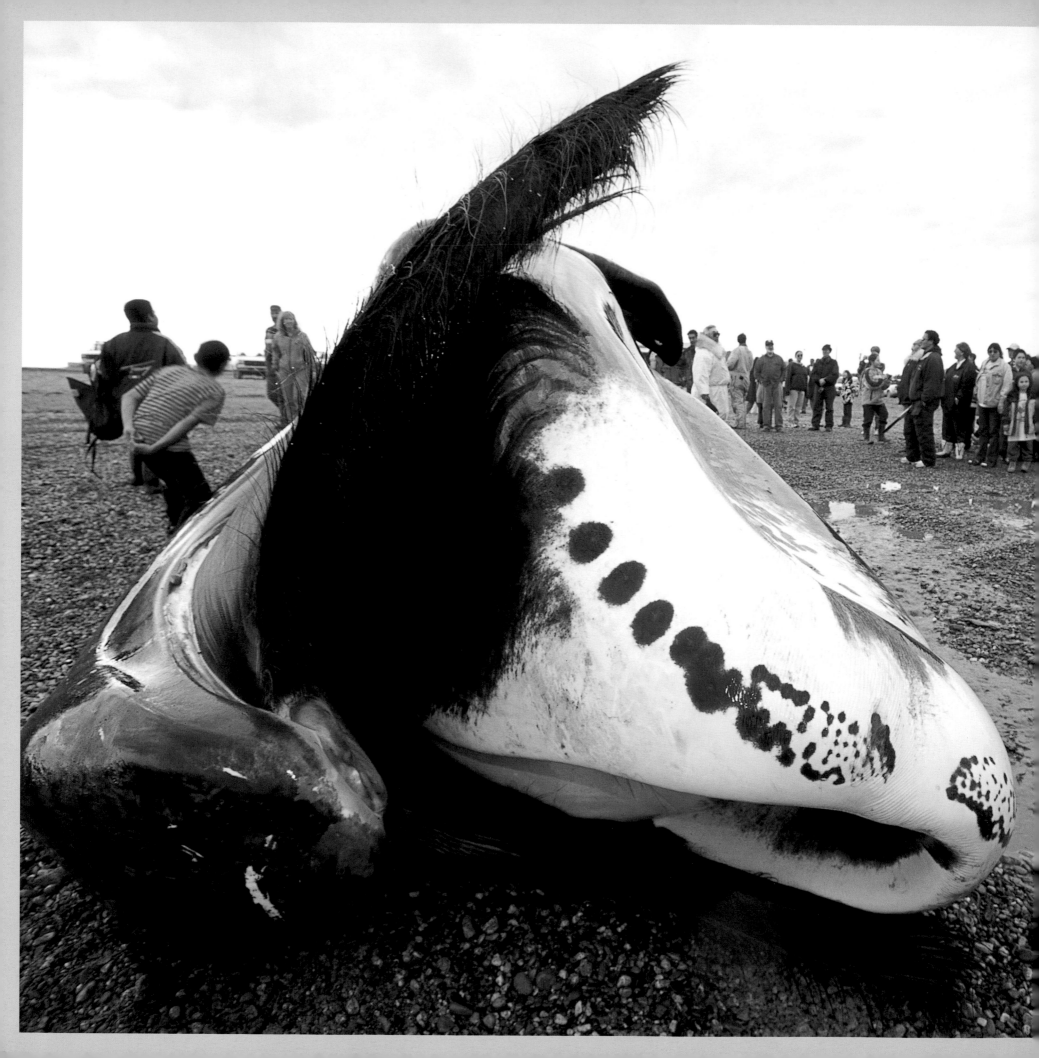

The Sacred Inupiat Whale Hunt

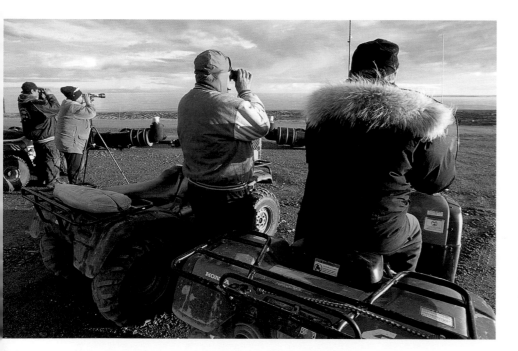

November 3, 2001. On a cold, crisp morning, I leave Robert's house to visit the cemetery only a few hundred yards away. The tundra is covered with snow and a faint sundog spans the fog-shrouded Brooks Range. The cemetery is marked by a pair of bowhead whale jawbones; the scene is silent. This is a sign of reverence, I think; a sign of the relationship the Inupiats have with the whale. A few weeks later, during Thanksgiving, whale meat and *maktak* is shared among the community members. It is not until almost a year later that I experience an actual whale hunt at Kaktovik.

September 1, 2002: I arrive at Kaktovik on Labor Day weekend, the first day of whaling. The hunters leave with the first rays of sun and will return in the evening after a day-long search. Every day for the next seven days the whalers go out, but come back empty-handed. News comes that Nuiqsut, a village about 150 miles west of Kaktovik, got their first whale.

September 9: Papa Tagrook wakes me at six in the morning and says, "Let's go, they got a whale."

People are gathering at the beach, listening to CB radios as the whalers communicate the news back to the village. After a whale dies, all the boats gather around the whale and the hunters give a prayer, thanking God and the whale for providing food for the community. The prayer, in Inupiaq, is broadcast back to the village. It is James Lampe's crew that brought down the whale, and congratulations from around the village are broadcast out to the boats. "We are about eight miles out, we will be on the shore in two hours," I hear on the radio.

The hunters bring a forty-two-foot bowhead whale onto the shore. Elder Isaac Akootchook offers up a prayer, and afterward children begin climbing the whale, jumping up and down, singing songs—simply celebrating, having fun. Eventually the children climb down and a loader dumps water over the whale. Then the hard work begins: Men start butchering the whale, while women cook fresh *maktak* in the nearby whaling shack. Children provide helping hands where they are needed. The festivities go on for hours. A thick fog rolls in from the north, bringing in cold air. When the butchering is finished in the early evening hours, the remains are left on the beach for the polar bears.

The next day is the community lunch at James Lampe's house. Everyone is welcome to the feast of freshly cooked whale meat, *maktak*, Eskimo doughnuts, and an assortment of other food. More and more polar bears come to the Bernard Spit to feed on the whale remains and wait for the freeze up of the ocean.

I leave on September 14. Kaktovik has been my second home for the past two years. My heart is filled with a tremendous sense of gratitude for the community, for their hospitality and for providing me with a window to learn about the Inupiat culture and their relationship to the whale, the sea, and the land.

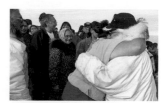

—S.B.

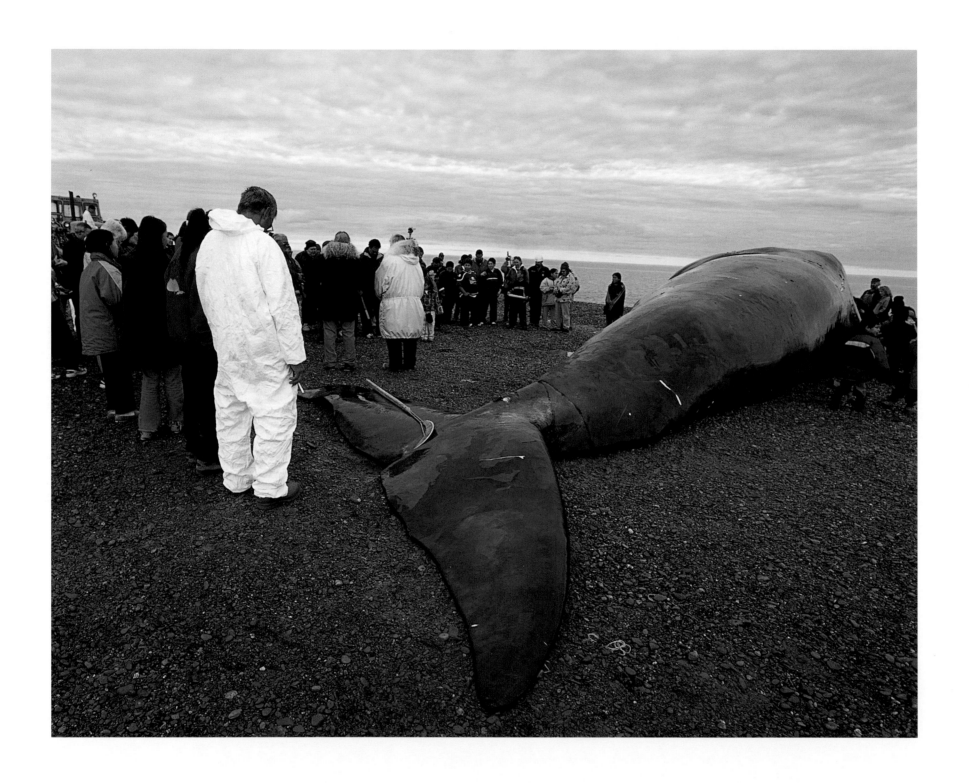

Elder Isaac Akootchook and Captain James Lampe offer a prayer after the whale is brought to shore.

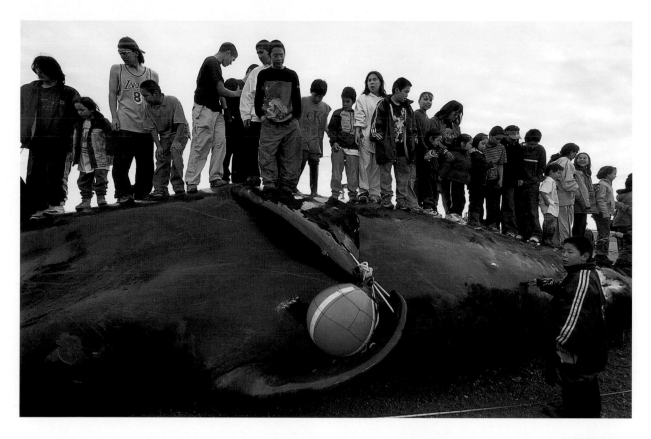

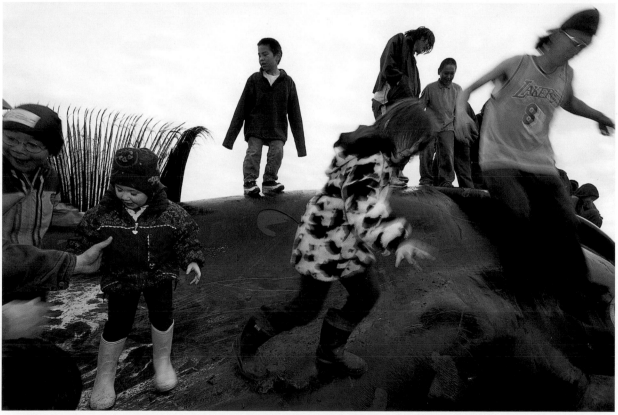

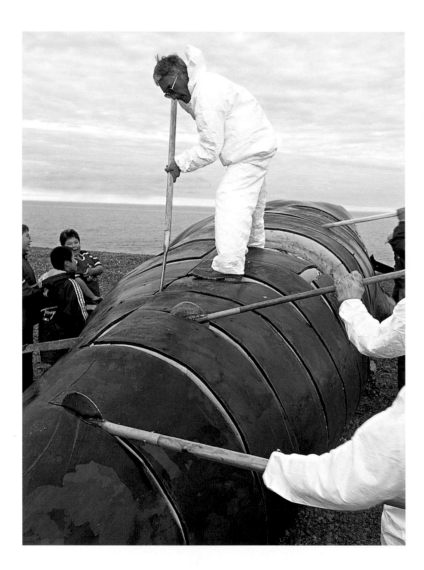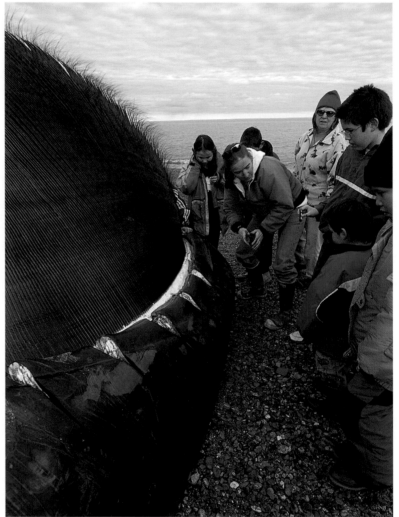

Nathan Gordon and others butcher the whale; Alaska Fish and Game biologist Gay Sheffield teaches children about bowhead whales.

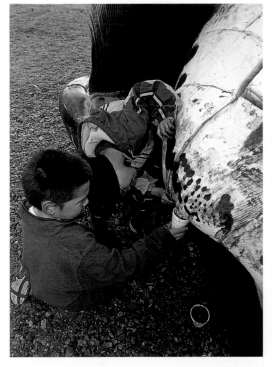

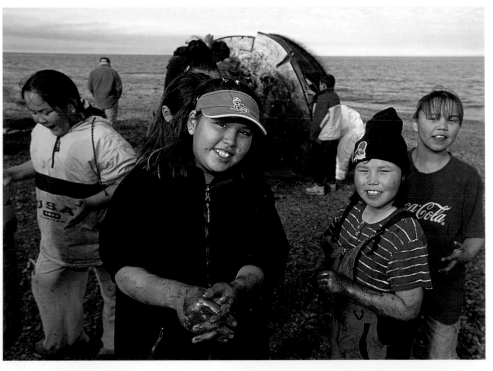

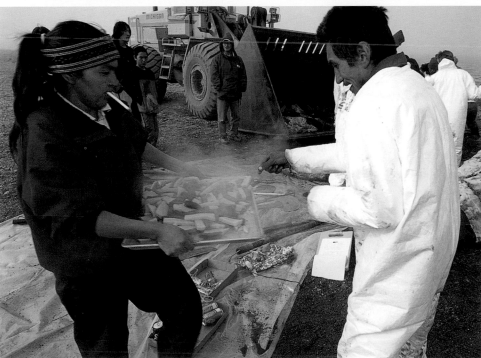

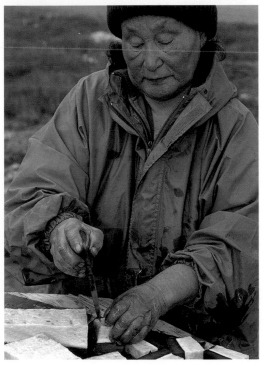

Children play during the celebration of the successful whale hunt.

The first slices of freshly cooked *maktak* (whale blubber and skin) are brought to the men as they continue to butcher the whale;
Lillian Akootchook cuts *maktak* into small pieces that she will boil and freeze for the winter.

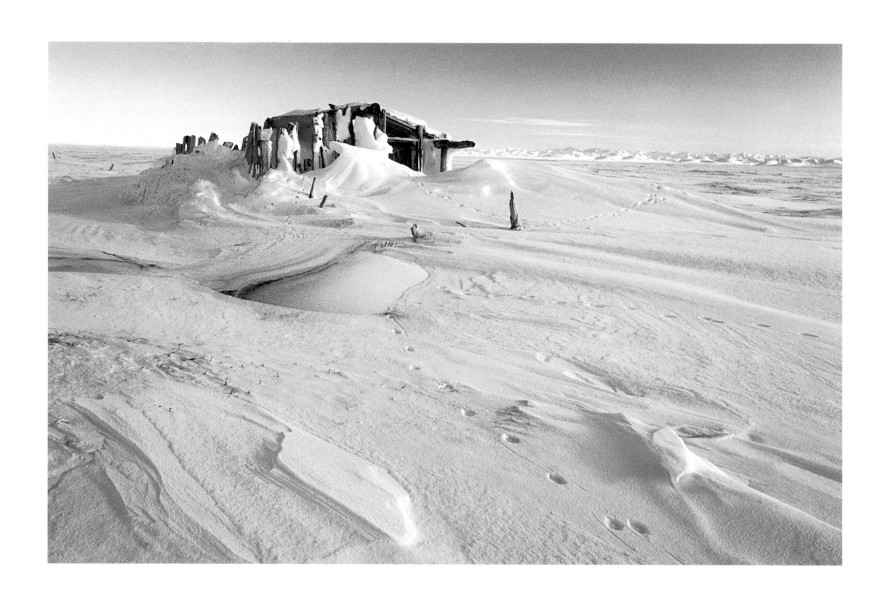

Life then and life now: Inupiat sodhouse and fox tracks on the coastal plain near Pokok Lagoon. According to Kaktovik elders, this house was last inhabited in 1929.

Opposite • Inupiat cemetery marked with bowhead whale jawbones in Kaktovik

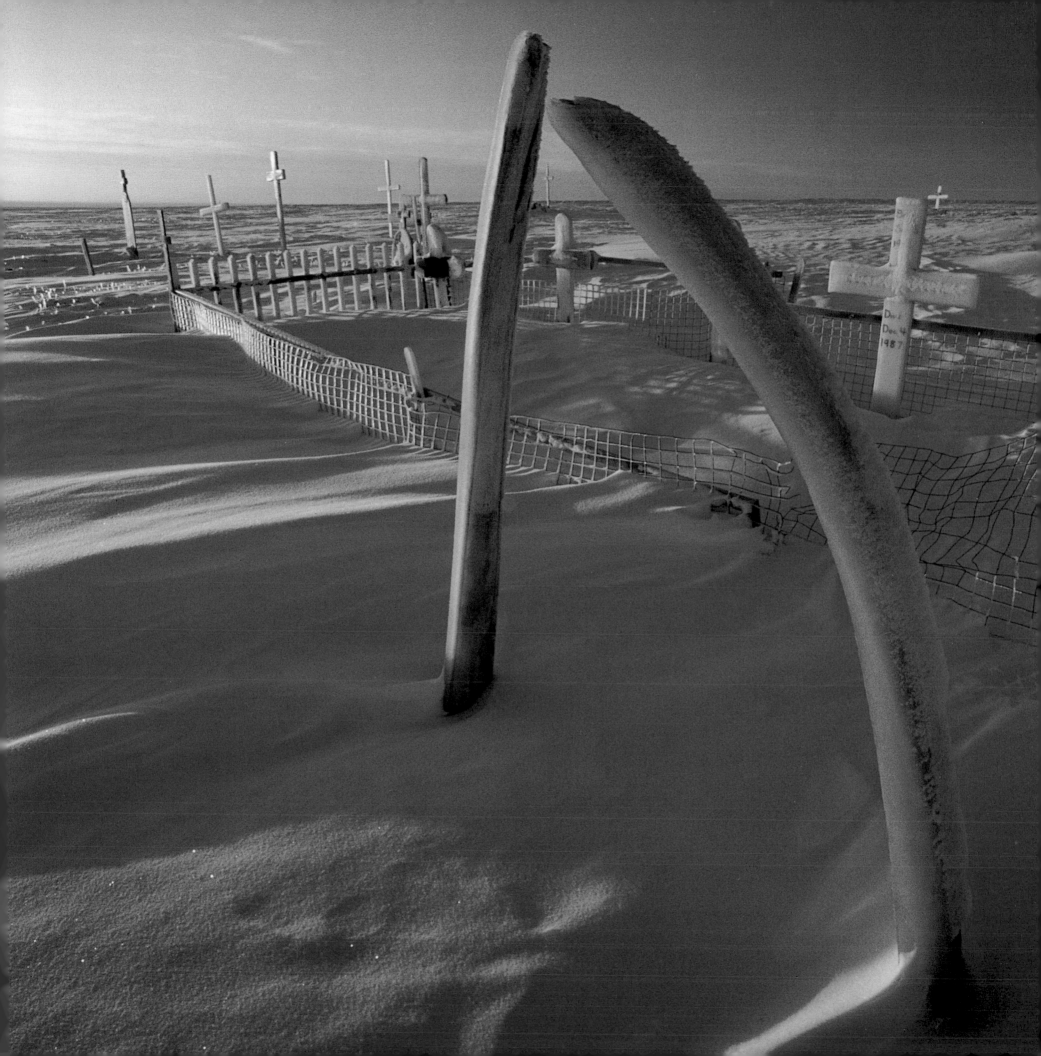

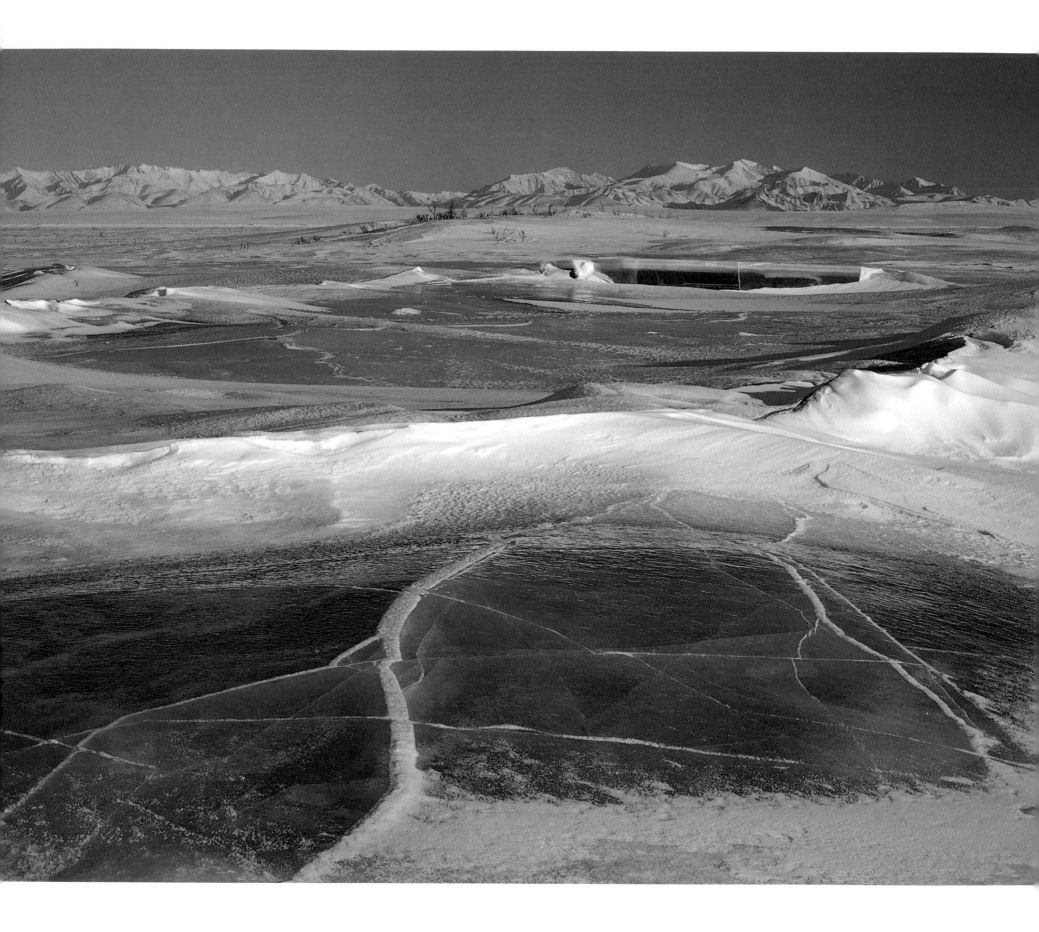

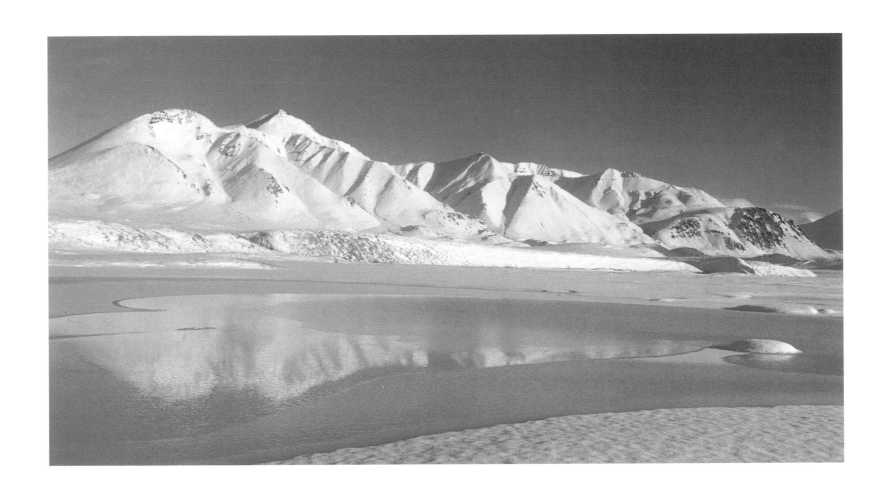

Winter reflection of the Romanzof Mountains on overflow water of the Hulahula River

Opposite • Aufeis along the Sadlerochit River

Paintings on an Arctic Sky

November 5, 2001: Robert Thompson, his cousin, Perry Anashugak, and I load our sleds and leave Kaktovik around ten in the morning on three separate snowmobiles. Six hours later we reach our destination: Old Man Creek, in the Hulahula River valley. The Hulahula River comes out of the Brooks Range here, and the overflow water creates a broad ice field half a mile across. From the east the river is joined by Old Man Creek, and from the west, a few hundred yards south at a steep angle from the hillside, Old Woman Creek joins the Hulahula. Both of these creeks are lined with significant willow patches that provide food and shelter for a variety of animals, including moose, muskox, ptarmigans, and porcupine. The willow patch is also a good place to pitch a tent because it breaks up the notorious arctic wind, which can be excruciatingly strong at times.

While Robert and Perry set up the tent, I notice the sky is catching a faint pink tint, not something I had seen before. At first I think it is the color of the sunset but soon realize—no, this color is actually *moving*. I am seeing the beginning of an aurora borealis. The sky is deep midnight blue, with stars galore across the northern horizon. I forget about food or going inside a shelter. I have never photographed an aurora before, and I am nervous. I take out my camera gear and find a comfortable spot at the edge of the willow patch. For the next four hours I am mesmerized as the faint pink display turns deep pink mixed with bright white, and then becomes deep red with bright yellow highlights.

The color palette in the sky and across the land is amazing. The moon is at its half phase, casting light and shadow on the snow-covered Romanzof Mountains. The Hulahula ice field catches the red of the aurora. Amazing shapes form and disappear in the sky.

Around eight in the evening the temperature drops to about minus fifty degrees F, and we turn in for the night. I got my first frostbite, on three fingers and the tip of my nose.

The next evening the sky presents us with a dramatic display of the more common green aurora. Unlike the previous night, where the shapes formed and disappeared slowly, the green display moves and changes shapes at a furious pace. The moon stays behind thin, wispy clouds, casting almost no light on the land.

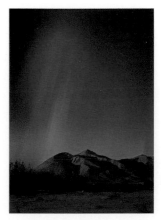

We camp out along the Hulahula River valley for the next thirteen days. Robert and Perry are here for autumn sheep hunting. Thanksgiving is approaching and they want to bring fresh meat home to share during the community feast. Each night I look up to the sky for yet another display of aurora, but never again see anything like the amazing red aurora of November 5.

—S.B.

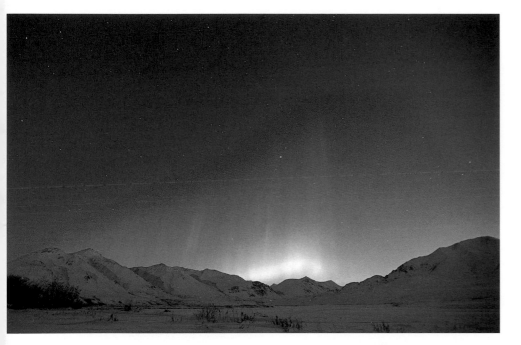

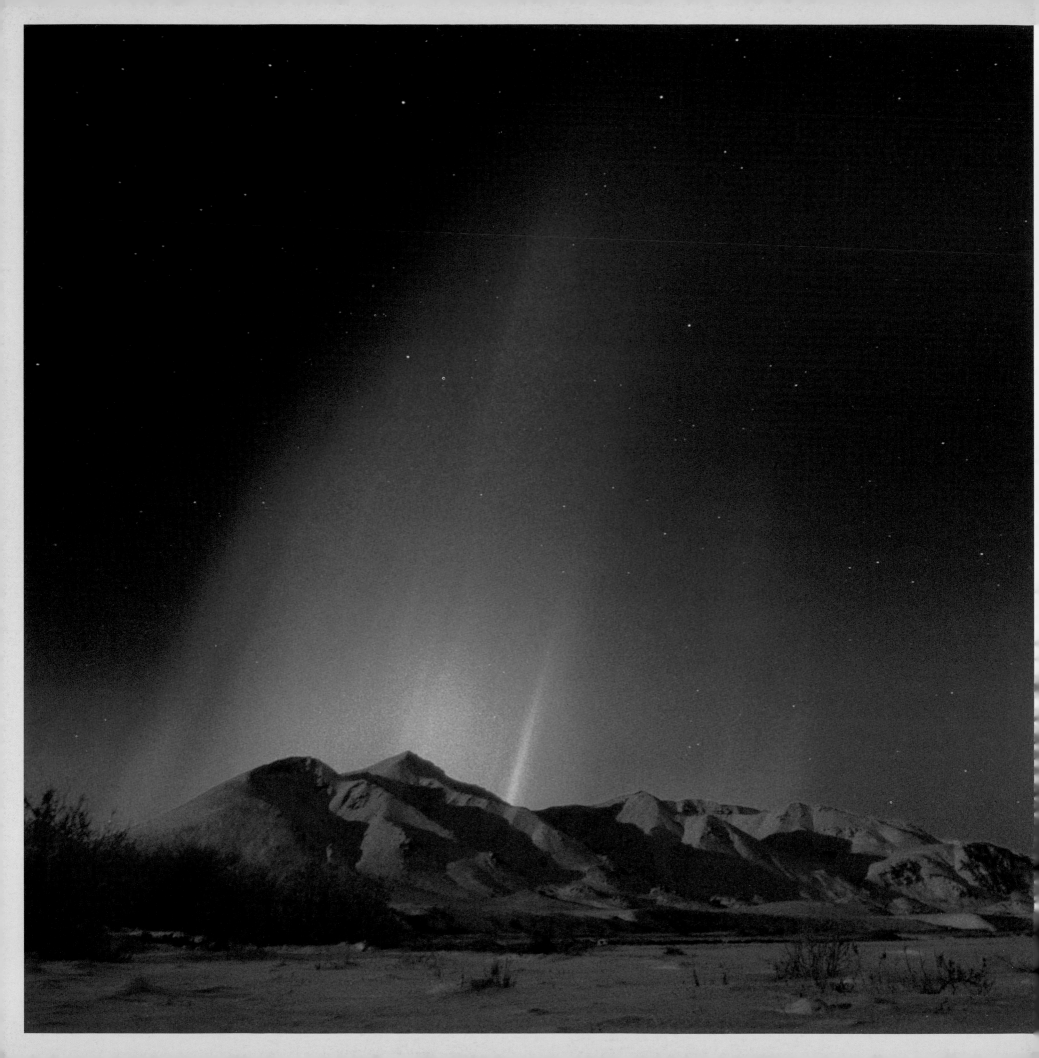

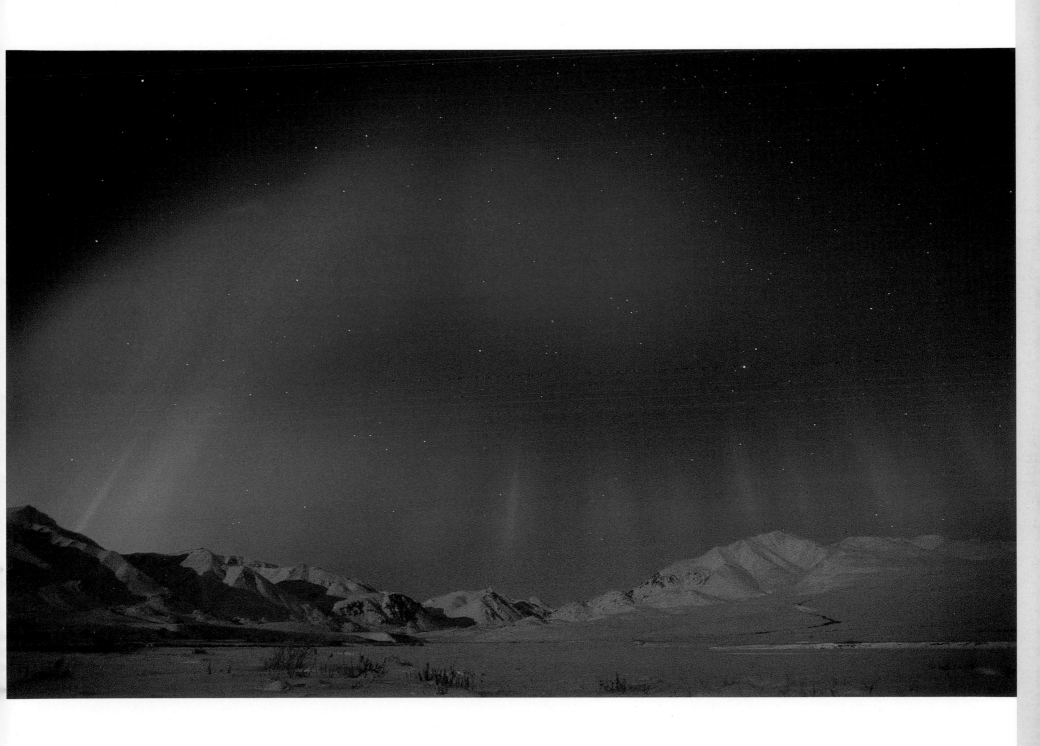

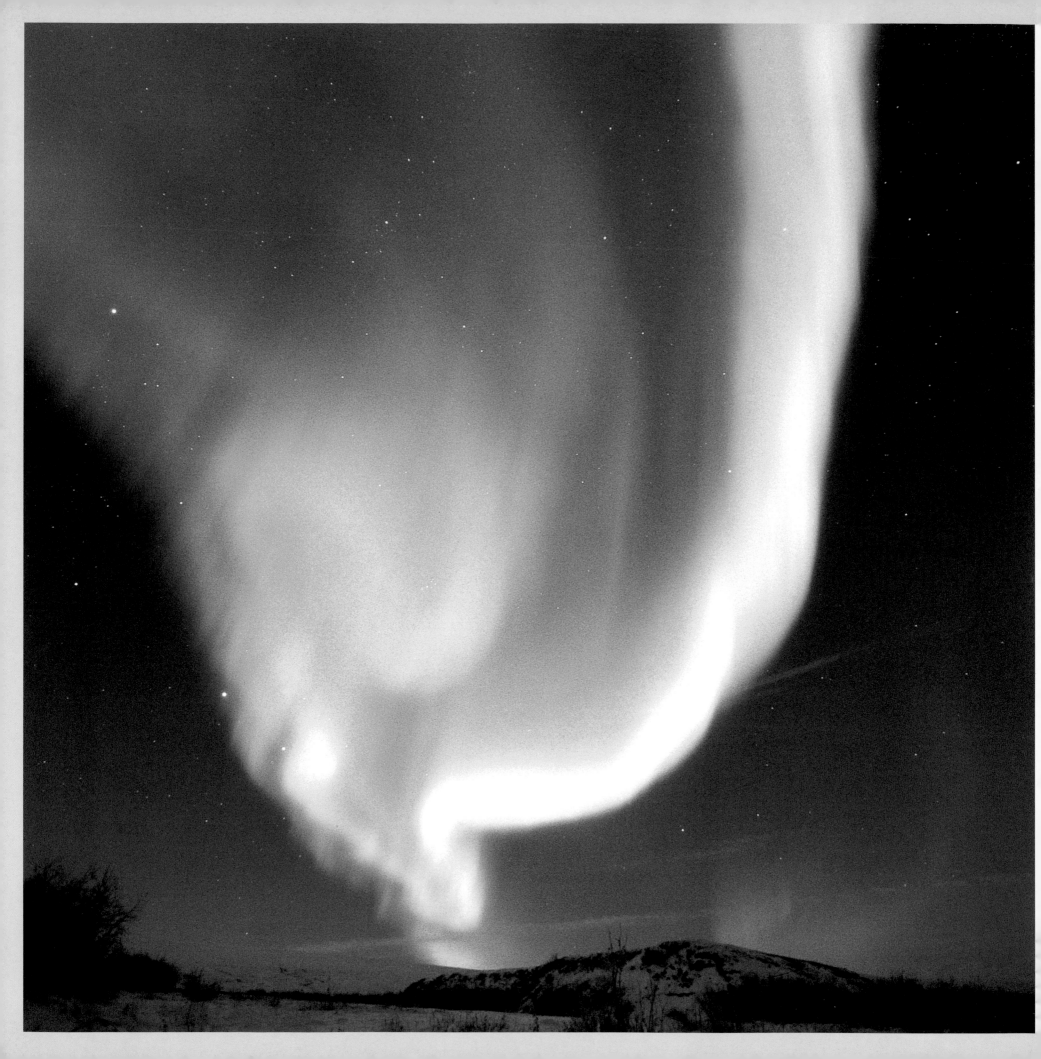

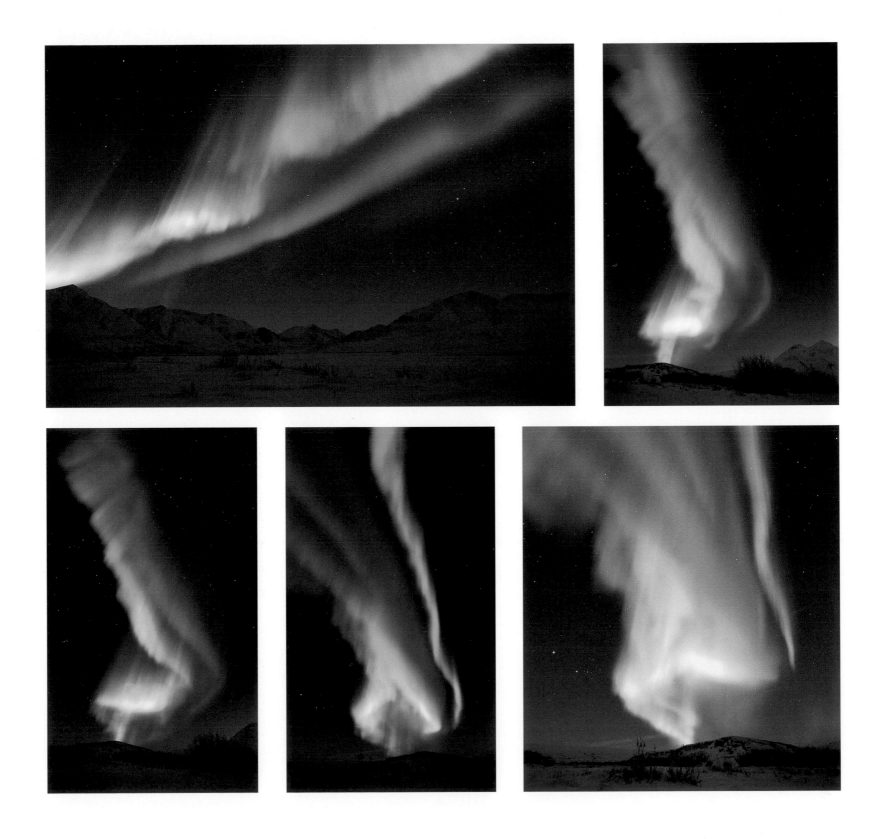

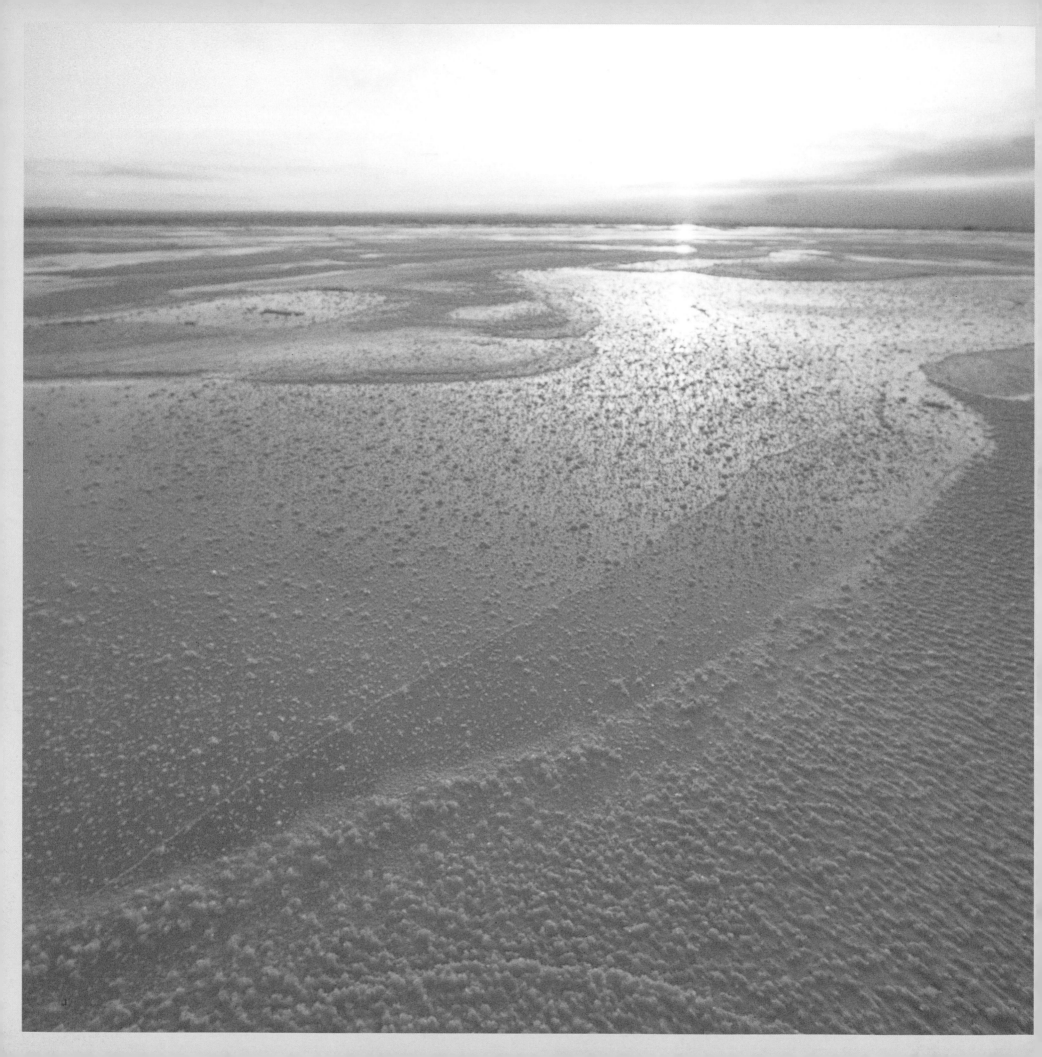

terry tempest williams

WILD MERCY

The eyes of the future are looking back at us and they are praying for us to see beyond our own time. They are kneeling with clasped hands that we might act with restraint, leaving room for the life that is destined to come.

To protect what is wild is to protect what is gentle. Perhaps the wilderness we fear is the pause within our own heartbeats, the silent space that says we live only by grace. Wilderness lives by this same grace.

We have it within our power to create merciful acts.

The act of restraint by the United States Congress in the name of the Arctic National Wildlife Refuge would be the most powerful act of all. Call it The Act of Wild Mercy, an interval of silence sustained in the twenty-first century.

Terry Tempest Williams

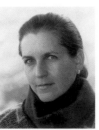

Photo by Ann P. Tempest

TERRY TEMPEST WILLIAMS *is the author of a dozen books on our relationship to place. Her books include* Refuge, An Unspoken Hunger; *and, most recently,* Leap. *She is the recipient of a John M. Simon Guggenheim Fellowship and a Lannan Literary Fellowship, and is a member of the Rachel Carson Honor Roll. She lives in Castle Valley, Utah, with her husband, Brooke. Together they are working with the Castle Rock Collaboration to preserve wildlands along the Colorado River corridor.*

Opposite • Winter morning on the Sadlerochit River

PHOTOGRAPHER'S NOTES

During the many lectures I have given across the country, one question is always asked: "What camera and survival gear did you use to cope with the extreme cold of the Arctic winter?" Working in one of the harshest climates imaginable was a challenge and the equipment I used was critical, both for my survival and for the success of my photography. By no means are the items noted here the only equipment available; this is just what worked well for me during this project.

If I am not warm enough in the field, the photography becomes meaningless. My outer layer was a heavy down parka and down pants, with 800-weight goose down and PTFE lining, made by Feathered Friends in Seattle. It worked flawlessly for me. Lillian Akootchook added a wolf ruff to the hood for me. This type of ruff is used throughout the Arctic and is essential for protecting the face from extreme blizzard conditions. Occasionally I also used the traditional Inupiat parka called a *tigi,* made out of sheepskin with a wolf ruff.

Since wind is the biggest challenge on the Arctic coast, I wore multiple layers of windproofed polypropylene beneath the down parka and pants. Layering is always a good idea; you can take unnecessary layers off when it warms up and then replace as needed.

I wore a balaclava and liner gloves from Outdoor Research, incredibly high-quality products. On top of the balaclava I wore a hat that Jane Thompson made by hand for me, then pulled up the parka hood when necessary. Over my liner gloves I wore sheepskin mittens Robert made, filled with loose *quiviut* (muskox wool). No matter how frustrated I felt with the clumsiness of using gloves, I never took them off to use my camera; touching metal surfaces with bare fingers in minus forty degrees F inevitably results in frostbite.

I tried to wear the "bunny" boots (vapor-barrier boots) commonly used in Alaska, but they froze solid each night and took a long time to warm up, so I switched to an extreme-weather boot from Cabela's rated at minus 100 degrees F. At times I also used toe warmers to keep my feet warm.

I used an extreme-weather down sleeping bag rated at minus seventy degrees F made by Feathered Friends; I never got cold after I got inside it. I used a ThermaRest sleeping pad. Robert and I used an Arctic Oven tent made by Alaska Tent and Tarp, which sets up quickly. During the Arctic winter, you are unable to do anything in a hurry—you cannot walk fast or you will generate sweat; you plan elaborately before taking out your camera to start shooting. This tent worked well for us in these conditions.

As an environmental photographer my goal is to capture images that evoke emotion and inspire the audience to care about threatened landscapes, wildlife, and indigenous cultures; because of this, my images are driven almost entirely by esthetic sensibilities rather than technical considerations. However, you need to be technically ready so that when the time arrives you can capture the image on film. I used both 35mm SLR as well as 645 medium-format cameras. In the extreme cold of the Arctic winter none of my latest electronic cameras worked, but my older-version Nikon cameras—including Nikon F4s and Nikon FM2— and my Mamiya 645 ProTL manual cameras worked without any problems.

The challenge is to keep the batteries alive. For the Nikon cameras, I first tried to use a DB6 battery pack. However, I found it inconvenient to be attached to the camera body through the cord, which restricts movement; in minus temperatures, it is important to keep moving in order to stay warm. Instead I used easily interchangeable battery holders, and kept two extra battery holders warm inside my parka. For my Mamiya I did not have a battery holder; instead I changed the batteries before every session and hoped the batteries wouldn't die, which worked fine.

In the summer months I also used a Nikon F5 camera body. For Nikon I used 17–35mm f2.8, 28–70mm f2.8, 80–200mm f2.8, 80–400mm f4.5–5.6 VR, 500mm f4 lenses, and occasionally a 1.4x teleconverter. For my Mamiya 645 I used 35mm f3.5, 45mm f2.8, 80mm f2.8, 150mm f2.8, and 500mm f5.6 lenses. For some of the summer wildlife and bird photography I used a Cannon EOS3 camera with a 600mm f4 lens and 1.4x and 2x teleconverters.

During the Arctic winter the sky casts a deep blue hue across the land. To cut this I used a warming 81A filter or a warming 81A circular polarizing filter. In the summer I occasionally used a circular polarizing filter. For the rare circumstances when I photographed a reflection I used a graduated neutral-density filter with two-stop strength.

In the winter I used primarily Kodak E100VS film and occasionally Fuji Velvia; in the summer I used mostly Fuji Velvia and occasionally Kodak E100VS. For photographing wildlife I used both Kodak E100VS and Fuji Provia 100F films, occasionally pushing them one stop. For photographing people I used Fuji Provia 100F; for photographing the northern lights I used Fuji Provia 400F pushed 1 stop. I flew in a Cessna 206 with the back door off or in a Supercub with the window lifted for my aerial photography, and used my Mamiya camera with the 80mm or the 150mm lens with both Kodak E100VS and Fuji Provia 100F film.

Having a mastery of the tools and knowing how to use them efficiently and effectively are essential in making great images, but this is just the first step. The most important aspect of creating emotionally moving images is how you feel about and relate to your subjects. Images are like words; they can be a powerful medium with which to inspire those who view them. I hope this book inspires you not only to take beautiful pictures, but also to use your images to join me in saving the last remaining wild places on our planet.

SELECTED REFERENCES

Books

Brower, K. *Earth and the Great Weather: The Brooks Range.* Friends of the Earth. New York: McCall Publishing Company, 1973.

Calef, G. *Caribou and the Barren-Lands.* Canadian Arctic Resources Committee. Ottawa: Firefly Books Ltd., 1981.

Craighead, C., and B. Kreps. *Arctic Dance: The Mardy Murie Story.* Portland: Graphic Arts Center Publishing Company, 2002.

Douglas, W. O. *My Wilderness.* New York: Doubleday, 1960.

Garner, G. W., and P. E. Reynolds. *Final Report—Baseline Study of the Fish, Wildlife, and Their Habitats.* Arctic National Wildlife Refuge Coastal Plain Resource Assessment. Anchorage: U.S. Department of the Interior, Fish and Wildlife Service, 1986.

Jacobson, M. J., and C. Wentworth. *Kaktovik Subsistence: Land Use Values through Time in the Arctic National Wildlife Refuge Area.* Fairbanks: U.S. Fish and Wildlife Service, Northern Ecological Services, 1982.

Lentfer, H., and C. Servid, comp. *Arctic Refuge: A Circle of Testimony.* Minneapolis: Milkweed Editions, 2001.

Lopez, B. *Arctic Dreams: Imagination and Desire in a Northern Landscape.* New York: Vintage Books, 2001.

Madsen, K., and N. Kassi. *Under the Arctic Sun: Gwich'In, Caribou, and the Arctic National Wildlife Refuge.* Englewood: Westcliffe Publishers, 2002.

Marshall, R. *Alaska Wilderness: Exploring the Central Brooks Range.* Berkeley: University of California Press, 1956.

Miller, D. S. *Midnight Wilderness: Journeys in Alaska's Arctic National Wildlife Refuge.* Portland: Alaska Northwest Books, 2000.

Murie, M. E. *Two in the Far North.* Portland: Alaska Northwest Books, 1997.

Peter, K. *Neetsaii Gwiindaii—Living in the Chandalar Country.* Fairbanks: Alaska Native Language Center, University of Alaska Fairbanks, 1992.

Pielou, E. C. *A Naturalist's Guide to the Arctic.* Chicago: University of Chicago Press, 1994.

Pratt, V. E. *Field Guide to Alaskan Wildflowers: Commonly Seen Along Highways and Byways.* Anchorage: Alaskakrafts, 1990.

Rennick, P., ed. *Arctic National Wildlife Refuge.* Anchorage: Alaska Geographic Society, 1993.

Sibley, D. A. *The Sibley Guide to Birds.* New York: Knopf, 2000.

———. *The Sibley Guide to Bird Life and Behavior.* New York: Knopf, 2001.

Truett, J. C., and S. R. Johnson, eds. *The Natural History of an Arctic Oil Field.* San Diego: Academic Press, 2000.

Ward, K. *The Last Wilderness: Arctic National Wildlife Refuge.* Santa Cruz: WildLight Press, 2001.

Watkins T. H., et al. *Vanishing Arctic: Alaska's National Wildlife Refuge.* New York: Aperture, 1988.

Weller, G., and P. A. Anderson, eds. *Assessing the Consequences of Climate Change for Alaska and the Bering Sea Region.* Workshop Proceedings, Center for Global Change and Arctic System Research. Fairbanks: University of Alaska Fairbanks, November 1999: 1–94.

Articles

Amstrup, S. C., and C. Gardner. "Polar Bear Maternity Denning in the Beaufort Sea." *Journal of Wildlife Management* 58 (1994): 1–10.

"Birds and Oil Development in the Arctic Refuge." *Audubon Alaska* (2001): 1–8.

Brackney, A. W. "Abundance and Productivity of Tundra Swans in the Coastal Plain of the Arctic NWR." In *Annual Wildlife Inventories: 1002 Area—Arctic NWR Annual Progress Report 1989,* edited by T. R. McCabe, 14–16. Anchorage: U.S. Fish and Wildlife Service, 1990.

———. "Distribution, Abundance, and Productivity of Fall Staging Snow Geese on the Coastal Plain of the Arctic NWR." In *Annual Wildlife Inventories: 1002 Area—Arctic NWR Annual Progress Report 1989,* edited by T. R. McCabe, 11–13. Anchorage: U.S. Fish and Wildlife Service, 1990.

Caulfield, R. A. "Subsistence Land Use in Upper Yukon–Porcupine Communities, Alaska." Alaska Department of Fish and Game, Division of Subsistence, *Technical Paper No. 16* (1983).

Collins, G., and L. Sumner. "The Northeast Arctic: The Last Great Wilderness." *Sierra Club Bulletin* 13 (October 1953): 12–26.

Fancy, S. G., and K. R. Whitten. "Selection of Calving Sites by Porcupine Herd Caribou." *Canadian Journal of Zoology* 69 (1991): 1736–1743.

Hupp, J. W., and D. G. Robertson. "Potential Impacts of Petroleum Development on Lesser Snow Geese Staging on the Arctic Coastal Plain." In *Terrestrial Research: 1002 Area—Arctic NWR Interim Report 1988–1990,* edited by T. R. McCabe, et al., 207–230. Anchorage: U.S. Fish Wildlife Service, 1992.

Kaye, R. "The Arctic National Wildlife Refuge: An Exploration of the Meanings Embodied in America's Last Great Wilderness." *USDA Forest Service Proceedings,* RMRS-P-15 vol. 2 (2000): 73–80.

Murie, O. "Wilderness Philosophy, Science and the Arctic National Wildlife Range." *Proceedings of the 12th Alaska Science Conference,* Alaska Division, American Association for the Advancement of Science, Fairbanks, AK. 1961: 58–69.

Reynolds, P. E. "Winter Distribution, Movements and Habitat Use of Muskoxen on Potential Petroleum Lease Areas of the Arctic NWR." In *Terrestrial Research: 1002 Area—Arctic NWR Interim Report 1988–1990,* edited by T. R. McCabe, et al., 130–147. Anchorage: U.S. Fish and Wildlife Service, 1992.

Schneider, D. "On Thin Ice." *Alaska Magazine* (October 2001): 40–45.

Sumner, L. "Arctic National Wildlife Refuge Address: 25th Anniversary." An unpublished letter from the files of the Arctic National Wildlife Refuge. Fairbanks: U.S. Fish and Wildlife Service, 1985.

West, R. L., and E. Snyder-Conn. "Effects of Prudhoe Bay Reserve Pit Fluids on Water Quality and Microinvertebrates of Arctic Tundra Ponds in Alaska." U.S. Department of the Interior, U.S. Fish and Wildlife Service, *Biological Report 7* (1987).

Whitten, K. R., and R. D. Cameron. "Distribution of Caribou Calving in Relation to the Prudhoe Bay Oilfield." In *The Proceedings of the First North American Caribou Workshop, Whitehorse, Yukon,* edited by A. M. Martell and D. E. Russell, 33–39. Ottawa: Canadian Wildlife Service, 1985.

RESOURCES

Following is a list of organizations where more information can be obtained about the Arctic National Wildlife Refuge. Many of these organizations have been working for decades to protect the coastal plain of the refuge from oil exploration and industrial development. They are a good source if you would like to learn more about conservation issues and how you can help to protect the Arctic Refuge.

Alaska Wilderness League
122 C Street Northwest, Suite 240
Washington, DC 20001
Phone: (202) 544-5205
www.alaskawild.org/

Arctic National Wildlife Refuge
101 12 Avenue, Room 236, Box 20
Fairbanks, AK 99701
Phone: (907) 456-0250
arctic.fws.gov

Defenders of Wildlife
1101 14 Street Northwest,
   No. 1400
Washington, DC 20005
Phone: (202) 682-9400
www.savearcticrefuge.org

Gwich'in Steering Committee
122 1 Avenue, Box 2
Fairbanks, AK 99701
Phone: (907) 458-8264
www.alaska.net/~gwichin/

National Audubon Society
700 Broadway
New York, NY 10003
Phone: (212) 979-3000
*www.audubon.org/campaign/refuge/
   alaska.html*

National Wildlife Federation
11100 Wildlife Center Drive
Reston, VA 20190-5362
Phone: (703) 438-6000
www.nwf.org/arcticrefuge/

Natural Resources Defense Council
1200 New York Avenue Northwest,
   Suite 400
Washington, DC 20005
Phone: (202) 289-6868
www.savebiogems.org/arctic

Northern Alaska Environmental Center
830 College Road
Fairbanks, AK 99701
Phone: (907) 452-5021
northern.org/artman/publish/

Sierra Club
85 Second Street, Second Floor
San Francisco, CA 94105
Phone: (415) 977-5500
www.sierraclub.org/wildlands/arctic/

The Wilderness Society
1615 M Street Northwest
Washington, DC 20036
Phone: (800) THE-WILD
(202) 833-2300
www.tws.org/wild/arctic

The Wildlife Conservation Society
2300 Southern Boulevard
Bronx, NY 10460
Phone: (718) 220-5100
www.wcs.org

U.S. PIRG
218 D Street Southeast
Washington, D.C. 20003
Phone: (202) 546-9707
www.SaveTheArctic.org

ACCESS AND OUTFITTERS

Below is an abbreviated list of commercial recreational guide and flight service companies currently authorized by the U.S. Fish and Wildlife Service to operate within the Arctic National Wildlife Refuge. Contact the U.S. Fish and Wildlife Service for a current and complete list. The information provided in this book does not constitute an endorsement by the U.S. Fish and Wildlife Service, Subhankar Banerjee, or The Mountaineers Books.

ABEC's Alaska Adventures
1550 Alpine Vista Court
Fairbanks, AK 99712
Phone: (907) 457-8907
www.abecalaska.com

Alaska Discovery
5310 Glacier Highway
Juneau, AK 99801
Phone: (907) 780-6506
www.akdiscovery.com

Alaska Flyers
Box 67
Kaktovik, AK 99747
Phone: (907) 640-6324

Alaska Wildtrek
Box 1741
Homer, AK 99603
Phone: (907) 235-6463
www.alaskawildtrek.com

Arctic Connections
519 West 8 Avenue, Suite 206
Anchorage, AK 99501
Phone: (907) 272-1909

Arctic Treks
Box 73452
Fairbanks, AK 99707
Phone: (907) 455-6502
www.arctictreksadventures.com

Arctic Wild
Box 80562
Fairbanks, AK 99708
Phone: (888) 577-8203
www.arcticwild.com

Coyote Air Service
Box 9053
Coldfoot, AK 99701
Phone: (907) 678-5995
www.flycoyote.com

Equinox Wilderness Expeditions
618 West 14 Avenue
Anchorage, AK 99501
Phone: (907) 274-9087
www.equinoxexpeditions.com

Kaktovik Arctic Adventures
Box 35
Kaktovik, AK 99747
Phone: (907) 640-6119

Wilderness Birding Adventures
Box 103747
Anchorage, AK 99510-3747
Phone: (907) 694-7442
www.wildernessbirding.com

Yukon Air Service
Box 84107
Fairbanks, AK 99708
Phone: (907) 479-3993

FACTS ABOUT THE ARCTIC NATIONAL WILDLIFE REFUGE

The Arctic Refuge was established in 1960 as a promise to the American people to preserve "wildlife, wilderness and recreational values." Vast and remote, this 19.5 million-acre refuge is the size of South Carolina. While 8.9 million acres are designated as wilderness, the 1.5 million-acre coastal plain, the biological heart of the refuge, does not yet have wilderness designation. Oil drilling has been proposed on the coastal plain.

The refuge shares a common border with Ivvavik and Vuntut National Parks in Canada, which in combination constitutes one of the largest conservation areas in the world.

North to south, the refuge extends 200 miles—from the Arctic coast, across the tundra plain, over glacier-capped peaks of the Brooks Range, and into the spruce and birch forests of the Yukon basin. The refuge preserves a continuum of Arctic and sub-Arctic ecozones.

It contains the greatest variety of plant and animal life of any conservation area in the circumpolar north. It is home to thirty-six species of land mammals; nine marine mammal species live along its coast; thirty-six fish species inhabit its rivers and lakes; and 180 species of birds converge here from six continents.

The 120,000-strong Porcupine caribou herd migrates throughout the refuge and northwestern Canada. The pregnant females come to the coastal plain to give birth in late May and early June. The annual migration of this herd is the reason the refuge is sometimes called "America's Serengeti."

All three species of North American bear (black, grizzly, and polar) range within its borders. The refuge is the only national conservation area where polar bears regularly den, and it is the most consistently used polar bear land-denning area in Alaska. The pregnant bears dig their dens in November, then give birth to one or two tiny cubs in December or January. The mothers nurse and care for the young at the den until March or early April.

The once-endangered muskox, an Ice-Age relic, live year-round on the refuge coastal plain and give birth to their young from mid-April through mid-May, when the coastal plain is still fully covered in snow.

The refuge contains North America's northernmost Dall sheep population. A year-round resident, they have lived in the Arctic Refuge since the Pleistocene.

The refuge contains North America's northernmost moose population.

Millions of birds come to the refuge each year. Their migrations take them to each of the fifty states, and they cross great oceans and follow distant coastlines to reach the lands and waters of six continents. About seventy species of birds nest on the narrow Arctic Refuge coastal plain.

Each autumn, the coastal plain of the refuge supports up to 300,000 snow geese, which leave their nesting grounds in Canada and detour here to feed on cotton grass to build fat reserves and gain energy before heading south to their wintering grounds.

It is a place of wildness, where timeless ecological and evolutionary processes continue in their natural ebb and flow. The refuge is a place where the mystery of nameless valleys remains alive, where one can experience solitude, self-reliance, exploration, adventure, and challenge. The spirit of wilderness prevails here.

The majestic Brooks Range rises from the coastal plain here only ten to forty miles from the Beaufort Sea. The refuge includes the four highest peaks and most of the glaciers in the Brooks Range. More than twenty rivers flow through the refuge, and three are designated as wild: the Sheenjek, Ivishak, and Wind. It contains North America's two largest and most northerly alpine lakes—Peters and Schrader.

Numerous prominent geological formations, including a range of permafrost and glacial features, are found here. It contains several warm springs, which support plant species unique to the area.

In this land of seasonal extremes, the summer sun remains above the horizon for months; in winter, the dark sky is enlivened by the multicolored aurora borealis.

The refuge has been a homeland for thousands of years to the Inupiat Eskimos of the north coast and the Gwich'in Athabascan Indians of interior Alaska. The Inupiat people primarily depend on bowhead whales and other marine mammals for food. The Gwich'in people depend on the Porcupine caribou herd for food, clothing, tools, and cultural identity.

Compiled from Arctic National Wildlife Refuge reports of the United States Fish and Wildlife Service

THE MOUNTAINEERS, founded in 1906, is a nonprofit outdoor activity and conservation club with fifteen thousand members, whose mission is "to explore, study, preserve, and enjoy the natural beauty of the outdoors. . . . " The club sponsors many classes and year-round outdoor activities in the Pacific Northwest, and supports environmental causes through educational activities, sponsoring legislation and presenting educational programs. The Mountaineers Books supports the club's mission by publishing travel and natural history guides, instructional texts, and works on conservation and history.

THE MOUNTAINEERS FOUNDATION is a public foundation established in 1968 to promote the study of the mountains, forests, and streams of the Pacific Northwest, and to contribute to the preservation of its natural beauty and ecological integrity. The Mountaineers Foundation fulfills its mission by stewardship of important preserves and by grant-making. Through these means, it actively supports conservation in the Pacific Northwest. Although The Mountaineers Foundation has close ties to The Mountaineers, the foundation is a separate corporation with separate volunteer officers and trustees. The Mountaineers Foundation gratefully welcomes your financial contribution to continue and extend its vital conservation work. Because The Mountaineers Foundation is a 501(c)(3) charitable organization, contributions are tax deductible to the extent allowed by law. Please contact *www.mountaineersfoundation.org* for more information.

Send or call for our catalog of more than 500 outdoor titles:

The Mountaineers Books
1001 SW Klickitat Way, Suite 201
Seattle, WA 98134
(800) 553-4453
mbooks@mountaineersbooks.org
www.mountaineersbooks.org